THE ADVENTURE

The Quest For My Romanian Babies

George C. Klein

Hamilton Books
A member of
The Rowman & Littlefield Publishing Group
Lanham · Boulder · New York · Toronto · Plymouth, UK

Copyright © 2007 by
Hamilton Books
4501 Forbes Boulevard
Suite 200
Lanham, Maryland 20706
Hamilton Books Acquisitions Department (301) 459-3366

Estover Road
Plymouth PL6 7PY
United Kingdom

All rights reserved
Printed in the United States of America
British Library Cataloging in Publication Information Available

Library of Congress Control Number: 2007922031
ISBN-13: 978-0-7618-3704-6 (paperback : alk. paper)
ISBN-10: 0-7618-3704-3 (paperback : alk. paper)

∞™ The paper used in this publication meets the minimum
requirements of American National Standard for Information
Sciences—Permanence of Paper for Printed Library Materials,
ANSI Z39.48—1984

*To Susie and the kids,
and to all my friends in
the United States and Romania
that made my adoptions possible.*

Contents

Preface   vii

Part I: The Story

Chapter 1	Turning the Corner	2
Chapter 2	From Korea to Kovno	3
Chapter 3	First Contact	23
Chapter 4	The Revolution	29
Chapter 5	AIDS	31
Chapter 6	Welcome to the Balkans	39
Chapter 7	Bread and Newspapers	49
Chapter 8	*Schiene Kind, Starker*	54
Chapter 9	The Little Olive-Skinned Girl	63
Chapter 10	"Your Babies Are Waiting!"	75
Chapter 11	My Babies!	81
Chapter 12	The Odyssey	87
Chapter 13	"Everything Vill Be Just Fine"	112
Chapter 14	Afterward	113

Part II: The Analysis

Chapter 15	Introduction: The Adoption Story	117
Chapter 16	Analytical Autobiography	120
Chapter 17	Analysis: The Historical Context: The Revolution	128
Chapter 18	Analysis Levels	138
	Individuals & Institutions	138
	National: The Romanian Communist Party (RCP)	143
	Global	146

Bibliography   149
Index   177

Preface

I had not planned on telling anyone my adoption story, but in 1990, on my second flight home from Romania, I realized that I had had an interesting experience. So I began to write notes on the back of an airsickness bag. Over the next year whenever a recollection flashed through my mind I grabbed a napkin or a page from a desk calendar, wrote the thought down, and stuffed the paper in my pocket. At the end of the year I dumped all my crumpled notes on to my desk and sorted them chronologically. Then, instead of writing out my story, which seemed rather tedious, I decided to take a shortcut. I decided to dictate my story into a tape recorder and let my secretary type it. I thought that one edit would produce a finished manuscript. However, reality intruded. My first problem was that it took 30 hours to tell my story. This was far longer than I had anticipated. And then my "one edit" became many edits, and this process stretched over six years.

However, before I could even begin my writing I agonized over how to tell the story. I wasn't a professional writer. However, I was a professor and that made me a professional storyteller. In fact, I often told my students that my job was to "inform and entertain." So, I thought I could write the book as if I were telling the story to a student who came to visit my office. This device led me to tell the story entirely in quotes. And, even though my student is fictitious, all the information in the story is true. Also, the conversations that I quote within the text are drawn from memory. However, I have used such quotations sparingly and I reserved them for conversations that were striking. There are, however, two small caveats to note. One is that in order to avoid legal complications I have omitted or changed the names of the adoption agencies and attorneys with whom I have dealt. This is not an important point since who they were was far less important than how they treated me. Also, I have changed the names of my friends, both here and in Romania, to protect their privacy.

Also, let me explain the choice of my title, *The Adventure: The Quest For My Romanian Babies*. Adventure involves risk-taking. That is, adventure involves choices that take you down unexpected paths. The book details the choices my wife and I were forced to make concerning adoption. However, some of these choices were little more than a shrug of the shoulders. Others were more considered. And, some were long and tortuous. As a result of this there was a great deal of stumbling and bumbling as we headed down the adoption path.

There was also a great deal of learning that went on. And this learning, about adoption and about Romania, is presented in the way that I learned it—haltingly, as I groped my way in the darkness.

My story, however, was not simply an adventure. It was also a quest. It was a journey that took me down a convoluted path to a distant land. This path was strewn with obstacles and was often hindered by powerful forces. However, in the end I attained my goal; and I also attained new insights into myself (see Stout, 1983: 87-103).

The goal here is to tell the readers an interesting story about my quest, and once that story is complete to interpret its meaning. However, that is more complicated than it appears. When I began this manuscript I thought this was "an adoption story." However, by the end of the manuscript what interested me was not adoption. Instead, it was the manner in which the Communist state had destroyed the psyches of Romanians through economic deprivation and police terror.

In order for this analysis to have meaning, however, it must be placed within a theoretical context. The appropriate context here is the case study method. This is commonly used in the life history school of sociology and anthropology. These studies are usually called *interpretive ethnography*. However, in a review of these studies I found them to be too humanistic. That is, too concerned with the researcher's feelings and not enough with the analysis of data. Also, my manuscript was not an ethnography. So, I decided to call my technique *analytical autobiography*. I discuss the details of this method in the last portion of the book.

My analysis of the Communist Party begins with the historical context. That is, the Anti-Communist Revolution in 1989. The second portion of the analysis is vertical. That is, I begin at the individual level and examine how economic deprivation and police state terror caused the breakdown of social bonds between individuals. The second level of analysis is institutional. Here, I focus on the economy and the (secret) police, which were the two institutions that most directly shaped the average Romanian's life. The third level of analysis is the Communist Party, and the dictators who controlled it. And, lastly, the global forces that sustained, and ultimately destroyed, Romanian Communism.

So, the purpose of this book is to inform, entertain, and analyze. I hope it is successful.

Part I
The Story

Chapter 1

Turning the Corner

I turned the corner. "Don! How ya doin'?"
"Fine. I just came to see my favorite prof."
"Come in. Have a seat."
"How do you like practicing law?"
"Okay."
"But, do you still want to be a black jazz musician? Do you still want to be known as 'Don Coolman'? Or, have you finally accepted the fact that you're going to be a Jewish Tax Attorney for the rest of your life?"
"I'll never accept *that*. But, even if I did, my *soul* will still be black."
"Did I ever tell you my *soul* was French?"
"Yes."
"Did I ever mention that I spent the best week of my life in Paris?"
"Yes. But, I've heard that story. What I'm here for is to hear about your babies. So, tell me the story. Tell me every agonizing detail."
"Every one?"
"Yes."
"Okay, here goes . . ."

Chapter 2

From Korea to Kovno

"I started by doing some research on adoption. The very first article I came across turned out to be the best one I read. And, of all things, it was in *Money* magazine (Harris, 1988). It said that the first large scale adoptions began in 1854 when 46 orphans from New York City were sent on an 'orphan train' to Dowagiac, Michigan. These starving and disheveled children were quickly adopted by local farm families. Over the next 75 years, as many as two hundred thousand abandoned children were shipped from city slums to farms. However, by the end of World War I social welfare agencies shifted to trying to keep troubled families together. Then in the 1920s, after infant formula was invented, it was decided that adoption was only suitable for babies. So, the last orphan train ran in 1929 (Harris, 1988; Dellios, 1993).

"Let me read you some statistics. In 1970, there were 89,200 adoptions, mostly of infants. However, after abortion became legal the number of adoptions dropped to about forty to fifty thousand domestic adoptions and ten thousand international adoptions per year. Today there are 40 infertile couples for every adoptable child. However, many of the children that are available are older, minority, or have problems. They are called 'special needs,' 'hard to place,' or 'waiting children.' These children are defined as mentally or physically handicapped, minority children over age eight, all children over age ten, or siblings. In 1984 there were about 7,500 special needs children waiting for adoption. But by 1987, the number had doubled to 15,000. A lot of these children are in foster care. However, most are not available for adoption. There may be as many as five hundred thousand of these kids shifted around endlessly in the foster care system (Harris, 1988; Stein, 1990: Dugger, 1991; Haynes, 1994; Richman, 1993a, 1993b).

"A number of organizations put out booklets with photographs and short biographies of waiting children. The best known one is the *CAP Book*. The organization that sponsors it is Children Awaiting Parents, Inc. Some of the kids in the *CAP Book* are American, and some are foreign; however, they're all either handicapped or the product of abuse, neglect, or abandonment. For example, some of these kids have 'congenital anomalies' and others have an 'unknown life expectancy.' Others have difficult behaviors such as 'lying, stealing, bed-wetting, fire-setting or occasional cruelty to animals.' A lot of these kids are older and suffer emotional scars from the loss of their parents. This makes it difficult for them to develop a sense of identity or attach themselves to others. With this type of child, up to 40 percent of these high risk adoptions fail. However, the vast majority of 'regular' adoptions succeed. And, a recent study showed that the vast majority of adopted kids were perfectly normal (Lewin, 1994). But, one article I read said that the adoptive parents of such children risk emotional and financial disaster. That is because you're turning your home into a psychiatric unit. And, the parents of these kids 'should not expect their affection to be returned in the normal way' (Fishman, 1992; Reitz and Watson, 1992; Lacayo, 1989). Also, 60 percent of all babies available are such special needs children (Fishman, 1992). And, then there were crack babies, and AIDS babies, and other sad stories. Now, I've been a social worker and Susie has been a special education teacher. We liked helping kids, but for *our* child we simply wanted 'a nice, normal, healthy baby.' From this initial research I stumbled upon the first truth in adoption: you must think about what you *really* want. And, what we wanted was not grief. We wanted 'a nice, normal, healthy baby.'

"There is one more complication in all this. It is a transracial adoption. For example if you are a white couple and you want to adopt a black baby, even a special needs black baby, they often won't let you."

"Really?"

"Yes, it's called 'racial matching,' and although it's now illegal it still goes on. Let me explain. Whites first began to adopt black babies in the 1950s or 1960s. But in 1972, The National Association of Black Social Workers called this 'racial genocide'. They insisted that black children should not be placed with white parents 'under any circumstances.' In fact, they felt that it was better for a black child to be in foster care or an institution rather than be with white parents. This is in spite of studies that show that interracial adoption did not destroy a black child's racial identity (Smolowe, 1995; Simon and Altstein, 1992). Implicitly or explicitly this was the policy in most states until a few years ago. In Illinois, for example, a 1985 lawsuit caused the Illinois Department of Children and Family Services to officially drop this policy. As a result, transracial adoption of wards of the state almost doubled from 32 in 1988 to 61 in 1992. However, they were still only 7 percent of the 835 adoptions the department handled in 1992. Nationally, the number of transracial adoptions has probably doubled in the last 10 or 15 years, to about twelve thousand. However, there are still many problems. I recall one television program in which a white family had been taking care of a black foster child. They had wanted to adopt the girl but the state refused. So, the family went to court. The judge decided that if the baby wasn't placed with a black family by a certain date the white couple could adopt her. At the last minute the state agency found a black family and yanked the baby out of the white couple's home. However, a few months later, the black couple beat the baby to death."

"What? Really?"

"Yes. Really. However, some black social workers say the real problem is that black families are screened out of the adoption process. They say this is because of 'institutional racism,' and there is some support for this point. For example, a National Urban League study found that out of eight hundred black families applying for adoption only *two* were accepted. That's 0.25 percent, whereas the overall national average for all families is 10 percent. This situation prompted Congress to pass a bill that changed the law on racial matching. This was a good thing since 40 percent of the 440,000 children in foster care are black, and 74 percent of the 22,000 babies abandoned in hospitals; by comparison, only 12.5 percent of the United States population is black. The original bill, which was sponsored by then Senator Howard Metzenbaum, said that agencies should not delay the placement of children in order to racially match them. However, the bill was watered down. The final language said that agencies that receive federal funds should not 'unduly' delay such placements. Also, the original bill said a transracial placement is better than long-term foster care. However, the final language said that adoption 'may be' a preferable alternative (Thomas, 1991a, 1991b; Richman, 1993a, 1993b; Goodman, 1993; Page, 1993; Holmes, 1995; Richardson, 1993; Chira, 1994; Jones, 1993; Horowitz, 1995a, 1995b; Williams, 1995; "New Rules Try To Ease Interracial Adoption," 1995; Davis, 1995; Lewin, 1994; Beck, 1995; Smolowe, 1995)."

"This all gets curiouser and curiouser."

"Yes. So, let me go on. I found another article that said that there were about sixty thousand adoptions of non-relatives in 1986. However, traditionally, adoption was considered a stigma in the United States. Such words as 'promiscuous,' 'barren,' and 'illegitimate' were commonly used in discussions of adoption; as recently as the 1970s, some delivery room nurses covered the mirrors or blindfolded the woman giving up the child. In the nursery these infants were marked DNS, Do Not Show to the mother, or DNP, Do Not Publish the mother's name. Adoption was considered sick to be . . . sick (Gibbs, 1989; Lacayo, 1989)."

"With the legalization of abortion the number of babies, at least white babies, fell. Foreign adoptions then became a popular alternative. One article commented that 'adoptive parents will practically go to the ends of the earth to find healthy, white, or perhaps Asian, infants.' In Illinois, for example, international adoptions jumped 750 percent from 1980 to 1988, from 51 to 388. Overall, there have been sixty to seventy thousand foreign adoptions over the last ten years by United States couples, and there are probably nine to ten thousand a year now (Gibbs, 1989; Pahz, 1987; McNamee, 1989b; Michelman and Schneider, 1988). This produces a supply and demand problem. As a result, prices have doubled or tripled for international adoptions over the last decade, they now average $10,000 to $20,000 a child."

"Since the 1950s, the main source for foreign adoptions was Korea. Korea has sent 120,000 orphans overseas since the Korean War ended. In the 1980s alone, more than forty thousand Korean children were adopted in the United States. Recently, however, the Koreans have begun to be embarrassed by all this, and, during the 1988 Olympics, they suspended all adoptions. The Korean government then stepped up its promotion of birth control and urged Korean families to adopt. As a result of this the number of Korean babies that were adopted here fell from about 6,000 a year in 1986, to about 3,500 in 1989, and about 1,800 in 1994. Many of the children that are being sent here now are older or handicapped. As a result of this, adoption has shifted to other countries. Currently, Chile, Ecuador, Paraguay, Peru, Guatemala, Columbia, and especially Russia and China are hot (Little, 1994; Louie, 1995; Iherjirika, 1994; Wills, 1994; Oloroso, 1994; Warren, 1995; Schmetzer, 1995a, 1995b; WuDunn, 1991; Daday, 1993; Mills, 1995; Huckshorn, 1992). However, some couples prefer Argentina because the babies are 'whiter'."

"Hmm . . ."

"Yes, *but*, let me emphasize that most needy kids in these countries never have a chance. For example, there are seven million abandoned and homeless kids in Brazil. Bogotá alone has at least one hundred thousand children who are homeless. Many of these children subsist by selling and using, marijuana, glue, or *bazuco*, a highly addictive form of cocaine. For girls, prostitution is common. They make about $5 per client. A report I read said that over two thousand kids were murdered in Columbia in 1993. Hundreds, perhaps thousands, are killed by vigilantes in Brazil each year. This is called 'social cleansing.' Other street children die from violence, drugs, or AIDS. Almost none of these kids will ever be adopted (Serrill, 1991; Lewin, 1990; Eisenberg, 1990; "Intercountry Adoptions Up in FY 1994," 1995; Brooke, 1994; Mercer, 1993; "Child Prostitution Growing in Brazil," 1993; Sheppard, 1991).

"Once we knew that babies were available, somewhere, we decided to adopt. The first thing we did was to tell our friends and relatives. One day a relative from the East Coast called and said that she knew of a lawyer in Maryland who could get us a baby. So, with guarded optimism, we called the lawyer. She said she would be happy to help. All we needed to do was find a baby. I immediately realized that adoption was going to be a long, and tedious process. And, a process with a lot of aggravation.

"A few days later some friends called us and said that they knew of a couple who had gotten a baby through a lawyer in Chicago. We called the couple and they said that the lawyer was 'a wonderful man.' We called him and he said that he did private, that is, non-agency adoptions (see McNamee 1989a, 1989c; Luft, 1995; Mansnerus, 1989; Petrakis, 1994). The lawyer told us that the way you get babies these days was to advertise in newspapers. This seemed odd to us, but that is what he had said. We mentioned to him that one of the gynecologists that my wife had been seeing suggested that we send our photograph and a letter to every obstetrician and gynecologist in the United States. He said that sometimes that worked, but doctors often received thousands of these letters and they usually ignored them or simply threw them out. Instead, he suggested that we call a woman he worked with who would put ads in the newspapers for us. We also asked him how much a typical adoption would cost. He said that his fee was usually $4,000, and hospitalization for the mother was usually $6,000. However, it could run a lot more if there were complications during birth, but usually, he said, the total cost was $10,000 to $12,000.

"We then called the woman he had recommended and asked her how to proceed. She said to write up a brief biography of ourselves and to send it to her with a $250 check. That was her fee. Then she would advise us on how to place the ads. Later, we found an article in the local newspaper on this lawyer. It began with the kind of ads that he and this woman were suggesting that we place. They said: *'Pregnant? Need help? Let us adopt your baby. We are a happily married, financially secure couple;'* or *'Adoption. A baby is our dream. Successful, married couple will give your baby love, security, and the best of everything. Expenses paid;'* or *'Wanted, baby. We want to adopt your normal white infant newborn to four years old. My wife will stay home and be a full-time mom. Help us to become a family, please. Desperate, please.'* The article said that with the help of these ads the lawyer had completed 43 adoptions in 1988. The lawyer was quoted as saying that he probably did more private adoptions than anyone else in the Chicago area. His adoption practice had begun when one of his clients came up with the idea to put an ad in the classified section of the local newspaper. From that one ad alone he placed six or seven babies (Miller, 1989; Sullivan, 1991; Gibbs, 1989; Michelman and Schneider, 1988).

"The article also talked about agency adoptions. This was the traditional way to adopt babies in America. In an agency adoption you applied. If they accepted you, you waited. You waited from a few months to a few years; and then, if you were lucky, you got a baby. Then you made a 'donation' to the agency of $5,000. But, nowadays, babies are scarce, and one private agency in the area charges $23,000 for an adoption. Two thousand dollars of that is a nonrefundable 'initial service fee.' The article quoted the director of this agency as saying that 34 percent of their clients got babies within six months of applying, and 100 percent of them got babies within 18 months. However, if they didn't find you to be a suitable client for their agency, you lost your 'initial service fee' (Miller, 1989; Godwin, 1989).

"Another option the article mentioned was 'facilitators.' This is halfway between an agency and a private adoption. For about $2,000, these facilitators help people who have been rejected by various agencies. These are people who have 'problems.' That is, these are people who were Jewish or 'too old,' that is, over 39. These facilitators help couples write biographies. Then the biographies are shown to birth mothers. These birth mothers have contacted the facilitators from newspaper and phone book ads. Then the birth mothers chose, anonymously, what biography they are most comfortable with. People who act in this role emphasize that this is not a sleazy, black market operation. What they are doing is helping couples to 'market themselves.' One agency official said, 'In all candor, we're involved in an extremely competitive business, and we're very much into marketing strategies.' But, another agency official added: 'A couple that presents poorly is going to have a tough time in today's economy' (Miller, 1989; Ogintz, 1989; McKay, 1989; Talaly, 1994b; Sullivan, 1994; Crossen, 1989).

"Now getting back to newspaper ads, Susie and I were uncomfortable with this approach. It felt . . . odd, and mercenary. It was as if we were buying a baby. So we decided not to place any ads. Instead, we began to call agencies.

"I had always assumed that when someone wanted to adopt a baby they simply called an agency. Then a year or two later they got a baby. In fact, that turned out not to be the case. I was disabused of this idea with my very first call to an agency. When the receptionist said was, 'How old are you?' I told her that my wife and I were both 43. She said, 'You're over the hill,' and hung up."

" Really?"

"Yes. This happens because there are so many people who want babies. This allows the agencies to set arbitrary limits, and the first arbitrary limit on adoption is being over 39. I then called the Jewish Children's Bureau. I asked if they had any babies available. They said, 'No. And, besides you are too old.' But, they said they would be happy to help us with an 'identified adoption.' I asked what was an identified adoption. 'Do you identify a baby and then we get it?' 'Oh no, no, no!,' she said. 'You find the baby, and then we do all the paperwork.' I thought, this wasn't a great deal. I then said that my wife and I had talked about adopting a Korean child. Did she know anything about this? Yes, but the best way to find out about Korean adoptions was to call the international adoption coordinator for the Illinois Department of Children and Family Services in Springfield. I thanked her and called Springfield.

"The international adoption coordinator told me that three agencies in the states did most of the Korean adoptions. One was in the southwest suburbs, one was in the western suburbs, and one was downtown. So I called one of the suburban agencies, and they said, 'Oh no, we don't have any babies available now. We've had a lot of cutbacks lately in the number of children coming to America.' They told me that I should call back after April 1. Then I called the other suburban agency, and they said, 'No! We don't have any openings.' But, they did suggest that I call back 'in a few months.'

"I then called the downtown agency. One of the secretaries said there were babies available from Korea and began to read through all the rules and regulations concerning these adoptions. At one point she asked me my age. I told her.

She then said in a jaunty voice, 'Oh! You qualify for a three to ten year old.' Then, there was a *very* long pause, as if she was looking through her manual to find the next thing to say. Finally she said, 'Should I go on?' 'Why not?' I asked and she replied, 'Because people usually hang up now.' So, a bit dumbfounded, I said, 'No, no. Go on.' After several more minutes she finished reading me the regulations. She then told me that an orientation meeting was required and that there would be one in a few weeks, but more on this later.

"The international adoption coordinator in Springfield had also mentioned that I might be interested in an organization called Stars of David International, Inc. that is a support group for Jewish adoptive parents. She gave me the number and I called. They said that they had a meeting the next day. So, I went. Their meetings usually have a speaker for an hour. The speaker discussed topics such as private adoption or how to raise your adopted child. But what was useful about the organization was not the speakers, instead, it was the emotional support and inside information that people gave you after the meeting. Most of the people in the organization had already adopted. So they could tell you the truth about the adoption process. For example, they would tell you that this lawyer was a crook or that agency would not help you because you were Jewish. In fact, I was told that some of the agencies I had called were Evangelical Christian agencies. They might take your money, but often would not help you because you were Jewish. I was told that one of these agencies had been sued by a Jewish couple in order to get a baby. So, suddenly, I began to realize there was a whole 'subculture of adoption,' and if you weren't involved in it you'd never know anything about it.

"At this time we also joined RESOLVE: The National Infertility Association. This is a national organization that is for people with infertility problems. However, they also have programs about adoption. I went to a few of the sessions. However, Resolve's sessions were often things I had already heard at a Stars of David's meeting. So, we dropped out of Resolve, and continued to go to the Stars of David meetings.

"The third organization we heard of was called Adoptive Families of America (AFA). It also runs local support groups, but we didn't join it as we felt that we'd already been saturated with information. However, it does have a very good reputation and a wonderful magazine to which we still subscribe.

"After a few meetings of Stars of David I realized that I needed to talk to a lawyer. So, I did some library research and found a book by Stanley Michelman, a prominent adoption lawyer (Michelman and Schneider, 1988). His book covered how to find a lawyer and how to do a private adoption. Michelman suggested that you search for an attorney who commonly does adoptions. Then you need to ask the attorney exactly how he or she handles their cases.

"I then began to research adoption law. I found that the key to every adoption is 'the permanent legal termination of the parental rights of the natural parents.' The first step in this process is for the natural parents to give their consent to the adoption. Then a 'home study' of the adoptive parent's fitness must be done by a licensed social agency. Once this is successfully completed every state requires the adoption to be finalized in court. This usually takes six months or more. Each state has its own statutes for governing adoptions. However, adoption between states requires one to go through a legal process called the 'interstate compact' (McKay, 1989).

"I then asked some friends, who were attorneys, of a recommendation for an adoption lawyer. Two of them recommended the same lawyer. So, I called him to make an appointment. But, we were both busy so I put it off. A few weeks later I went to a Stars of David meeting and there he was. He had come to talk about Illinois adoption law. And, I wouldn't even have to pay him a fee to hear it. He spoke for two hours. Now, all this legal information was 'interesting' and 'useful.' However, in passing, he said two things which I thought were . . . striking. One, was that 80 to 90 percent of all adoptions were the product of word of mouth. I thought that was astounding. I had always assumed that people simply applied to an agency. Then a year or two later they got a baby. In fact, that's not the case. And, secondly, he said, 'Be *tenacious*. Tell *everybody* you know that you're interested in a baby.' And, that's exactly what we did. We told everybody.

"As a result of this we got a call one day from Bill, my barber. My wife answered the phone, I wasn't home. He said, 'I'm afraid this is a little embarrassing, but I talked to your husband about adoption, he said you were interested. Are you still interested?' 'Yes', she said. He told her that one of the women in the shop knew a lawyer who had a baby available. So my wife said that I would call him after work.

"That night I called the lawyer and asked about the baby that was available. He said, 'The mother is six months pregnant. She is a typical 27 year old city Italian girl with a typical 27 year old city Italian boyfriend. She wants to give up her baby. And, she will be willing to have any tests you want to guarantee that the baby is healthy.' So, I said, 'An AIDS test?' 'No problem, she's healthy.' I said, 'Does she take drugs?' 'No! Oh . . . not for years, and then just a little.' 'Smoking?' 'Yes, she does smoke.' After several minutes of these kinds of questions I finally said, 'Why does this woman want to give up the baby?' 'Well, she wants to quickly and definitely arrange an adoption so that she can go to Cook County Jail and serve her term for burglary. Then she can get on with her life.' 'Oh,' I said, 'and how much will this cost?' 'It will be $17,000 for her and me.' Which meant $30,000 with my lawyer and the medical expenses. That is the going rate for private adoptions, under the table. 'But', the lawyer said, 'we have to know *today*.' So, I called my lawyer, the one from the Stars of David meeting. He was out of town for a few days. I finally got a hold of him, and told him about my conversation. Now, my lawyer is a very nice, affable fellow, and a very straight arrow—that's why we hired him. So, I began to tell him what the other lawyer had said. But, in the middle of the story he cut me off. He was furious. He yelled, 'This sounds like baby selling to me!' He then paused and said, 'But, I'll call and see what he has to say. Maybe, we can work out a deal.'

"An hour later he called me back and said, 'I talked to the lawyer and he told me the same story that he told you. So, I told him, that I'm advising my clients not to become involved.' He then went on to explain that this was baby selling, which was a felony. And since you were committing a crime, anytime this woman wanted her baby back she could file a lawsuit and automatically get the baby back.

This reminded me of the story of some Israeli couples. They adopted babies who were kidnapped off buses in El Salvador during the civil war or snatched from public markets in Brazil. Then, with some cash to the right officials, paperwork of 'dubious validity' appeared and the kids were 'adopted,' actually, smuggled out. However, a British television crew uncovered this and some of the couples had to give their babies back (Jaffe, 1991; "Israeli Couple, Six Brazilians Arrested For Alleged Baby Smuggling," 1993; "Brazil Charges Israelis in Baby Scam," 1993; Fieweger, 1991; "Israelis Hear About Bribery In Latin American Adoptions," 1988; Peters 1988a, 1988b; Neubauer and Germund, 1988; Schmetzer, 1995).

Also, we didn't want to get involved in a situation in which the birth father arose from the primordial ooze and took our baby. And, this whole story could have simply been a scam (Stevens and Tennison, 1993; Franks, 1993; Drell, 1994; Enstad, 1993).

"Incidentally, when our lawyer told the other lawyer that he was committing a crime the other lawyer said, 'Oh, I didn't know that. I do real estate.'

"By turning down this baby we had done the 'rational' thing. But, we gave up *my* baby. And, it was hard to do.

"The day after my initial call to the lawyer I got a second call about a baby. A friend of mine was sitting in the beauty shop next to a lawyer. The lawyer told her that she knew of a baby that was available. This lawyer, I was told, knows a guy, let's call him, 'Izzy from Indianapolis.' And, Izzy know of a baby. So, are we interested? 'Sure,' I said. So, I called Izzy. I said that I had gotten his number from so and so and I had heard that there might be a baby available and was it true. He said, 'Yes.' He explained that he has two biological children and two adopted children; and he was very, very, happy with his adopted children. And, he liked to help other people adopt. So, he knew this doctor who has babies that become available from time to time. So I asked, 'Well, can you tell me the story of the current baby that is available?' He said, 'This doctor I know has a patient, a young woman, who is six months pregnant. She's having twins, and she wants to give up her babies.' 'How come?' 'The usual story. Some guy knocked her up and left town. Now she's at sea. So, she wants to give up her babies.' And, now, being wise to the ways of the world, I said, 'And, how much will all this cost?' He replied, 'The usual market value for an NWI times two, $50,000 to $60,000.'"

"What does that mean?"

"These things are talked about in code—in the adoption subculture. What it meant was: 'Everybody,' at lease most of the white people in the suburbs, want an 'NWI', a Normal White Infant. And, usually it costs $30,000 for an NWI—under the table.

"So, I said to him 'Well, why don't you have the doctor call me and we'll talk some more.' I asked a number of other questions about money. I think I asked too many questions about money. That was because at one point he said, 'Of course you know it will cost $50,000 or $60,000, but we won't tell the judge that.' So, again I said to have the doctor call me. But, the doctor never did.

"Incidentally, there are 'gray market' adoptions—barely legal adoptions. And, this and the Italian baby were 'black market' adoptions—illegal. But, it happens *every day*. That's because people come to a lawyer and say, 'Get us a baby, we don't care how you do it.' It's supply and demand. And, the lawyer produces—for $30,000. He gets an NWI. It happens every day (see McNamara, 1975: 75-84). By the way. A couple of years ago a lawyer told me that female Jewish babies in California go for $70,000 each. And, male Jewish babies are $100,000 each. I don't believe it. But, that is what he said."

"Really?"

"Well, that is what he said. Anyway, we continued to be . . . tenacious. For example we were sitting in a restaurant with some friends. They said, 'Oh, there is Doctor So and So. He's somebody we know.' So we said, 'What kind of doctor is he?' 'An obstetrician.' So I said, 'Let's go say hello.' We went over and chatted. Then I said, 'Oh, by the way, we are interested in adopting. Do you know of any babies that are available for adoption?' He replied, 'No, today girls, women, feel they have an *absolute moral obligation* to keep their baby. It doesn't matter what age they are and whether they are married or not. So, I never see any babies for adoption.' In spite of this I gave him my card, just in case.

"Another time a friend called us and said, 'I know this woman whose mother is a missionary in Ecuador. She knows a lot of rich people. And, she has access to 'white babies' that are normally reserved for the upper class. So, she can get you a white baby from Ecuador. Here's her name and number.' I was uncomfortable with this white-baby talk. But, we called and spoke to her. We thought we might be able to get a baby out of this, of some color. However, we made our Romanian connection before anything developed.

"As our search broadened we met someone who knew the deputy director of family services at the local naval base. They suggested that I give him a call. So I did. I asked him if he knew of any babies that there were available. He said, no, but, I gave him my number anyway. Then I spoke to a friend whose daughter went to a local Catholic girls' high school. I asked him if they ever had any spare babies. 'At Saint Sybarite by the Lake?' he exclaimed, 'No, never!' But, I asked him to pass my name on to the nuns, in case.

"One day we spoke to a women who ran a home health care agency that brought over Polish women to work as domestics. We mentioned that we were interested in adopting. She said, 'It's too bad I didn't know sooner. Sometimes some of these women get pregnant. But, they can't take their babies back home because they're already married. This happened not long ago. And, the woman had to get rid of the baby before she went back to Poland.' 'Well, keep us in mind for the next time,' I said. But then she added, 'I also happen to know someone who can get you babies from Poland.' 'But, I heard Poland requires you to be Catholic, to be no more than two generations out of Poland, and speak some Polish.' 'No. He's Jewish and he has contacts in the hospitals.' His name was 'Lech.' I called Lech and I asked him to give me the details. In a heavy Polish accent he said, 'I think you need come in. I don't want talk over phone.' He sounded like a crook. We didn't pursue this either because we made our Romanian connection shortly thereafter.

"I also called the family doctor of a friend of mine. She had told me that he had gotten her a baby a few years ago. I explained to the nurse that I was a friend of so and so and did the doctor know of any babies that might be available. She said, 'Oh, no! We *never* have that kind of information. Oh, no! No, no!' My friend is a judge's daughter. So, perhaps, the nurse thought that I was really a cop.

"We were also given the name of a lawyer in New York, I'll call him 'Stanley Milgram.' He's very well-known in adoption circles. The name was given to us by a friend whose wife was an adoption worker. We had heard some vague story that he recruited pregnant women in Appalachia. When they gave up their babies he then placed them 'up north'. From these girls he produced large quantities of white babies for adoption, at inflated prices. Later, I ran across an article about adoption in Texas. It turns out that he is involved in Texas and not in Appalachia. The article said that what Reno once was to divorce, San Antonio now is to adoption. The number of Texas-born children adopted by out of state couples jumped from 500 in 1986 to 810 in 1989. This had occurred because Texas has extremely permissive adoption laws. As a result of this lawyers import pregnant women into the state. San Antonio, which has less then one million people, has 14 adoption agencies, which apparently, is a large number. Six of these have opened since 1984. The article said that one adoption agency worker commented, 'The girls know they can shop around here. They pick the agency that can give them the nicest place to live and the most money.' The article went on to explain that 'unlike the years of bureaucratic maneuvering required to open an agency elsewhere it is easy to get a license in Texas.' One state official said that applicants must meet the standards, but that the standards are 'rock bottom.' This all began in 1984 when an agency called 'The Adoption Services Associates,' or ASA, opened in San Antonio. Since then they've become 'Babies 'R Us.' They've placed 750 infants in just three years. And, almost all of them have been out of state. These babies are both 'precious' and 'pricey.' ASA charges adoptive parents $4,500 to $5,500. And, then adds $10,000 for the upkeep of each pregnant woman. With about 250 adoptions a year the agency makes $1 million annually (Gordon, 1991a; see also Gubernick, 1991).

"At this point in my search I got a call about an orientation meeting for Korean adoptions. So I went downtown for the meeting. There were about 50 people there. The agency had invited three couples with their Korean babies to show off—advertising. These children were two or three years old. They ran around the room endlessly. And, they were *so* cute. During the orientation we were told that a Korean adoption would cost $10,000 or $12,000. And these children were *so* cute I was ready to write a $30,000 check on the spot. But, sadly, they were 'not available.'

"So, I listened to a talk. During the meeting they gave out the guidelines for Korean adoptions. The guidelines were: parents must be married for three years, one parent must be a United States citizen, and the family must make $20,000 a year or more. The applicants must also be in good mental and physical health and have medical coverage. They expected one parent to be in the home for the first six months after the child was placed. Both members of the couple must be between 25 and 45 years of age. Couples under forty could adopt an infant; but, couples over forty could only adopt a three to ten year old. And, couples over 45 needed the Korean government's special permission to adopt. Also, couples could have up to four children and still adopt a Korean child. But, if the family already had five children, then an older or a handicapped child would be the only possibility. The 'agency fee' for such an adoption was $3,000, but, then there was a $250 'application fee,' $1,125 'office interview fee,' $1,125 for a home visit, and $500 for visits after the child had arrived. There was also an 'overseas agency fee' of $2,580 which covered the cost of child care and documentation in Korea. There was also a $630 'donation' to the Korean agency to assist other children still in orphanages in Korea. And, there was an 'escort fee' of $1,100 to bring the child over.

"During the meeting they mentioned that the number of children coming from Korea had been cut back, dramatically. As a result of this it was much easier to get older, handicapped, or male children. I understood why it was easier to get older or handicapped children, but, I didn't understand why it was easier to get males. So, after the meeting I went over to one of the social workers and asked why males were easier to get than females. She said that 80 to 90 percent of all the people adopting Korean children asked for a female infant. 'Why?,' I asked. 'The *China Doll Syndrome*,' she replied. Everyone wants their own China Doll.'

"I asked her if we could have any input into the choice of a child. That is, could we ask for a child who was say, affectionate or sociable, versus one that was quiet or shy. 'No,' she replied. I also asked her a number of other questions. Then I said, 'By the way, what if I were to get a job in Washington? Can I start the process here and transfer my application to your Washington office?' She suddenly got very cold. She said, 'You really have to decide what your priorities are. Do you *really* want to try and get a job in Washington. Or, did you *really* want a baby?' I was not impressed with her response. I had thought the process was about adopting babies, not about . . . being assholes!

"I sense you had a bad reaction to this."

"Yes. But, let me go on. Before I filled out the application I thought I should call the other two agencies in the Chicago area that did Korean adoptions, just one more time. One agency said that they now had Korean children available. They were from seven to 16 years old. They also had Amerasian children from 10 to 16 years old. The waiting period was approximately one to three years. Since we wanted a baby and it was too long a wait, we forgot about that agency.

"I then called the other agency and they sent out some literature. It was rather thoughtful. They asked if you wanted your family to be interracial for generations to come? That was something people rarely thought about (see Boyle, 1992; Isaacs, 1989). However, the Korean adoption program was on hold at that time. But, they did have children available from Columbia, India, and Thailand. Apparently, it was much easier to get non-Korean foreign children because there wasn't as much of a demand. In fact, during the orientation meeting the caseworker said that she had a brother and sister waiting in India to be adopted. And, they were only a *little* malnourished. There was not a great wave of enthusiasm for these sad little children. In any case, a few months later I called one of these agencies and they said that applications were now open for Korean children. They had 'handicapped children and boys' available. I said, 'You mean handicapped boys?' She said, 'No, just boys.' This confirmed the China Doll Syndrome.

"By this time we had also contacted a number of well-known, out-of-state agencies about Korean and other foreign adoptions. One large agency in Minnesota said that since we were from Illinois they could only offer us Korean children that were 'older, siblings, and those with correctable defects, such as deformed arms and legs.' However, they had healthy Korean girls who were 10 to 14 years old, healthy boys from seven to 14, Amerasian children over two, and sibling groups of three or more. They also had programs for children from Hong Kong and a number of Latin American countries. There were also new programs for Greece and India. However, the Indian children were often premature, low birth weight, and between the ages of four and seven.

"We also received some literature from a well-known agency in Michigan. They said they had placed 2,300 children in the last 14 years. However, these children were often premature, had low birth weights, and the mothers usually had had no prenatal care. For Korean children they took applications only for 'waiting children.' These were kids who had medical conditions such as cleft palate, heart defects, orthopedic conditions, and so on. Also available were Korean kids who were school age siblings, or older children, such as boys over five or girls over nine. They also had children from Taiwan, India, and Honduras. These programs ranged in cost from about $4,500 to $7,000 per child.

"With the Michigan agency's application they included a questionnaire which asked about your feelings on the acceptability of adopting a child with 37 different medical problems. They asked about our willingness to accept a child with: low birthweight, birth mark, heart defect, Hepatitis B carrier, blood disorder (thalassemia, sickle cell anemia, hemophilia), a child needing a sex change operation, a child with a missing limb, a child requiring wheelchair living (due to spina bifida, cerebral palsy, polio, orthopedic problems, or congenital hip defect). It went on and on and on. They asked questions about the acceptability of children with malformations, webbing of the fingers, seizures, diabetes, cleft lip, severe malnutrition, kidney failure, burns, developmental delay, and syphilis. It was too depressing. I could not make these decisions. So, I put their applications away. I felt that if we already had had our own kids, then adopting a handicapped child would have been an option. But, for now, we just wanted 'a nice, healthy baby.'

"One Sunday afternoon, Susie and I went to a Stars of David party. We met a couple that had gotten a baby through surrogacy. They told us that they had been hesitant about surrogacy because they had been horrified by the Baby M case in New Jersey where the surrogate mother had refused to give up the baby. They had heard that the lawyer involved in the case had a bad reputation because 'he wasn't very careful' in recruiting surrogates. So, they did some research and found agency in California. The agency was well thought of because they were very careful about their screening of surrogates. As a result, the couple told us, the agency had never lost a baby because the surrogate had changed her mind and refused to give up the baby.

"This couple's story was fascinating. They told us that they had been matched with a woman that already had a husband and two or three children. When the surrogates cycle came up the 'future father' had to run to the doctor's office that night and give a 'specimen.' Then at midnight they had to air express a vial of his semen to California. On the first attempt the woman became pregnant. And without any difficulties she gave them the baby. Not only that, the surrogate's family was so happy for the adoptive parents that they threw them a baby shower. The experience, the couple told us, couldn't have been more wonderful. And, this had cost $20,000, which had included $10,000 for the surrogate mother.

"After the couple left Susie and I talked about their experience. Although they had a good experience the procedure seemed to me to be . . . extreme. An extreme, and expensive, way to propagate ones own genes. As if your genes were better than anyone else's. This seemed rather narcissistic.

"Later, I did some reading on surrogacy. Although the numbers are small, a few thousand babies have been born this way, the moral and ethical complications are large. In the Baby M case, William and Elizabeth Stern paid Mary Beth Whitehead $10,000 to allow an egg of hers to be fertilized by William Stern's sperm. She was to carry the child and then turn it over to the Sterns. In March 1986, the baby was born. Ms. Whitehead then changed her mind and refused to give up the baby. Eventually, the courts ruled that Ms. Whitehead was the mother but gave the Stern's custody. However, Ms. Whitehead was allowed visitation rights.

"This process leads to troubling ethical issues. For example: In surrogacy who is the 'real' mother? Is it the woman who gave birth? The woman who married the sperm donor? The woman caregiver? Or, the woman who can pay the most for the child? Is the biological mother just that, a biological mother? Or, is she merely a 'surrogate uterus?' Is a baby a 'thing' that people can fight over in court? Should such a court decision be made 'in the best interests of the child'? And, what are the child's 'best interests?' Are they primarily economic? Will this lead high income women to 'use' low-income women for 'breeding' when it is 'inconvenient' for high-income women to have children (see Johnson, 1993; Hanley, 1989; Chesler, 1988). This all seemed too morally ambiguous for me.

"Later, at that Sunday afternoon party, Susie told me that she was hesitant about adopting a Korean child. She feared other people's prejudices would hurt the child. In fact, I mentioned to a friend that we might adopt a Korean baby. He said, 'Oh, they're very cute. But, they grow up to be chinks.'

"So, Susie and I watched the kids at the party playing. There were children of all shapes, sizes, colors, and nationalities. There were Peruvian Jewish children, Chinese Jewish children, and Black-Hispanic Jewish children. They all were attractive and delightful. In the end Susie simply said, 'I'm confused.'

"Over the next few months Susie and I talked a great deal about adopting Korean children. Susie teaches on the northwest side in Chicago. She had Korean kids in her class. She thought they were bright, very well-behaved, and pretty. She said that there were a lot of Christian Korean children and a lot of Buddhist Korean children, but there were very few Jewish Korean children. And, what were to happen, say, 20 years down the road, if our son were to call up some princess and say, 'How about a date?' and she'd say, 'Oh, I'm not going to go out with you, you aren't really Jewish, you're Korean.' So, she felt it would be better, for all concerned, to leave the Korean children for Christian and Buddhist families, and for us to try to find a white baby. I didn't agree, but I understood. Besides, we wanted baby. But, we only qualified for a three to ten year old Korean child. Also, I recalled reading studies that showed that children over four tended to have psychological problems once they were adopted.

This was because they had a memories of their previous life. I didn't want that to happen. So, we decided not to pursue Korean adoptions.

"A few weeks later I thought to myself, if we could do an international adoption from Korea, why couldn't we do one from anywhere else? So, I took the Chicago phonebook out and turned it to the page marked 'Consulates.' I also dug up an old Washington, DC phonebook I had, in case I got a job in Washington. I opened that book to the page marked 'Embassy.' I put both books on my desk and I began to call. I usually had to talk to a specific consular official. This meant that I had to repeatedly call the consulate or embassy in order to reach that particular individual, who, of course, was never there. So, I made phone call, after phone call, after phone call. In fact, I spent my entire spring break on the phone making hundreds of phone calls.

"The first call I made was to the Romanian Embassy. That was because my wife had a bilingual Romanian class in her school. Several years ago the two Romanian teachers had told her: 'There were lots of babies in Romania. Why don't you adopt?' My wife said, 'When we're ready.' Well, now we were ready. So, I called the Romanian Embassy dozens of times, and nobody answered. When I told a Romanian-American friend about this he said, 'Hey, they're Communists. They don't care. They get paid whether they answer the phone or not.' Well, finally, they did answer. I then asked them who was in charge of adoptions. They said, 'Mr. Council Blaiken.' But, he was never in. After many, many calls, dozens, in fact, I finally was able to get a hold of 'Mr. Council Blaiken.' I had a little speech prepared. I said, in a perfectly modulated voice, 'How do you do. My name is George Klein and I am calling from Chicago. My wife and I are in our early forties and we don't have any children and we're interested in adopting. And, since my wife's grandparents came from Romania,' which was true, but a coincidence, 'might there be some children available?' He replied, 'I no understand. Please repeat.' So, I said, 'We wannum baby! You have um?'

"You really said that?"

"No. But, it was almost that bad. In any case, he said, spitting the words out as if he were a machine gun, 'Program suspended July 1988.' So, I said, 'When will the program be open again?' He replied, 'I do not know.' So, I then said, 'Well let me give you my name and address in case it does open up again. Thank you. I'll call you again.' I began to make other calls. I called Italy. No, no they said. No babies available. Denmark, no. Netherlands, no. Sweden, oh no, they said, they import their babies from Third World countries. Canada, no. Portugal, no. Australia, no. Austria, no, no, no! I called Hungary. One set of my grandparents were from there. So, I gave my speech. I said in my perfectly modulated voice, 'How do you do, my name is George Klein, I'm calling from Chicago. My wife and I are in are early forties and we don't have any children, and since my grandparents came from Hungary, might there be some babies available for adoption?' He said, 'It's *very* difficult to adopt in Hungary, even if you are Hungarian. No, no, I'm sorry. I can't help you.' So, I called the Greek Embassy. The gentleman said, 'Well, it is easy. You just find a Greek baby. Then you go to court and adopt it.' This was not helpful.

"I then called the Belgium Embassy. They said, 'Oh, we'll send you some literature.' They sent out a little brochure that mentioned an agency to write to. So, I wrote a letter, and our French instructor translated it. I offered to pay her, but she refused. So, I gave her several pounds of Hershey Kisses in payment. A few weeks later we received a nice little packet of information from the agency, in French, telling me about all the Third World children that could be adopted through this agency. This was not what we were looking for.

"I then called the German Consulate here and made my little speech. They said they would send out a brochure. It said: 'Adoption. Please contact the following agencies: Group I for Catholic children; Group II for Protestant children; and, Group III for Catholic and Protestant children.' I put the brochure in a drawer. I then called the Swiss Embassy and they gave me the address of an agency. I wrote a letter and had one of our faculty translate it for me into German. They wrote back and said, 'We only take German-Swiss children, and we only let German-Swiss people adopt them.' The Germans are a little arrogant, you know.

"I then called the Spanish Embassy and they said they would send out a list of all the adoption agencies in their country. There were only 24 agencies in the whole county. It's not like here, it is centralized. So, I wrote a letter and went to one of our Spanish instructors. I said to him, 'Could you translate this, and we'll send it out to all of the agencies?' He said, 'No, no, no. Don't sent it out to the ones in the south.' 'Why?' 'Because, you don't want any Gypsy babies.' 'I don't?' 'No, you don't.' 'Oh.' So, he picked 11 of the agencies in central and northern Spain and I sent out the letters. But, we had no luck.

"I called the French Embassy. They really did not want to bother with me but they said, 'Oh, let me mail you out the list.' We received the list. Again, it was centralized, so there were only 27 agencies in the whole country. So, I wrote a letter and took it to the French instructor. I said, 'Can you translate this for me, and then we'll send it out to all these agencies.' She said, 'Oh, no, no, no. You don't want to send this out to all of them. You might get Gypsy babies. We'll just send it to the agencies in central and northern France.' 'Oh,' I replied."

"What did your letter say?"

"Well, the French letter was different than all the others. Did I ever mention to you that when I went to Paris I realized that my soul was French?"

"Yes, *many times*. Why don't you go on with the story."

"Well, my letter said, 'I love Paris, I love France, I love the French language, I love French culture. I want to retire to France. But, in the meantime, do you have any babies to adopt?'"

"So, what came of all this letter writing?"

"Nothing. However, I did get a letter from an agency in Paris which said, 'We thought your letter was charming. We passed it around the office. But, we don't have any babies.'"

"Did you make any other calls?"

"Yes, I called Israel. They said that they imported Third World babies. So, I had no luck there. I called Ireland and I said, 'Do you have any red-haired, freckly faced babies?' They said, 'No.' I called Great Britain and said, 'Do you have any red-haired, freckly faced babies from Northern Ireland?' They said, 'Well, if you want to move here for three years, then we'll talk about it.' I said, 'Thanks anyway.'

"I also called the embassies of Latvia, Lithuania, and Estonia. One set of my grandparents had come from Lithuania. This was before Russia broke up. I had always assumed that their embassies were simply fronts for the Russian Government, but, in fact, they weren't. They were independent of the Russians. They were the product of the pre-World War II governments, and they lived off of the bank accounts frozen before World War II. In fact, in 1989 we still recognized the 'independent' governments of Latvia, Lithuania, and Estonia. It was all a diplomatic sham. So, I called the Estonian Embassy and gave my little speech. The gentleman said, 'Well, you know, Estonia is under Communist domination.' I said, 'Yes, I do know that.' He said, 'No, I'm sorry, I can't help you.'

"I then called the Latvian Consulate and they said, 'Oh, no, we don't know anything about this. You have to call the American Latvian Association.' So, I called them. They said, 'Oh, no, we don't know anything about this. You have to call this lawyer in Cleveland.' So, I called this lawyer in Cleveland and he said, 'Funny you should call. I am leaving for Latvia next week to try and set up an adoption program.' 'Oh', I calmly said. However, I told him there were two problems. One was that my grandmother came from Lithuania, not Latvia. And, secondly, that we were Jewish. He said, 'Oh, don't worry, there are lots of Jews in Riga. I'll see what I can do.' Many weeks later he hadn't called back. So, I called him. He said, 'Sorry, I can't help you. The same old gang is still in charge. There aren't going to by any adoptions.'

"In Lithuania my grandmother had lived between the two main cities in Lithuania, Vilna and Kovno* now called Vilnius and Kaunus. I called the Lithuanian Consulate and I said in my perfectly modulated voice, 'How do you do. My name is George Klein. I'm calling from Chicago. My wife and I are in our early forties and we don't have any children. We are interested in adopting. And, since my grandmother came from Kovno, and since we're interested in *renewing our cultural heritage*, might there be some babies available?' There was a very long pause and the women said, 'God bless you!' I said, 'Well,

---

* pronounced: Vil-neh and Kov-neh

thank you,' I said, 'But, might there be some babies available?' 'Well', she said, 'I don't know, why don't you write me a letter.'"

"Let me interrupt. Was that 'renew our heritage' line sheer *schmaltz*?"

"I'm afraid so. In fact, Lithuanian Jews call themselves *Litvaks* and are raised in the Jewish community. Whereas, Lithuanian gentiles, they're mostly Catholic, call themselves *Lugens*. And, we don't have anything to do with the them. Let me explain. My grandmother came to America as a teenager. And, in my youth I remember my *baube* saying, 'You have to deal with the *goyem* until five o'clock. But, after five the gates to the ghetto close; and, you don't have to deal with those people anymore.' Also, when I was a kid, my grandmother would talk about World War II and how all our relatives that had stayed behind had been murdered. In these stories she always said the word, *geharget*, murdered, in Yiddish. I heard those stories over, and over, and over, again. I still *tingle*, literally, when I hear that word. And, it was the *Lugens* that helped the Nazis. So, there is little contact, and little love lost, between the *Litvaks* and the *Lugens*. But, that would have nothing to do with *my* baby. So, I wrote the letter.

"Several weeks went by, and the woman from the consulate finally wrote back. She said that she was sorry, but she couldn't help.

"In spite of her answer I thought that I might pursue this Lithuanian connection a bit further. Chicago has a lot of Lithuanians. In fact, about hundred thousand of the eight hundred thousand people of Lithuanian descent in the United States live in the Chicago area. Chicago sometimes is called Lithuania's second capital. So, I called the Lithuanian American Cultural Center and they gave me the name of the Honorary Lithuanian Consul General in Chicago. I called him and asked if it might be possible to adopt a child from Lithuania. He said, 'No, no. I don't think so. But, perhaps you could adopt from a Lithuanian American social agency.' I said, 'Okay.' Eventually he called me back and said that nothing could be done.

"About this time I happen to catch a story about a 'Free Lithuania' demonstration downtown. But, I didn't catch the name of the organizer. However, the next day there was an article in the paper that a Lithuanian editor had come to Chicago and he was being shown around town by a local Lithuanian American doctor (Warren, 1989; see also McRoberts, 1989; Johnson, 1991; Zabell, 1991; Zabell and Kiernan, 1992). So, I called him. I said in my perfectly modulated voice, 'How do you do. My name is George Klein. My wife and I are in our early forties and we don't have any children and we're interested in adopting; and, since my grandparents came from Kovno, might it be possible to adopt some children from Lithuania?' 'Lithuania, SSR*?,' he incredulously asked. So I said, 'Yes, why not?' He said, 'Well, I'll check into this.' Sometime later he called back and said the person I had to talk to was the Lithuanian representative in the Russian Embassy in Washington. He gave me his name and phone number. So I called, and called, and called. But, no one ever answered the phone. I eventually found out that he was only in Washington on Tuesday mornings. The rest of the week he was in New York at the United Nations. Even though I called every Tuesday morning for weeks, I was never able to reach him.

"Also, right before I made my Romanian connection, there was a press conference sponsored by the Jewish Federation in Chicago (Jouzaitis and Kass, 1991). One of the speakers said that Lithuania was 'an island of freedom' in a sea of Russian antisemitism. The press conference had been sponsored by the Jewish Federation and some congressman. So, I called the congressman's office and asked one of his staffers if he could help me get a baby from Lithuania. He never called me back. However, one of the fellows I called from the Jewish Federation had contacts in 'Friends of Seudis.' Seudis was the name of the independence movement in Lithuania. From Friends of Seudis he got me the name of someone to write to in Lithuania. But, I didn't write to him because I made my Romanian connection just then. However, later on I wrote, in order to help others adopt, but he never answered. So, in the end, nothing ever came of the Lithuanian connection."

Chapter 3

First Contact

"All of this went on for months. And, nothing came of it. It was very discouraging. However, by pure chance I happened to have a Romanian American student in one of my classes. I'll call him, Raymond Floriescu.* He was 35, had traveled widely, was very worldly, and very smart. So, we often chatted after class about politics or world affairs. One day, in the spring of 1989, he was sitting in my office. I said to him, 'By the way, do you know anything about adopting Romanian babies?' I thought he'd say, 'My father is an engineer,' or, 'My father is a plumber, I don't know anything about this.' But, when I asked him the question his face, literally, turned white. And then, just like in a cartoon, his jaw went 'clunk.' Then he said to me, 'Yes, I do know about babies in Romania. My mother-in-law was a doctor in orphanages for 20 years; and, she's visiting Chicago right now.' Now, I was the one who was shocked. My face turned white and my jaw dropped open, clunk. After the shock subsided, we made a date to get together for dinner with his mother-in-law.

"Raymond arrived at the restaurant with his wife, Elena, and his mother-in-law. His wife was a professional musician who had been a violinist in the Bucharest Philharmonic. His mother-in-law, Floriana, was a short, stocky, sweet-faced woman of about sixty. Floriana didn't speak English, but we were able to communicate through her daughter. We chatted and it was all very pleasant. However, after an hour she asked *The Question*: 'What kind of baby do you want?' We said that we wanted 'a nice, healthy baby.' She said, 'I think I can help you.' We were delighted. Cautious, but delighted.

"We went out with Raymond, Elena, and Floriana a few more times before Floriana returned to Romania. In the fall of 1989. Floriana went back to Romania. She soon called Elena and told her that all adoptions were currently frozen. That was because Nicoli Ceausescu, the president of the country, had been caught selling babies in Western Europe for $30,000 each. There had been a

---

* Many names in Romania end in 'escu' or 'eanu.' This ending means, son of, as in, Johnson.

scandal and all adoptions had been frozen. However, she hoped that when the Party Congress met at the end of the year they would quietly open up adoptions. Then she could help us.

"So, with cautious optimism, I went to a bookstore and picked up some travel books on Romania. One of them said that 'a trip to Romania, population 23 million, is somewhat like an expedition to the Arctic: both cost a lot and combine few comforts with many challenges.' However, Romania offered 'picturesque towns nestled among mountain ranges where peasants continued to thrive much as they did 100 years ago.' There were 'beautiful monasteries built in the Middle Ages richly decorated with colorful frescos in Moldavia.' And, 'remote swamps in the Danube Delta were filled with wildlife.' It said that in many ways Romania differed from the rest of Eastern Europe. That was because its language was a Romance language. And, it was Eastern Europe's least developed country. Although Romania had 'charming medieval towns' the guidebook recommended the country only to 'experienced and adventuresome Eastern European travelers.' This was because there was a scarcity of budget hotels, mediocre dining, and poor transportation. Also, tourism officials were often not willing, or able, to help. They concluded that a visit to Romania could prove to be a 'trying,' but 'unique' experience (Tanner, 1989).

"Also, hotels are often in poor condition and that transportation could prove to be a 'grueling experience.' They went on to say that 'long and bitter winters reign over Romania. Many hotels, as well as, private homes lack heat because of oil shortages. By March, however, the situation improves. Minimal heating exists and food is more plentiful; so spring can be a pleasant time of year to visit, as can, fall.' For those bothered by hot weather, they should avoid Bucharest in July and August as air-conditioning is almost nonexistent. And, they added that airline, train, and auto travel are slow, unpleasant, and chaotic (Tanner, 1989).

"I then began to look into Romania's history. One guidebook gave a brief summary of Romanian history (Fodors, 1989). It pointed out that Romania is quite different from the rest of Eastern Europe because of the Roman conquest of the area by the Emperor Trajan in 106 A.D. When the Roman's withdrew, about 200 years later, much of the Roman language and culture had been absorbed by the native Dacian population. There were a number of invasions over the next several hundred years but the Dacians retained the language and customs of the Romans. An alternate argument is that Romania was settled by a Latin-speaking tribe called the Vlahs a thousand years after the Romans; and from their name came Wallachia, "Land of the Vlahs." However, historians are still arguing about this.

"In the early Middle Ages the three ethnically Romanian states emerged: Transylvania, in the north; Wallachia, in the south; and Moldavia, in the northeast (Candurachi and Dricoviciu, 1971). After the fifteenth century, these states were subjected to continual Turkish attacks. One of the princes who held off the Turks in the mid-1400s was Prince Vlad Tepes. He was known as 'Vlad the Impaler' or 'Count Dracula.' Impaling was a nasty, but common, form of execution at the time. However, his reputation was transformed into one of a vampire by Bram Stoker's novel. However, many Romanians still consider him a great hero for holding off the Turks (Kozma, 1995).

"In 1600, the three Romanian states were briefly united. However, it was not until 1881, at the Congress of Berlin, that Wallachia and Moldavia were combined into the nation of Romania. The country was ruled by King Carol. After World War I, Transylvania was united with Romania. During World War II, the fascist Iron Guard took control and Romania joined the Axis.

"At the end of World War II, the Russians invaded and took control. In 1947, King Carol's son, Michael, formally abdicated and Romania became a communist state. Under communism Romania was industrialized, much like the rest of Eastern Europe. However, Romania was unique among Eastern European nations in its independence within the Warsaw Pact. For example, Romania's last participation in the Warsaw Pact military maneuvers was 1962. And, even through the Romanian government was Communist it prohibited any Soviet troops to be stationed in the country. In 1984, Romania sent athletes to the Los Angeles Olympics even though the rest of the Warsaw Pact boycotted the games.

"In 1965, Nicoli Ceausescu took control. He was the General Secretary of the Communist Party, Supreme Commander of the Armed Forces, and President of the State Council. He developed a cult of personality that was the most highly developed in Eastern Europe. Ceausescu's wife, Elena, was the first deputy prime minister, and his children and other relatives held other important positions in the government. This led some to say that they enjoyed 'socialism in the family.'

"The guidebooks pointed out that Romania had great financial problems. Although Romania boasted rich energy supplies and fertile farm lands they suffered from a 'faltering economy.' That was because much of their food supplies and oil were exported. This resulted in 'erratic shortages of consumer goods.' This export policy was the product of Ceausescu's obsessive desire to eliminate the country's foreign debt. In the Gorbachev Era, many Eastern European nations had experimented with some form of liberalization and private enterprise. Romania had not. Ceausescu declared that such policies were in total contradiction with 'socialist principles' (Tanner, 1989).

"One of the travel books pointed out that in many regions of Romania the way of life was barely different from that of a folk museum you could find elsewhere in Europe (Fodors, 1989). It then gave some details on the country. It mentioned that Romania had an area of 91,700 square miles. It was the 12th largest country in Europe, about the size of Yugoslavia, West Germany, Great Britain, or Oregon. In its population of 23 million, 88 percent considered themselves to be ethnic Romanians, 8 percent Hungarians, and 4.5 percent Germans. There was also a smattering of Slavs, Jews, Gypsies, Tartars, and Turks.

"This book then went into a more detailed history of Romania. It emphasized the Roman invasion and on how the Roman and Dacian cultures had fused. This gave Romania a 'tenaciously Latin heritage.' And, although Rome withdrew in 275 A.D., the culture was kept alive by soldiers and colonist who remained behind. In the fourth to the ninth century, there were many barbarian invasions. However, the Romanians were able to keep their cultural identity. Around this time there was a gradual penetration of Transylvania by the Hungarians. Over the centuries Hungarians, Turks, and the Hapsburgs ruled Romania. This lasted until 1918. (Fodors, 1989).

"Only in the mid-1800s did modern Romania begin to emerge. In 1859, the head of the army was elected the ruling prince of Moldavia and Wallachia. These two provinces were then united. Although Romania had considerable local autonomy, it was still officially part of the Ottoman empire. This ended in 1877 when Russia and Turkey went to war and Romania entered the conflict on Russia's side. The Treaty of Berlin in 1878 recognized Romania's full independence, however, Transylvania remained outside the new state. In 1918 after World War I, Transylvania was incorporated into Romania (Fodors, 1989).

"The years between World Wars I and II were chaotic. Economic crisis, bitter political strife, and the rise of fascism all intermingled. In the 1930s, the fascist 'Iron Guard' arose. In 1940, Romania was carved up as a result of the Hitler-Stalin Pact. Romania lost Bessarabia and Northern Bucovina to the USSR, the southern province of Dobruja to Bulgaria, and one-third of Transylvania to Hungary. King Carol was forced to abdicate in September 1940. Pro-Nazi Marshal Antonescu, backed by the Iron Guard, took control. In January 1941, the Iron Guard tried to oust Marshal Antonescu and seize power. But, Antonescu rallied the army and crushed the revolt. However, he soon led Romania into the war on Germany's side. On August 23, 1944, when the tide was turning against Hitler, Antonescu was overthrown and later executed. The group that took power was a coalition including King Michael and a number of antifascist parties, including the Communists. Romania then entered the war on the Allied side. As a reward for this Transylvania was restored to Romania after the war. However, Dodbruja, Bucovina, and Bessarabia were not. After the war King Michael was restored to his throne. However, in 1947 he was forced to abdicate. Romania then became a 'Marxist republic.' Since World War II, the Communists had made progress in education, medicine, industrialization, housing, and so forth. But by 1973 the rise in world oil prices had badly hurt the economy. Also, the development of a large petrochemical industry proved to be a costly miscalculation. As a result, Romania was saddled with a massive foreign debt that Ceausescu decided to repay at 'breakneck speed.' A vast percentage of all products were exported. As a result of this, Romanians suffered chronic shortages of 'everything' including food, fuel, medicine, and consumer goods. It also lead to interminable lines, rationing, and a thriving black market (Fodors, 1989; see also Goetz, 1990; Bair, 1991).

"All this was 'interesting' but it was utterly meaningless. My eyes would glaze over when I read it. It didn't mean anything to me. This was just 'information,' in the worst sense of the term.

"After I finished my reading, I began to look around for a travel agency that could get me to Romania. I opened the phonebook and found an agency that specialized in Eastern European travel, and particularly, Romania. So, I called and had a brochure sent out. The cover letter said that they were the 'Official Romanian Tour Company' in the United States. Pretty impressive, I thought. That was until I looked at the tour they sponsored. 'Dracula, Tour to his Homeland for Halloween' for $1,599. I called a friend who worked at a travel agency and asked her for material on Romania. She replied, 'I don't know what you are talking about. But I'll go look in our files.' She found a few pages of material and sent them off to me. Attached was a note that read: 'This is from a 1982 Pan Am book.' Later, she sent some brochures about 'the colorful countryside'. It showed peasants in their 'colorful costumes' and the 'colorful' tourist hotels on the Black Sea.

"I then stopped by the office of a big, national travel firm. Their brochures said that I could take 'The East European Grand Tour.' This would allow me to go to Bucharest with its 'tree lined boulevards and terraced restaurants which were curiously reminiscent of Paris.' I called the Chicago Council on Foreign Relations and they sent me a brochure on their Danube cruise. It said that during the cruise we would stop in Bucharest, 'the Paris of the Balkans.' Another travel agent offered a tour of 'The Bewitching Balkans.' During the day I could go sight seeing. At night I would have 'gracious dining' in a 'splendid hotel' featuring 'colorful Romanian folk dancing and music.' Many of the travel agents I spoke to seemed to think I was asking about, the moon.

"Since Romania seemed so foreign I thought I would call Lindblad, which advertises about 'exotic destinations.' In fact, they offer a trip called, 'Adventure: Mongolia.' I received a brochure from them about a 'Blue Danube Cruise' where I could visit Bucharest, 'the Paris of the East.' I stopped by the office of another national chain of travel agencies and asked for their literature on Romania. The woman looked dumbfounded. She went to her files and pulled out three brochures from 'Love Holidays—Uni-World.' A few pages after 'Central Asian Adventure' was 'The Grand Tour of Eastern Europe-Deluxe,' 22 days. On Day 14 I would be in Bucharest. There I could shop for 'beautifully embroidered blouses and other handi-crafts.' I said to the woman, 'Could I have copies of these brochures?' 'Take them,' she insisted. I said, 'But, it's your only copy.' 'Take them!' she ordered.

"I then called the Romanian National Tourist Office in New York. I asked them to mail out some information. Many weeks later I received a page cut out of a magazine about 'How to enjoy your stay in Romania.' I also received a brochure on the spas of Romania, and a badly printed brochure with fuzzy pictures. I dutifully read all of this material. But, as I mentioned earlier, none of it meant anything to me. It was just like the moon to me."

Chapter 4

The Revolution

"One night, in December 1989, I went down to the basement to work out. I put on my sweats, my headphones, and climbed onto my exercise bike. I then rewound the tape in my VCR. I hit play. I saw that there was a revolution in some god forsaken Eastern European country. In . . . Romania! Blood rushed to my face and I gripped the handle bars. I peered intently at the TV screen. The reporter said that the revolution had been sparked by the attempted arrest of Lazlo Tokes.* Tokes, a Lutheran minister, was the leader of the ethnic Hungarian minority in Timisoara.** On December 15, 1989, the secret police, the Securitate, had come to arrest him. However, a large crowd had gathered. When the Securitate had moved towards his house someone in the crowd shouted, 'Down with the dictator!' There were several seconds of stunned silence. Then everyone joined in. The crowd grew, but the police did nothing.

"The next day large crowds gathered. They denounced Ceausescu. But, again the police and the military did not respond. On the following day, Sunday, December 17, one hundred thousand people poured into the main square in Timisoara. It was warm, and the crowd was festive. However, the army was called out; early in the evening the soldiers were ordered to fire on the crowd. Some refused and threw down their weapons. They were immediately shot by Securitate officers. Some people held up children in front of them, so the troops would not fire. But they fired anyway. The children and their parents were both killed. Thousands were reported to have been killed.

"The next few days I rushed home from work and clicked on the news; but, Romania was quiet. A few days later there was rioting in Bucharest. It began when President Ceausescu called a mass rally in the square in front of the Central Committee Building. Such rallies were routinely organized by the Communist Party. But, this time large numbers of ordinary Romanians joined in with the party faithful. Ceausescu gave a speech. At one point he called the

---

* pronounced: To-kesh.
** pronounced: Tee-mee-shwa-rah.

demonstrators in Timisoara hooligans. A murmur began in the crowd. Then shots were fired. Shouts of 'Murderer' and 'Give us back our dead!' were heard. Ceausescu was stunned. His mouth dropped open. The television cameras went dead, and he fled.

"Thousands of demonstrators then poured into the Central Committee Building. They made speeches and burned thousands of volumes of Ceausescu's books. The demonstrators, tears streaming down their faces, danced around the flames. Thousands of other demonstrators marched to University Squares. There was a confrontation in the square with the army and several people were killed. A large group of demonstrators marched to the television station. The station was seized and the revolution was announced over the air. One speaker declared, 'God has turned his face towards Romania again.'

"At the urging of 'Free Romanian Television' a million people poured into the streets of Bucharest. Many of them were students. As the demonstration grew snipers suddenly began to fire into the crowd. Many were killed. Soldiers, who had joined the revolution, fired back. Civil defense armories were looted and citizens formed armed 'patriotic guard' units. The army and patriotic guards fought side by side against the snipers. They flew the Romanian tricolor flag, with the Communist symbol cut out. This was called, 'the flag with the hole in the middle.'

"As the battle raged the National Salvation Front took power. The Front was a coalition of anti-Communists and former Communists who had fallen from Ceausescu's favor. Ion Iliescu emerged as its leader. Although the National Salvation Front had taken control of the television and radio stations, the situation in the streets was chaotic. For three days there were pictures of soldiers and civilians crouched in corners, firing at snipers.

"Then Ceausescu was captured. He and his wife had fled from the Central Committee Building and flown off in his helicopter. But, the pilot had landed and abandoned them on a lonely highway. A group of patriotic guards had then captured them. They were taken to an army base and driven around in a tank so that the Securitate could not locate them. Eventually, they were taken to Bucharest and put on trial. They were charged with genocide. After a brief trial they were convicted and sentenced to death. Three hundred soldiers volunteered to shoot them. The Ceausescus were led into a courtyard, stood up against a wall, and shot. It was December 25, 1989.

"The trial and execution had been filmed. The next day the film was played on television, over and over again. And there was the image of the Ceausescu's bodies, with little trickles of blood coming from their ashen faces. Soon, the fighting died down. Within a few days the revolution was over. Romania was free!"

Chapter 5

AIDS

"Shortly after the revolution shocking, bizarre, articles began to appear about Romanian babies. The first was on January 10, 1990. It said that before 1966, contraceptives in Romania were shoddy and in short supply. As a result of this abortion was very common. In 1965, for example, there were 274,000 live births and over 1.1 million abortions. President Ceausescu was unhappy with the country's shrinking workforce. So, he banned abortions in 1966. In just one year, live births doubled to 528,000. However, as the number of births went up, the standard of living began to go down. Soon illegal abortions increased dramatically. Also, maternal deaths shot up. They went from 235 in 1966 to 506 in 1968. By 1983, the birth rate had fallen back to its 1966 level. The government responded to this by further restricting abortions, banning contraceptives, instituting monthly pregnancy exams for women, and heavily taxing single persons and childless couples. As a consequence of such policies births again began to go up; but, so did the number of unwanted children. Orphanages were soon overflowing with abandoned babies. Also, healthcare was inadequate. As a result of this, the infant mortality rate was high—about 80 deaths per 1,000 infants. In Sweden, however, it was 7 per 1,000 (Burke, 1990; Reaves, 1990c).

"On January 11, 1990, there was an article about an orphanage in Plataresti.* This home was one of 28 established to house the disabled. The home lacked adequate heat, light, food, and medicine. That was because Ceausescu had decided that his people no longer needed 'social assistance.' One government official explained that it was difficult to ask for money for a problem that did not exist. As a result, the children were starving and dying from the cold. A quarter of the children in the home died each year. For those who survived, many did not know how to speak, play, or even watch television. Some teenagers did not even function at the level of even one year olds. The staff consisted of untrained peasants who could not read or write. And, after sundown the orphanage was dark because the staff stole the lightbulbs (Sudetic, 1991b).

---

* pronounced: Plah-tah-resht.

"Dr. Barbara Bascombe, an American pediatrician working in the orphanages, painted a similar picture. She counted that there were over 100,000 children in orphanages in Romania. Many of these children were developmentally disabled. Four and five year olds often functioned like two year olds. Other children hid in corners, rocked on their hands and knees, or banged their heads on pipes. Some children had grotesque deformities because there was no one to treat them. This was the result of the Ceausescu's 'peculiar' ideas about healthcare. For example, the entire profession of psychology was disbanded because it was seen as a cult. Also, specialization for physicians beyond medical school was seen as a waste. And, medical school professors were often uneducated political hacks. Because of this lack of training, staffing, and minimal physical care many children simply died. Without adult nurturing some of those that survived became amoral psychopaths (*Morning Edition*, 1991; Battiata, 1990b; see also Ingram, 1992b).

"On January 15, 1990, I read an article that gave more details. In 1966, a year after Ceausescu came to power, Romania adopted legislation mandating a prison term of from one to five years for any illegal abortions. Abortions were permitted only if a woman already had five children. In 1986, the law was tightened so that an abortion for any woman under 45 became illegal unless her life was in danger. The result of these laws was frequent self-abortions. The most common method was to push a rubber tube up into the uterine cavity. However, such methods often produced life-threatening medical crises. For example, Bucharest Municipal Hospital alone handled 3,000 failed abortions in 1989. And, 200 of these women required major surgery. Furthermore, every one of these patients was examined by a commission that included a policeman and a public prosecutor. In order to avoid a jail term many women never went to the hospital for help. As a result of these self-abortions it was estimated that 500 to 1,000 women a year died in Bucharest alone. This abortion related mortality rate was ten times higher than the European average. It has been estimated that at least ten thousand women died from unsafe abortions under Ceausescu. In the first year after the revolution, however, once abortions became legal, the maternal mortality rate fell 50 percent. This was the result of one million abortions being performed in 1990. One study concluded that Ceausecu's policy was not pro-natalist but, actually anti-natalist. That was because there were fewer healthy women alive who could bear children (Dobbs, 1990: Stephenson, et.al., 1992; Sudetic, 1991a; Reaves, 1990c; Barringer, 1991).

"On January 22, 1990 there was an article in *Newsweek* entitled 'Over-Planned Parenthood: Ceausescu's Cruel Law.' It said that when Ceausescu had decided that he wanted to increase the population of Romania from 23 million to over 30 million people he decreed: 'The fetus is the property of the entire society, anyone who avoids having children is a deserter who abandons the laws of national continuity.' Ceausescu then made books on sex education state secrets. Women under 45 were rounded up at their work-place every month and taken to clinics where they were examined for signs of pregnancy. These doctors were called the 'menstrual police.' Although abortion was illegal, 60 percent of all pregnancies probably ended in abortions or miscarriages. And, because abortions were illegal, they were expensive. They cost from two to four months salary. However, if something went wrong, the woman was usually afraid to go to a hospital (Breslan, 1990).

"In 1986 members of the Communist Youth League were sent to quiz citizens about their sex lives. They asked, 'How often do you have sexual intercourse?' 'Why do you fail to conceive?' Women who did not have children, even if they could not, had to pay a 'celibacy tax' of 10 percent of their monthly wages. Also, about 10 percent of all babies were born underweight. Newborns, weighing under 3 pounds 5 ounces were classified as 'miscarriages' and denied treatment. And, many unwanted babies ended up in orphanages. One doctor said, 'The law only forbade abortion, it did not promote life' (Breslan, 1990; see also Churchill, 1991).

"A couple of weeks later, the first article on AIDS among babies in Romania appeared. The article noted that tests by Romanian and French virologists had revealed that of over 1,000 children under age 13 tested for AIDS in Romanian orphanages 367 had tested positive. The children were the victims of direct transfusions of unchecked blood, and repeated use of unsterilized hypodermic needles. Also a common practice in Romania was for 'body to body' transfusions, and a single adult might give blood for up to 15 children. Also hypodermic needles might be used hundreds of times. Romania had only one blood screening machine in the entire country and that was in Bucharest. Further, disposable syringes and plastic surgical gloves were nonexistent. One doctor commented, 'Nothing which is normally done in other places is done here, that's why these children had AIDS' (Lethwaite, 1990a).

"A front page article in the *New York Times* soon followed. It began with a story about sixty babies on the third floor of a drab hospital, the only AIDS facility in Romania. In some rooms there were two babies to a crib. In one small cubicle four infants close to death lay in a row under a single blanket. Amid the cries and moans of the children the nurses scurried about. But they could not keep up. Many of the babies lay in wet clothes. The ones with shrunken, wrinkled faces died without anyone noticing (Bohlen, 1990g).

"Throughout the country two thousand children had been checked so far for AIDS. Two hundred and fifty of them had AIDS, and two hundred others tested positive for the HIV virus. The AIDS epidemic among Romanian babies seems to have been the product of an old practice—that of injecting blood into the umbilical cords of infants to stimulate their growth and give them immunity to diseases. Since the practice only required a small dose of blood, one pint of AIDS contaminated blood could be used for many babies. This practice of injecting blood from adults into infants and small children fell out of use in the 1930s in the United States and Europe (Bohlen, 1990g).

"In Romania, however, the story of AIDS wasn't just about outmoded medical practices. It was more perverse than that. When the first hint of AIDS occurred in Romania, Ceausescu declared that the virus did not exist in his country. So, there was almost no AIDS testing and all information about AIDS was considered to be a state secret. As a result of this policy there was no official acknowledgment of the AIDS virus in Romania until after the revolution in December 1989. However, Ceausescu's policy began to crack about six months before the revolution. The first evidence of AIDS among children had occurred in June 1989, when a doctor tested a 12 year old girl and unexpectedly found that she had AIDS. He did more testing and the results surprised him. Of the 150 children that he tested, 31 were positive for the HIV virus. Twenty-nine of the 31 were under three years old. This finding was unexpected because these children had been chosen as a control group. All these children seemed to be suffering from pneumonia, diarrhea, and infections. When the physician reported his findings to the authorities, the Ministry of Health instructed him not to do any further testing. These children were then moved from one clinic to another. Eventually they were sent home to die.

"Physicians then went to Constanta,* on the Black Sea coast, and to Giurgiu,** directly south of Bucharest on the Danube, to test for AIDS. They found children who were suffering from persistent infections, but a diagnosis of AIDS never occurred to them. One doctor said, 'If you were told there was no such virus in Romania, why would you expect to find it?' However, there was further testing. It was found that 138 out of 192 babies that were tested were HIV positive. At that point the authorities' said, 'Stop, you are playing around.' So, the doctors stopped their testing; and, they never sent their findings to the World Health Organization. In the fall of 1989, a conference on AIDS for Romanian pediatricians was cancelled.

"Since the revolution, however, testing has begun. This time it has been done by primarily French physicians. However, in early 1990 more than two thousand samples of blood were waiting to be tested at Bucharest's Virology Institute. However, the doctors there had only 500 test kits. Also, early in 1990, at Victor Babes Hospital in Bucharest, two nurses said they had recently seen 20 or 25 babies die of AIDS; and two or three children, whose limbs were as thin as sticks, would die that very night. One of the nurses said that these children had no parents and they attach themselves to them as if they were their real mothers. One nurse said that 'it's a work of big love' (Bohlen, 1990g).

"The following day another article appeared in the paper. It pointed out that only 138 adults were infected with the HIV virus in all of Romania. How-

---

* pronounced: Cos-tan-za.
** pronounced: Jir-ju.

ever, out of 2,184 children tested, 706 had been found to be infected. And, in Cerevoda, near Costanta, one-third of all the children at the orphanage were infected with AIDS. However, treatment was very limited. At Victor Babes Hospital in Bucharest, for example, there were only ten bottles of penicillin to treat all the children with AIDS (Castelnau, 1990).

"In May 1990 there was another article in the *New York Times*. It showed a picture of a nurse covered in a gown and mask bathing an AIDS baby. The baby's body was limp and lifeless. However, the baby's eyes were filled with terror. The article pointed out that Romania was hampered by a shortage of equipment and a sluggish bureaucracy that had made only 'halting strides against AIDS in infants.' And, even as late as May 1990, only 20 percent of all the blood donations in the country were being screened for AIDS. However, blood transfusions to babies had been stopped. Also, blood donations by high risk groups, such as homosexuals, prostitutes, and people infected with hepatitis, had been curtailed. However, the situation for children with AIDS had improved, somewhat. AIDS babies now had their own cribs, received disposable diapers, and were getting some individual attention (Bohlen, 1990f).

"The mothers of a number of AIDS babies were tested for the illness. Only 6.7 percent of the 193 mothers located and tested for the virus showed they were infected. Also, almost half of the diagnosed cases came from the area around Costanta, Romania's main port on the Black Sea. It was assumed that the disease took root there among sailors and then spread by transfusion (Bohlen, 1990f).

"In June 1990, another dreadful article appeared. It said that foreign doctors had recently found 75 orphanages in Romania that they did not know existed. Some of them were no more than bare rooms in village houses with naked children huddled on the floor. These children received no professional attention during Ceausescu's 'Era of Light.' At the orphanages the children were divided into two groups, the normal and those with handicaps or 'incorrigible behavior.' The handicapped and incorrigibles were sent to other institutions to die. The remaining children received slightly better care until they were capable of working (Bohlen, 1990g, 1990f; Battiata, 1990b; Rothman, 1990).

"In June 1990, there was a photo essay in the *New York Times* magazine section entitled 'Romania's Lost Children' (Nachtway and Hunt, 1990). The photos were touching, but I had seen many similar images before: the boy screaming in his prison-like crib, four teenage boys crowded together in a tub of filthy water, a boy tied to the bars of a dirty bed, and babies, looking 80 year olds, dying of AIDS. But one photograph haunted me. It was a picture of three children in an orphanage. In the background a boy sat laughing in a crib. Below the crib was a girl who lay flat on her back on the floor, as if in a coffin. And, in the foreground, there was a boy in ill-fitting pajamas who played with the head of a doll. His piercing brown eyes stared directly at the camera. He did not ask, 'Why me?' He was too innocent for that. But, if he had asked, what could one have said to him? A madman condemned you to birth.

"Finally, in November 1990, the 'New York Review of Books' had a long article on how AIDS came to Romania. It described images of 'cadaverous' Romanian babies with the disease. This was Ceausescu's 'grisly legacy.' The article pointed out that Ceausescu was a 'single-minded' Communist who made 'production' the sole goal of the state. This included people, as well as, products. So, in October 1966, he simply declared that all women had to have four and later five, children.

"These policies had an uneven effect. Professional women had the power to simply refuse to cooperate with such policies. The urban middle class were able to get around these restrictions by getting contraception on the black market. And, although abortions were illegal, the middle class could secretly arrange for them through local doctors. They cost about $50. However, the urban working class was not so lucky. Doctors were sent to the factories every four months to examine all women of childbearing age. If a woman was pregnant she was 'registered.' If she terminated her pregnancy, she would probably go to jail. The peasants were relatively unaffected by this policy because the Romanian Orthodox Church forbade birth control and abortions. Thus, the brunt of the policy fell on the women of the urban working class. Some of these women tried to induce their own abortions or went to 'back alley abortionists.' As a result of this, abortion-related deaths increased 600 percent. It is also believed that some women committed infanticide. Many others carried their babies to term and abandoned them (Rothman, 1990).

"The regime's response to these large numbers of unwanted children was to create a system of orphanages. These orphanages probably held 150,000 children. One group, the '*leagane*,' was for newborns up to three years old. These probably held a total of ten to fifteen thousand children. A second group were for normal three to six year olds. Older, normal children went to a third group of orphanages. There were about forty thousand children in these institutions. However, one group of orphanages were for the handicapped, and the 'irrecoverables' (Rothman, 1990).

"The institutions for the irrecoverable, holding thirty thousand children, were for those who were 'abnormal.' These were children with problems such as cleft palate, clubfoot, paralysis, blindness, or mental disability. They also were for children who were too noisy, too quiet, troublesome, or, simply, 'bad.' In the United States many of these medical and behavioral problems were easily treatable. The children in those institutions lived in bare rooms on concrete floors. They had their heads shaved and they were kept in cages. They were fed very little. These orphanages were like Nazi concentration camps. As a result of these conditions, one-quarter to one-third of these children died each year (Rothman, 1990; Bohlen, 1990i).

"The article then went on to analyze the AIDS epidemic in detail. The AIDS epidemic began with the use of 'micro-transfusions' in babies. In this technique three to six tablespoons of whole blood from an adult were transfused into each baby. These transfusions were given to babies who were 'weak.' Instead of these micro-transfusions, the doctors could have fed the children preparations of powdered milk and fats. However, if they had done this they would have been subjected to questioning by state investigators. So the simple solution was to give micro-transfusions. Further, almost all illnesses in Romania were treated through the injection of antibiotics. For example, one epidemiologist found that it was not uncommon for a child to have 120 injections over a four-week period if they were ill. Also, needles were in short supply so they were frequently reused. So, micro-transfusion, repeated injections, and repeated reuse of needles made the AIDS epidemic in Romania inevitable (Rothman, 1990; Neely, 1991; Lynch, 1990; Kenny, 1990).

"In February 1990, a relative of ours, who is a doctor, called us and said that we should definitely not go to Romania. He said that AIDS was rampant. He knew this because he read it in numerous articles. That is, articles that I had sent him. Furthermore, he said that we would be foolish to go because 'those who are desperate are ripe for exploitation.' I didn't think that I was 'desperate' and I didn't think that I was 'ripe for exploitation.' But, I was very depressed about the Romanian AIDS situation. And, I wondered if there were healthy babies who could be adopted.

"I decided it was silly to keep guessing. So, I called Dr. Anthony Fauci, the director of the United States government's AIDS program. I thought, why play around, let's go to the top. When I called he wasn't in. So, I said that I really didn't need to speak to him, personally. What I needed was information about AIDS in Romania. So they transferred me to their international division. I spoke to its director. He said that he wasn't really *the* expert on Romanian AIDS. But, there was an epidemiologist who had been in the State Department and he was an expert on Eastern Europe. So, I was transferred to him. He explained that the AIDS epidemic was primarily localized in the south and east. In particular, it was in Bucharest, Costanta, and Ghirgui. There were only a few scattered cases elsewhere in the country.

"He went on to explain that you had to examine the medical records of any child you wanted to adopt. And, the key thing to find out was whether the child had had any transfusions or vaccinations. If they had, then you had to give them hepatitis and AIDS tests. Now, there were many French physicians in the country who were testing children for AIDS in all the orphanages. If a child tested negative on an AIDS test then the odds were that they were healthy. But, the virus didn't manifest itself immediately, and children grow very rapidly, so there needed to be a second AIDS test a few months later. That is, if you wanted to be sure. If the child tested negative on the second test then they were almost certainly healthy.

"I was relieved and thanked him for the information he had given me. And then I said, 'Well, the next time you're in Chicago, I'll treat you to a steak dinner. I really appreciate this information.' He then said, rather intensely, 'Well, if you *really* want to thank me, why don't you let me know how all this turns out.' I said, 'Sure.' But, the intensity of this request struck me as rather odd.

"About two weeks later he called me. He began by blurting out, 'Do you think you can get me some Romanian babies?' Aha! 'Well, first you have to do a family study,' I told him. 'And then you have to do the paperwork for Immigration. And, once that's all finished, I can give you some contacts.' Several months passed and I didn't hear from him. So, I called and said, 'How are things going?' 'Well,' he said, 'we've decided on what family service agency we are going to be calling to do the home study.' 'Oh,' I replied. I never heard from him again."

Chapter 6

Welcome to the Balkans

"In January 1990, two weeks after the revolution, Raymond called me and said, 'Maybe you should go to Romania, now.' I said, 'Well . . . I don't know what to do first. Let me look into this.' I knew you needed a family study so I called a local social agency. They said it usually took two or three months to complete a family study. Then I called the Immigration Service. I asked them what was involved in doing a Romanian adoption. They then began to pepper me with questions. For example, they asked, 'Have you filled out an I-600 or a I-600A yet?' 'No, I'm afraid I don't know what that is.' And they laughed at me, as if I were a fool."

"They actually laughed at you?'

"No, they chuckled . . . derisively."

"Jeez. Go on."

"Then they asked if I had death certificates from the orphan's parents? I said, 'Well, there is no orphan . . . yet.' They laughed, again. Then they asked, 'Do you have evidence that the orphans sole or surviving parent can not provide for the orphans care and, have you in writing proof that the parent, forever and irrevocably, has released the orphan for immigration and adoption?' I said, 'Well, there is no orphan . . . yet.' And, then they asked, 'Do you have a final decree of adoption?' 'Well, no, because there's no orphan . . . yet.' And, then they asked, 'Do you have evidence that the orphan has been unconditionally abandoned to an orphanage.' Well, after many, many of these types of questions, to which I had no answer, it was obvious that the adoption process was going to take a *very* long time.

"I soon learned it was even more involved than I anticipated. For example, as part of the application you have to submit your fingerprints to the Immigration Service. They then send them off to the FBI. The FBI fingerprint clearance, alone, takes three to four months. So I called Raymond back and told him that it would be impossible to go now. But, we could go on July 1. By that time the paperwork would be finished and Susie and I would both have completed our teaching for the year. Then we could go at our convenience, and stay as long as necessary. 'Fine,' he said.

"A week later the INS application arrived. I began to fill it out and chase around for documents. I also began the home study. The home study is conducted in order to satisfy the courts that the child is being placed in a suitable home environment. Most of it consists of questions concerning your lifestyle.

"I had no idea what agency to use for a home study. So, I called my adoption lawyer and he said, 'You're Jewish, aren't you?' 'Yes.' 'So, call Jewish Family Services.' So, I called them and spoke to their adoption caseworker. Our first appointment was a joint meeting with Susie and myself in the caseworker's office. It lasted an hour. Then Susie and I met separately with her for an hour each. And, then she came to visit the house and to talk with us further.

"For the first meeting we went to the caseworker's office. After waiting a few minutes the caseworker came out and called our name. I looked up and blurted out, 'You look like all the girls I went to high school with!'

"You really . . . you just said that?"

"Yes, but, it was true, and spontaneous. I think she laughed. I hope she laughed. Are you shaking your head?"

"Yes. But, go on."

"A couple of months later, at 8:30 am on Tuesday, March 2, 1990, the second day of my spring break, Raymond called. He said, 'Romania is flooded with French, Germans, and Italians. If you don't go today, you're not going to get a baby.' I said, 'Today?' He said, 'Yes, today.' 'Well, how about tomorrow?' I asked. 'Okay, tomorrow,' he said.

"Raymond then dug up a copy of a Romanian-American newspaper and looked up Romanian-American travel agencies. He found two in New York and one in Chicago. These were the agencies I needed to call in order to get a quick ticket on the national airline of Romania. And Tarom, because it was government subsidized, was one-half to one-third the cost of a regular carrier. So, he gave me the number of the Chicago agency and I called. I asked when the next flight to Bucharest was leaving. They said, 'Tomorrow, leaving from New York at 10:00 p.m. And, the fare is $537. However, the cost to get you to New York quickly, is about $537.' So, I booked a Wednesday morning flight from Chicago and the ten o'clock flight out of New York. However, Tarom only flew back from Bucharest on Wednesdays, so I had to stay a full week. Since I had no choice I made a return reservation for the following Wednesday.

"Because of the flight schedule I needed three days off from school. I called the college and spoke to an administrator. I said that I was going to Romania to adopt a baby. But, because of the airline schedule I needed to take three personal days off after spring break. The administrator was already mad at me because I had recently said to him, 'Can I go to a certain criminology meeting? He had replied, 'I have no objection to that.' So, I went. When he found out that I had gone to the meeting he was enraged. He wrote me a memo which said, 'Just because I said I had no objection to you going to the meeting, that didn't mean I gave you *explicit permission* to go. Please come in so that I might sanction you.' So, now, just a few days later, I said to him, I needed time off to go to Bucharest. His response was, 'This troubles me.' But, he finally said that if I could arrange for substitutes to cover my classes, I could go. So, I began calling faculty members. But, I couldn't reach anyone because it was spring break. And those faculty members that I did reach wanted to know why I was going. I had to talk for awhile, and be chummy, in order to seduce them into saying yes. But, I had no luck. I made call, after call, after call, with no luck. However, eventually, I lined up some people to cover all my classes. It took eight hours of calls. I was exhausted.

"Now, in order to adopt a child you have to have a myriad of documents. So, in between calls about my classes, I called Susie and told her I was leaving the next day for Bucharest. I told her that she had to stop on the way home and pick up some medical records. I called the doctor and he agreed to type out a one-sentence letter saying that my wife and I were both in good health. She also had to stop at the bank and pick up my birth certificate, her birth certificate, and our marriage license. When she got home we took everything, plus a bank statement, and the listing agreement for our house, to copy. We made six copies of everything. We did this because we might adopt two kids. If we did this we might have to leave two copies of the documents at the orphanage, two copies with the lawyer in Romania, and two copies with the American Embassy. We also had to go to the local police station. The police had to do a computer check to see if we were criminals. If we weren't, then they'd give us a piece of paper saying that we were okay. After they checked they gave us a statement saying: 'They are not criminals.'

"Once we finished this we were able to go out to eat. Afterwards, we went shopping. Raymond had told us that Romanian money, the *lei,** was worthless. So, all transactions were conducted, or at least expedited, with 'gifts.' We were told to pick up, first and foremost, cigarettes. In fact, cigarettes were the real currency of the country. Kents were preferable, but Dunhill, Philip Morris, and Virginia Slims were also good. Also, nylons, razor blades, audio tapes, makeup, hand lotion, clothing, and all kinds of food, particularly coffee and pasta, were all nice gifts. So, we went to Walgreens and we spent about $100 on Kents, razors, cosmetics, nuts, chocolates, and gum. We got home at about 11:00 p.m. I then had to pack. It took awhile. Finally, at about two or three in the morning I finished, and I went to sleep. But, since I still needed more documents, I got up at 5:00 or 6:00 a.m.

"When I woke up, I saw Susie was getting ready for work. A question suddenly popped into my head. An 'important question.' A question that, incredibly, had not occurred to me until just then. Once before an 'important

---

* pronounced: lay

question' of this type had come to me. I had once said to Susie, 'Are you going to end up going nuts one day because you never had any babies?' 'No,' she ebulliently replied, 'I have my puppies!'

This time I said to her, 'Do you trust me to pick out the babies . . . myself?' 'Sure', she nonchalantly replied. I was incredulous. She usually didn't trust me to pick out bananas at the grocery store. '*Really*?' 'Sure. I trust you.' 'Are you sure you don't want to come with me?' 'No. I have to teach. And, besides, we don't have anyone to take care of the puppies.' I shrugged. I kissed her good-bye and she went off to work."

"Did you ever discuss how many children you wanted?"

"Yes. But it was all . . . pretty vague. I didn't know what I'd find there. Or, what they'd offer me. We had talked and decided that one baby would be fine, and that two babies would be wonderful. However, I had said to her, 'But, what if there are two more babies that are terrific? How about . . . four?' She just shrugged."

"So, it was all pretty vague."

"Yes. In my head, it was all pretty vague. But, it turned out well. This was a once in a lifetime opportunity. We took advantage of it, and now we're finished (see Bernstein, 1991). Maybe."

"Maybe?"

"Yes, maybe. We heard that our daughter's biological family broke up. We wrote our lawyer in Romania and offered to take her two brothers and two sisters. But, they had moved away so he had lost contact. So, nothing came of it. But, generally, I feel bad about all the babies we left behind."

"How many were left behind? Didn't most of them get adopted?"

"No, That's the impression one got from television. But, at that time only 7,000 Romanian babies were adopted, worldwide."

"Really?"

"Yes. And, that left 150,000 babies behind."

"That's sad."

"Yes, and times are very tough in Romania now. People are hungry. So, the number of babies in orphanages is starting to go up again."

"By the way, when a relative of ours heard we might go back for the four other kids he yelled at me: 'For Christ's sake . . . you'll . . . you'll be 50!' 'So, I'll be 50,' I coolly replied. However, there is an irony here. In 1900, life expectancy in the United States was 49."

"Really?"

"Yes. And, here I am starting a family, in my forties. Ain't modern life grand!"

"Yes, please go on."

"Okay. The crucial document that I needed for Romania was the home study. But, we were only half finished with the interviews. So, I called her and explained the situation. She agreed to write out a brief statement saying that we would be fine parents and in the near future the home study would be complete. So, I jumped in the car at 9:00 a.m., and went over to pick up the letter. When I came back Elena had called and left a message on the answering machine. I called her back. She said that she wanted to give me a package to take to her mother in Bucharest. Would I do it? 'Of course,' I said. And, I asked if she didn't mind driving me to the airport. She agreed.

"She arrived about an hour later. I hadn't yet finished packing all the little odds and ends that I needed to take with me. It was getting late and I was starting to get a bit frantic. I took the documents that were crucial to the adoption and put them on the dinning room table. This was to guarantee that I would not forget them. When I was finally ready to go we dragged my suitcases to her car. We hopped in and she drove me to the airport. I was really worried because we were late; but, I thought I would get to the ramp just in the nick of time. However, traffic was slow and I became more and more anxious. I didn't want to miss my flight to New York. Of course, if I made the flight I would have gotten there at two in the afternoon. And then I would have had to wait eight hours. But, still, I didn't want to miss my flight. Elena finally pulled up at the airport. By that time I was frantic. I ran to the trunk and grabbed my suitcase. Suddenly, I froze. My heart began to pound. 'I forgot the documents!' I screamed. So I threw the suitcases back into the trunk and I jumped back into the car. 'Hurry, hurry,' I screeched, 'let's go back.' So, we zoomed back to my house. And, there were the documents, on the dinning room table, right where I had left them—so I'd be sure not to forget them. I grabbed the envelope and we dashed back to the airport. By this time it was fair to say that I was, 'hysterical.' We pulled up at the airport; but, it was too late. So, I dragged my bags out of Elena's trunk and said good-bye.

"I lugged my bags over to the United counter. I told the agent that I had missed my flight and that I needed to make a connection in New York at ten o'clock. She said, with grand indifference, 'Oh, you have to go to another counter.' While waiting in line at the second counter the next flight for New York left. By the time I got to the front of the line the third flight was about to leave; and, there would be no more flights until much later in the day. When I finally reached the counter I was told, 'It's too late for our flight. Go to TWA.' So, I took my ticket and went to TWA. I told the agent, 'I missed my flight on United to New York. Can I give you my ticket and you put me on one of your flights?' She said, 'This isn't our ticket.' 'Yes, I know.' The supervisor glared at me and in an ice-cold voice said, 'Give me $328 and I'll put you on the next flight.' I said, 'But, I already paid for the ticket.' She then said with contempt, 'Well, you'd better call your travel agent.' So, I went to the phone and called.

"I told my travel agent what had happened and she screeched, 'You missed your flight?' I said, 'Well, it's not like I missed the plane to Bucharest. It doesn't leave until 10:00 p.m.' She said, 'Why don't you hold on.' A few minutes later she returned and said, 'I'll call you back. My supervisor will change the ticketing.' 'Fine.' In the meantime, the next plane left for New York. Several minutes later she called back and said, 'Everything is set, you can fly on TWA.' So, I went back to TWA and told them that my agent had changed my ticket. They punched my name into their computer and my new reservation came up. So, grudgingly, they put me on the next flight to New York. However, the next flight to New York was going to the wrong airport. So, when I arrived at LaGuardia I had to get on an airport bus. Forty-five minutes later I arrived at Kennedy.

"Even though I was 'late' I still had several hours to kill. So, I went up to the TWA desk and asked, 'Is there any nice Italian restaurants in the area I can take a cab to?' They said, 'You don't have to leave the airport, just walk all the way down to the end of this terminal and you'll find a nice restaurant.' So, I walked down to the far end; but, the restaurant was closed. They said, 'Oh, we don't have many flights at night. So, we just close at seven o'clock. But, you can go over to the International Terminal and there's a nice restaurant there.' So, I took the airport bus to the international terminal. However, that restaurant was closed, also. So, I took the airport bus back and went to the restaurant near the TWA desk. However, that restaurant was being remodeled so all that was open was a cramped cafeteria. I got in line and bought a couple of hotdogs, potato chips, a fruit cup, and a couple of Pepsis. It cost $15.52! I still have the receipt. After I finished eating I wandered over to the Tarom counter and waited for their departure lounge to open up. Meanwhile, I chewed stick after stick of Juicy Fruit gum. I was tired and bored. Finally, at about nine o'clock, the Tarom lounge opened.

"I wandered in and sat down in the back. I pulled out a newspaper and began to read. There were a lot of people milling around. All of them were talking quite loudly in Romanian. There seemed to be a particularly loud conversation going on behind a large pillar; but, I couldn't see what was happening because I was sitting on the opposite side of the pillar, about ten rows back. After a few minutes the arguing got louder. Then, suddenly, from the other side of the room came, 'The Rocketeer.' A body shot across the room and disappeared behind the pillar. From behind the pillar I could hear the fella' screaming, '*Communisti! Communisti!*' Then he and another man began screaming at each other. I looked over at the attendant at the check-in desk. My expression said, shouldn't we call the SWAT team? She just shrugged and went back to her newspaper. It was as if she was saying, this happens every day, don't worry about it. I listened intently as the two men argued from behind the pillar, in Romanian, of course. No one else, though, seemed particularly interested. However, every once in a while someone would jump up and run over and scream something at the invisible *Communisti*. Finally, The *Communisti* moved from behind the pillar. I saw that he was a skinny, 35 year old fellow in a blue suit with a little goatee. He had a striking resemblance to Lenin. After a few more minutes, the argument cooled down. Although it occasionally flared up most of the people in the lounge ignored it. They wandered around and chatted with each other. After about an hour of this The Rocketeer went over and shook the *Communisti*'s hand.

"A little later the attendant announced the boarding of the flight. Everyone stood up; and, then I noticed something interesting. There were a lot of people in the lounge wearing blue jean outfits . . . blue jean shirts, blue jean pants, blue jean jackets. All of them stood up and walked out. Those were the Romanian-Americans. Those that remained wore shabby, World War I overcoats. And, the women all wore babushkas. They were the Romanians. I felt sorry for them as they shambled towards the door. One after another they disappeared into the shadows. They were on their way back to Romania.

"As I walked down the jetway and into the airplane I could see that it was a rather old plane. As I stepped through the door I felt as if there was a sign over it that said: 'This is a Third World airline. Don't expect much.' When I entered the cabin my expectations were confirmed. The interior of the airplane, like the peasant's coats, was shabby. The aircraft had been an old SAS plane. It appeared that SAS had flown chickens in it. And, when they tired of that, they sold it to Tarom. However, in spite of this, it did have a 1950s chic. As I looked for a seat I realized that there was no first class on the plane. That was because the crew had thrown their baggage onto the first ten rows of seats. So, I sat down in the 11th row, behind the galley on the far side, in the no smoking section. However, as soon as the plane took off the crew pushed their bags aside, sat down, and began to smoke. They did this continuously, all the way to Romania.

"I also noticed something interesting. As we waited for the plane to finish boarding I asked the stewardess if I could have a Pepsi. She gave me one and I thanked her. However, when the Romanian's came over and asked her for a Pepsi, they handed her money. I didn't understand it then, but later on I realized that *nothing* is ever done for free in Romania. Everything is done for a 'gift.'

"After a long wait we were finally ready for take off. The stewardess picked up the mike and said, 'Would everyone please move to the back of the plane.' I was puzzled. But, dutifully, everyone moved to the back of the plane. I went up to the stewardess and said, 'Excuse me. I'd like to sit up front, in no smoking.' 'Fine,' she said, 'this is just for take off.' 'For take off?' 'Yes', she said slowly and deliberately, 'for balance.' 'Oh,' I mumbled. So, I shuffled towards the back of the plane. I plopped down into an empty seat; and, I thought to myself, what kind of airline is this?

"A little later the plane rolled down the runway. The nose went up, the tail went down, and the plane took off. Everyone was then allowed to return to their regular seats. As the plane flew eastward I couldn't fall asleep. I don't sleep well on airplanes. So, I read the newspaper—for a long time. In the middle of the night I finally started to get sleepy. Just then we landed at Shannon. That was so everyone could buy duty free watches. I went out and stretched my legs. I called Susie to say hello. I got back on the plane and we continue east. About 24 hours after I left Chicago, the plane finally arrived in Bucharest.

"The plane landed at Otopeni International Airport. As we taxied I could see that the terminal was a plain, boxy, modernistic concrete building. It looked like any modern small-town airport. We taxied towards the terminal, but stopped short, in the middle of the concrete. They pushed a stairway up and immediately all the Romanians ran off and disappeared underneath the airplane. I just sat there, perplexed. A truck pulled up. It was and old 1950s Russian flatbed. One of its two workmen climbed into the cargo bay and began tossing the bags onto the back of the truck. The Romanians grabbed their bags and ran to the terminal. I thought to myself, what kind of country is this? I shrugged and walked with the remaining passengers to the terminal.

"As the plane was landing I had seen armored personnel carriers and soldiers surrounding the terminal. I knew that the revolution had been over for only two months. But, it was unsettling. Not that I was afraid that I was going to be shot. I felt that civil society should be . . . civil—no soldiers, no guns. Ha! How naive. Most societies are not based on freedom and democracy; they are based upon oppression. We got it all wrong. Romania, Guatemala, the Congo—those are the norm; not freedom and democracy.

"When I returned home I did some reading in my favorite school of philosophy, existentialism. Existentialists say: there is no God, there is only choice. We make ourselves. There are no excuses. We will ourselves to be what we wish. We are the sum total of our actions. Each individual's destiny is within themselves. We are condemned to be free! (see Satre, 1989; Stumpf, 1989; Kaufman, 1956). We are condemned to be free. How naive. It seemed obvious to me that no existentialist philosopher had ever lived under the boot in Romania.

"Existentialists, however, did get one point right. They didn't believe there was 'a human nature'; but, they did believe there was 'a human condition.' And, this set 'limits' on the individual. Limits, what a benign word. Limits meant clawing at the earth to protect yourself from snipers in Sarajevo. Limits meant hoping to survive the next jolt of electricity to your testicles in Argentina. And, limits meant that your prayers will be answered and you won't be hacked to death in Rwanda. Limits.

"I walked past the soldiers into the terminal, and up the stairs. I went over to the visa desk. I handed the visa officer my application and the $37.50 fee. But, Raymond had told me what else I needed to give him. So I handed him two packs of cigarettes and I spoke the appropriate phrase, 'And this is for you.' He smiled. Boom! He stamped the form and sent me on my way. However, if I hadn't given him a 'gift' it might have taken six or eight hours to get my visa."

"Couldn't you have just given him a couple of dollars?"

"No. That would be, 'a bribe.' That would be . . . crude. Declasse. A 'gift' was appropriate here."

"So, I then walked to the other side of the terminal to the immigration desk. I handed the immigration officer my passport, visa, and two packs of cigarettes. And I chanted, 'And this is for you.' He asked, 'Reason for visit?' Raymond had told me that it would be too involved to explain that I was there to adopt a baby. So, I simply said, 'Tourist.' Boom! He stamped my passport and sent me on my way. I had just saved another six to eight hours. I then walked over to the luggage carousel. It wasn't a nice chrome one like we have in the United States. It was wood; and, when it moved, it klunked. But, then, it didn't move very often. And a lot of people stood there waiting for their bags. On the far side of the carousel was an opaque glass wall. I could see the shadows of a large crowd of people waiting behind the wall. But, no one was allowed past the guard. However, suddenly, through the crowd, came Floriana, my friend's mother-in-law. She ran up to me, threw her arms around me, and kissed me. A young fellow had accompanied her. He was a handsome, dashing, 23 year old with a cape, very Eastern European looking. He introduced himself to me, in English. His name was Gheorghe and he was to be my translator. He also introduced me to Ion,* who was going to be our driver. Ion didn't speak English. Since Floriana didn't speak English, either, she and Ion talked while Gheorghe and I chatted.

"I asked him what he did. He said that he was 'a poet.' So I said, 'What university did you go to to become a poet?' He said, 'I did not go to university, I am just a poet.' I said, 'Well, what does a poet do?' He said, 'I write poetry, I play the guitar, I smoke cigarettes,' and to paraphrase him, 'I flit from flower to flower.' I thought, it's a nice job if you can get it. Anyway, he explained that he spent most of his time working as a translator for journalists. He had been Russell Baker's translator, from the *New York Times*. He had also worked for several Dutch journalists. He was artsy and he had seen many Western films. So, we talked about films and literature. He was interesting, pleasant, even, charming. We had a nice chat, a long chat, because we had to wait two hours for my bags."

"Two hours?"

"Yes, Two hours. Let me explain.

"I asked Gheorghe, 'What's taking so long?' He said, 'You came at a bad time. When your plane landed it was the last hour of the shift. So the workmen had to sit for an hour and smoke their cigarettes. Then the new shift came on and they had to sit for an hour and smoke their cigarettes. So, you just came at the wrong time.' I concurred. Finally, after the two hours, my bags came up. I grabbed them and we headed for the custom's officer and the exit.

"There were eight exit doors. Seven were blocked by soldiers with Kalashnikovs. Now let me digress for a moment. In Romania 'soldiers' are

---

* pronounced: Yohn

actually just kids. There is universal conscription for males. So soldiers are mostly 18 year olds, with pimples. And, green felt uniforms. And, like all teenage boys they leered at the attractive women as they walked by. However, no matter how much they looked like horny teenagers, they did have Kalashnikovs. And, if they pulled the trigger they'd blow you apart. Later on I found out that a common occurrence was for soldiers to walk up to you and say, 'Help you with your bags?' If they helped you, you owed them a pack of cigarettes. If you said, 'No thank you,' they stood in front of you, blocking your way. So, you gave them a pack of cigarettes. That was because they had a Kalashnikov, and you didn't.

"Now, to go on. There wasn't a customs officer to be seen. Some of the tourists were waiting in line. However, most of the Romanians were running out door eight, where there was no soldier and no customs official. So, I said to Gheorghe, 'What's going on? Why is everybody running out door eight? Why don't the soldiers stop them?' He explained that each soldier was responsible for one door, and no one was responsible for door eight. But, we couldn't go out door eight because we were right in front of door seven, with the soldier looking right at us. However, after waiting a couple of minutes Gheorghe turned to me and said, 'Are you tired?' I said, 'Yes, I am *very* tired. I've hardly slept in 24 hours.' So, he walked up to the soldier and whispered to him. The soldier smiled and waved us through. I was surprised. I could have had cocaine, Stinger antiaircraft missiles, or plastic explosives in my suitcase. It didn't matter. He just smiled and waved us through. Once we reached the curb Gheorghe turned to me and said, 'What do you have?' I understood what he meant. So, I opened my 'gift' suitcase and reached in. The first thing I came up with was a package of a dozen packs of Juicy Fruit gum wrapped in plastic. I showed it to Gheorghe and he said, 'Fine.' He grabbed the package and stuck it under his arm. He then went back to the soldier and slipped it to him. The soldier smiled and saluted. I smiled and saluted. We got in the car and drove off. I turned to Gheorghe and asked, 'What was all that?' He turned to me with a smile and said, 'Welcome to the Balkans'."

Chapter 7

Bread and Newspapers

"Ion had pulled his car to the terminal's curb. This wasn't difficult since there were only a smattering of cars at the airport. So, we loaded the bags in the car, turned left out of the airport, and started towards Bucharest. The airport was out in a rural area so it took thirty or forty minutes to get to the city. Ion, early in the drive, turned to me and said, 'America.'* I replied, 'Yes, America.' Then his face lit up and he said, 'Hollywood?' I said, 'Yes, Hollywood.' Then cupping his hands in front of his chest he said, 'Bosoms!' 'Yes,' I said, 'bosoms.' After this, every half hour during the week he would turn to me and we'd repeat this conversation. Now, some might call him a sexist pig. But, what made his remarks funny was not the sex, but the cultural stereotype. America as the land of bosoms. Yes!

"As we neared the city the empty fields turned into strips of peasant cottages—no, hovels. They were small and drab. They were surrounded by seven- or eight-foot high walls. Behind the walls were gardens. All the houses were ramshackle and looked as if they had not been painted in years. And, they were all painted different colors. So, as we sped by patch after patch of faded color flashed by. When we approached the edge of the city old commercial buildings began to appear. As we entered the city proper, the streets were lined with large concrete public housing projects (see Rocks, 1993). These identical buildings, with their identical apartments, were interchangeable; and, for their Communist rulers, the people were interchangeable, too—for they had only one function, to serve The State.

"As we drove down the street I looked up and saw that almost every balcony was draped with colorful clothes flapping in the breeze. However, instead of making the projects look more hospitable, it simply made them look, shabby, oppressive. And, these buildings went on endlessly, block after block after block.

"As we entered the heart of Bucharest I could see the city had once been quite beautiful. It wasn't surprising that it had been called, the Paris of the East.

---

* pronounced: Ah-mare-ee-kah

The boulevards were wide and some of the buildings still had their old world charm. And there were many, many trees. But, it appeared as if the country had been frozen in time—somewhere between 1930 and 1950; and everything had then been allowed to deteriorate. Dust had settled over everything, buildings, trees, people. Everything was . . . gray.

"As we drove through town I was told that most of the cars were Dachas. They were little, squarish Romanian versions of the French Citron. And, they were all old. The city's streets were littered with broken down Dachas. Their trunks were open and their hoods were up as their drivers attempted to repair them with monkey wrenches. We also passed endless gas lines; some of them were several blocks long. 'How long do you usually wait for gas?' I asked. 'A few hours, usually,' they answered. 'However, sometimes before a holiday, the wait is a couple of days.' I also saw large numbers of dogs roaming the street. 'Do many dogs get run over?' 'Yes.'

"As we drove through the city I was told that much of it had been torn down during the Communist Era and replaced by drab Communist buildings. In the 1700 and 1800s, the city had been quite beautiful. Most of that was now gone. However, here and there I caught a glimpse of a street that looked like Paris. Also, there was a lot of German influence in the country. Many ethnic Germans had traditionally lived in Romania. But, now most of them were gone. I was told that there was also a very strong Italian influence. That was because Romania had been the northeast corner of the Roman Empire. And, many of the legionnaires had stayed on after their tours of duty and had intermarried with the native Dacian women. As a result, the language was 70 percent Italian. And, Romanians considered themselves to be an island of hot-blooded Latins in a sea of rather dull Slavs.

"As we drove through Bucharest, Floriana explained that her orphanage, Orphanage No. 1, had been the show place orphanage of the entire country. Many Communist officials had left their children there when they had gone on vacation. However, since the revolution, it, and all the other orphanages in Bucharest, had been picked clean by the French, Germans, and Italians. So, there weren't any 'nice' babies left in Bucharest. Also, the number of children coming in to the orphanages had fallen dramatically since the revolution. That was because abortion and birth control were now legal. Floriana explained that before the revolution there were 12 babies a day dropped off at her orphanage, alone. But, since the revolution, there had been only 12 babies left in over two months. So, because there were no nice babies left in Bucharest she said that we would fly to Arad, a town in the western edge of the country, to find a baby. We would leave tomorrow.

"I was told that I would be staying at Floriana's house that night. On the way to her house they wanted to show me some of the city. We went by University Square. This was where much of the fighting had occurred during the revolution. We went by the other major squares, also. And, in every one there were crosses with tall thin amber candles burning. These commemorated those that had been killed during the revolution. We drove to the television station. It had been the center of the revolution. We parked and got out. We walked past a building that was directly across the street from the station. It was a corner building with a curved facade. I remember it was salmon colored. It was riddled with thousands of bullet holes. Its windows were blown out and it had been gutted by fire.

"I crossed the street. I could see a five-foot iron fence surrounding the two-block-long media compound. In the compound was a tall building with numerous antennas on top. Next to it was a short, squat building. They were connected by a second floor bridge. There were armored personnel carriers and soldiers surrounding both buildings. Although it was more than two months after the revolution, the government still feared an attack by the Securitate. We walked to the corner. There, at the gate, was a large cross. This was a replica of the one that had been erected in Timisoara to commemorate those killed in the massacre. It was surrounded with many candles honoring the dead from Bucharest who had been killed in the revolution. As Gheorghe and I wandered around the area speaking English, someone came up behind me and tugged my sleeve. He then began speaking to me in English. Before I could say anything I was grabbed by the arm and pulled towards the car. 'Why did you do that?' 'He could be Securitate.' 'Oh.'

"We drove on to Floriana's house. Her house was in an old section of Bucharest. The outside of the house was nondescript. However, inside, it was designed like a French villa. When you entered there was a vestibule. Then a set of French doors opened on to a central room with a large piano. There were several doors off that room. To the left was a hallway going to the kitchen and bathroom. To the right were the bedrooms. In the center was the dining room. I could see that the house had once been grand. It had high ceilings and was decorated with many nineteenth century works of art. Raymond had said they used to call the house, *The Museum*. Even the moldings were intricately carved works of art. But nothing had been painted or repaired in years. Also, there was no central heating. However, there were seven-foot-tall, ceramic-tiled furnaces in every room. This was very important since it gets to be thirty below in the winter. And, because Ceausescu had decided to pay off the country's debt, all at once, everything exportable had been sent out of the country—food, medicine, and oil. So, for most people, there was only heat in the winter for two or three hours a day. It was lucky that I was staying with someone who was 'rich.'

"We were going to fly to Arad early the next morning. Since I hadn't slept for almost 24 hours I wanted to go to bed, immediately. But, first, I went to the bathroom to clean up. I turned on the light and the cockroaches scurried under the bathtub. Then I turned on the water in the sink. There was just a trickle. When I asked Floriana about this she said, 'Since the revolution the water pressure has been very bad.' I then went to the toilet. It was an old-fashioned one with the box high on the wall. When I pulled the chain nothing happened. I realized that there was no water in the tank. I found out that the only way to flush the toilet was to put a bucket in the bathtub before you sat down on the toilet. While you were on the toilet the water dribbled into the bucket. When you were finished you picked up the bucket and poured the water into the toilet. This flushed everything down.

"If you wanted to take a shower you also had a problem. The shower consisted of a flexible hose from which water dribbled out. And, unless you turned the water heater on early in the morning, you never had hot water. But, it didn't much matter, since the water just . . . dribbled out. As a result of this, I never felt clean in Romania.

"After I used the bathroom I laid down. Floriana's cat, Zadek, jumped up on the bed and lay down next to me. We both immediately went to sleep.

"The next morning we got up early and drove to the airport. This time we went to the national airport, not Otopeni. We drove up and were stopped by some soldiers. 'We're taking an *important American official* to the plane,' Ion said. The soldiers looked at me, shrugged, and waved us on. We drove in and pulled up in front of the terminal. The terminal was an old, beat-up building. We went inside and walked up to the ticket counter. We asked to buy some tickets to Arad. 'No, no. You don't need tickets, yet,' the woman at the ticket counter responded, 'you've got plenty of time. Besides, I have to finish my nails.'"

"She really said that?"

"Yes.

"Remember, she's a Communist, well, a former Communist, and she gets paid, just like the people at the embassy, no matter what."

"So?"

"So, we sat down and waited. It was starting to get late and we still didn't have our tickets. Finally, she finished her nails and she sold us the tickets. Then we had to go through security. They checked us with a magnetometer and then they searched us. I asked Gheorghe, 'What's all this for?' He said, 'Some crazy Arabs hijacked some planes a couple of years ago. So now they're very careful about security.' We then went through a black curtain and into the main terminal.

"As I entered the terminal it was as if I had been propelled back into a 1930s movie. There was a large central waiting room with a fountain in the middle. A fountain, that apparently had been dry for years. There was a large dome several stories above us. It had been painted with a dark paint that had not been cleaned in years. And, there were many people standing around smoking the local brand of Snagoff cigarettes. At any moment I expected to see Humphrey Bogart appear through the smoke. So, we sat down on the edge of the fountain and waited. I looked out the windows and saw packs of dogs roaming the airport. I asked Gheorghe about this and he explained that people tossed away a lot of food at the airport, unlike other places in Bucharest. So, that drew the dogs. Besides he assured me, they were harmless.

"I took out a book and began to read. Later, I asked Gheorghe if there were any newspapers in English that I could buy. 'No. Not yet. But, there are many Romanian newspapers available.' He then explained that Romanians devoured the many new newspapers that had appeared since the revolution. In fact, he told me that information had been so tight under Ceausescu that the last phonebook had been published in 1977. But, now, 'the only things people are interested in are bread and newspapers.'

"Finally, it was time to board the airplane. We walked out to the middle of the concrete to board the plane. We got on an old Russian airplane, about the size of a commuter plane, and we flew northwest from Bucharest. The flight took 45 minutes. Romania isn't a very large country. So, flying to Arad was like flying from Chicago to Detroit. During the flight we flew over the mountains and landed in Arad, which is in the western edge of the country.

"After the plane landed Floriana, Gheorghe, and I walked from the plane to the small terminal and collected our luggage. Outside the gate we were met by Alexandru. He was a short, stocky, yes, dare I say, pudgy, fellow with a large round face and a friendly demeanor. He hugged Floriana and shook everyone's hand. I was told that he was Floriana's nephew and the city attorney of Arad. After our introduction Alexandru turned to me and asked, 'Do you want to go to the under-three or the over-three orphanage?' 'The under-three orphanage,' I said, 'We want a baby.'

"We loaded up the car and sped off towards Arad. Arad was a provincial city of about one hundred thousand people. It was older and grimier than Bucharest. At least Bucharest had large boulevards that were sunny and open. Arad, however, had the worst of Bucharest, but none of its best. We drove through the downtown area. It had several blocks of old buildings with a trolley line running through the center of it. There was a lot of hurly-burly in the downtown. There were a lot of people, but, many of them were quite poor. The shops were sad looking. They were empty or had products in them that the average Romanian could never afford. After my brief tour of the downtown we turned down a side street and arrived at the orphanage. This was Leaganul Pentru Copii Arad—the Orphanage For Babies in Arad.

Chapter 8

"Schiene Kind, Starker!"

"The orphanage was a block-long building which looked like an old library; the kind that Andrew Carnegie built 100 years ago in the United States. There were two stairways into the building. We took the right one and went in. We entered and turned right again. The walls were institutional green. We went towards the director's office. Having been a social worker I immediately knew what kind of place this was. It was a 'public institution.' That is, it was an institution that was worn down—like most of Romania. We went through several doors and we were shown into the director's office. We sat down at a long conference table near the entrance to the office. At the other end of the conference table sat the director. She was an attractive and lively woman in her forties. She was a medical doctor and wore an open lab coat over her blue dress. She had a blue streak in her hair. During my stay I noticed that many upper middle class women in Romania had colored streaks in their hair.

"When we entered the office the director was involved in an animated conversation with a German couple in their early thirties. The director greeted us and then we sat down and waited while the meeting continued. It went on for a fairly long time, about 45 minutes. At the end, the German woman burst into tears and collapsed into her chair. She had to be carried from the room by her husband. I thought to myself, 'They didn't give her a baby. And, they're not going to give me a baby, either. I came all this way for nothing.' I turned to Gheorghe and said, 'What just happened?' He said, 'She's overcome with joy. The just gave her a baby.' 'Oh, that's nice.' I nonchalantly commented.

"After the German couple left I was again introduced to the director. We chatted for several minutes about my trip, the weather, and other insignificant topics. Eventually, our talk moved to more substantive matters. I was told that there were four hundred children in the orphanage. I later learned that each aide had to take care of twenty or thirty babies. As a result of this there simply wasn't enough time to take care of each child adequately. I had been told that at most orphanages an aide would go down the line of cribs at feeding time and give each child a bottle. Then the aide would come back and collect the bottles a few minutes later. When the feeding was over the aide would then change each child. There wasn't time to do much else."

"What did they feed the babies?"

"At the orphanage in Arad it was milk, sugar, and ground up cookies."

"That was . . . their food?"

"Yes."

"Go on."

"In other Romanian orphanages I've heard that they cut off the tips of the nipples of the bottles to make the feedings go faster. So, the milk just pours into the babies' mouths. If the kids are survivors they gulp it down. If they're not, they gag. In fact, when I got my kids home I found that Joel would clutch his glass of milk and not let it go until he had drained it. And, in feeding Ariel you had to rapidly shovel spoon after spoon of food into her mouth. If I hesitated, she screamed. That went on for about four months. Then it faded. But, it was as if they couldn't believe they'd ever get another meal."

"Wait, let me go back. What if the child went in their diaper after they were all changed?"

"Then the child just laid there in its urine or feces until the next shift when the aide fed and changed them. In fact, a charitable organization's literature showed a seemingly healthy baby wearing pajamas. This baby hadn't been changed for three weeks. As a result of this she had ammonia burns over 90 percent of her body. Let me read this from their literature:

Unclaimed children, some unnamed, some bearing their names on pieces of tape stuck to their foreheads, were deposited in the orphanages. Many of these places have staffs so meager that the babies learn not to cry because no one responds when they do. The infants are force-fed a steady diet of watered down gruel within one minute so that the caregiver can move on to the next overcrowded iron crib. Mattresses are permanently damp with urine and have holes where the ammonia has burned through. Wet, knotted rags used as diapers turn to ice during the winter in unheated rooms where many orphanages experience 30° F temperatures and have no blankets. For lack of plumbing, the children are periodically hosed down in masse. Children reach the age of five never having gone outdoors and are too short to see out a window. They know only the bars on their cribs.

Overwhelmed by what they view as a futile situation, with one individual possibly assigned to attend to hundreds of children, the caregivers simply withdraw into groups to sit and smoke. And as though these children are not suffering enough, thousands have hepatitis and AIDS.

"Now, the orphanage I was at was pretty good, by Romanian standards. It was clean, the kids seemed relatively healthy, and the staff seemed okay. They even had painted cartoon characters on the wall. And, because Arad was a small city, in a rural area, the kids seemed to have enough food. So, it appeared that this was a top of the line orphanage, by Romanian standards. But, their top of the line, was our bottom of the line.

"So, to resume the story. In the corner of the director's office were boxes filled with toys that had recently been delivered by aide organizations. Foreign aide had helped improve things since the revolution. And the government had doubled the daily spending per child to about $1.25 (Dumphy, 1990). But, many things were still not adequate. For example, there was only one crib in the courtyard for 400 children. As a result of this, each child went out for only an hour a week. Therefore, all the children looked . . . gray.

"The director explained that not many babies had been adopted from Arad, yet. That was because few foreigners knew of any towns outside of Bucharest. However, right after the revolution six large blue trucks had pulled up. On the sides of the trucks, in German, was written, 'Friends of Romania.' Six couples got out of the six blue trucks. They said, 'We wish to help. This is for you.' Then, they unloaded box after box of diapers, toys, and gifts. When they finished they said, 'By the way, can we have six babies?' 'Sure, why not?' the orphanage director had said.

"The director told us that she hoped many babies would be adopted. That was because the previous week a group of ethnic German students had demonstrated in front of the orphanage. They had wanted to take the building over and turn it into a German high school. So I said, 'But what about the babies?' She shrugged. 'They don't care.' If the orphanage closed and a baby's mother was known, then the child would probably be returned to her. If not, then the child would be transferred to another orphanage.

"We talked for about an hour with the director and her staff in her office. Then it was time to go look at the babies. She asked, 'What are you looking for?' My wife and I had talked a great deal about this. We had decided that we wanted a nice, normal baby. This evolved into a baby that was, 'healthy, smart, and cute.' So that is what I told the director. As we started to walk towards the wards the staff crowded around us. The staff, all women, wore white lab coats buttoned up to the collar, and little white Amish-style caps. We were a novelty to them. As we went from ward to ward a fairly large group followed us around. They would always ask the same question. 'What are you looking for?' 'What are you looking for?' That was because they wanted to be helpful. It was a little too complicated to keep saying, 'Healthy, smart, and cute.' So, I simply began to say, 'I want the best baby in the orphanage.'

"So, we began our tour. We entered the first ward. Near the doorway was a little dark-haired boy. He had dark skin and large eyes. He was sitting on a horse with wheels on the bottom. He was about 2-$1/2$ or 3 years old. He scooted over to me as I entered the room. He looked up at me with his large brown eyes. His eyes said, 'Please take me.' I smiled, reached out, and touched him. I was moved. I felt sorry for him. But, Floriana rushed up to me and said, 'No, no. This one, the intelligence is not so good.' I smiled again, touched the side of his face, and walked past him into the room. He tugged at my arm, and he tugged at my heart. But, I thought it was important to be 'rational,' rather than, emotional. Sounds odd to say that, doesn't it? But, that's what we had decided. By the way, did you see the *20/20* television shows on Romanian babies?"

"No, I missed them."

"In those programs there was a 15 year old blind girl that lived in an orphanage. And, a child whose leg was so deformed that it went up instead of down. She got around by sliding along the ground on her haunches. And, then there was a boy with cerebral palsy who was, literally, starving to death. He looked like a cadaver. People saw those children on television and made an emotional connection—simply from the picture on the screen. They went to Romania, found those particular kids, and adopted them. They're better people than I am. They're saints. I just wanted a normal, healthy baby."

"But, how did you find *your* babies?"

"I walked further into that first room and I saw four little boys, about 1-1/2 years old, jumping in a crib. One of the boys was a redhead. Since Susie and I are both redheads, I pointed to the redheaded boy and I said, in a booming voice, 'I want that baby!' I was kidding, but they didn't know that. So they said, 'We're sorry. But, that boy's adopted.' And, again I said in a booming voice, 'I want that baby!' They said, 'We're sorry, but he's adopted.' So, I said, 'Change the papers! I don't care.' I was being stupid, because they didn't know I was kidding. But, while I was being stupid, Floriana brushed passed me and went up to a cherubic little blond boy. She pointed to him. Then she raised her arms like a weightlifter. Since we spoke broken German up and back she said to me, '*Schiene kind, starker!*' 'Pretty child, strong one!' And, I said, 'Yes, yes . . . but I can't decide, yet. Let's go look some more.' She shrugged and we went on.

"We went from ward to ward. Each ward had 20 to 40 cribs. And, they were all lined up in neat double rows. As we walked down the aisles I looked at baby after baby. Some just laid there passively, others rocked endlessly in order to stimulate themselves. Some stood up and held out their hands. Some I touched for a moment as I walked past. Except for brief contact with the aides, that was probably the only human contact they would have that day.

"As we walked past each child Floriana would 'educate' me about each one. She'd say, 'No, no, mother's schizophrenic,' or 'No, handicapped,' or 'No, not this one, she's got such and such, no good,' or, 'Gypsy, you wouldn't be interested, too dark.' Someone else in Romania later said to me, 'The Gypsies, they steal, it's not their fault, it's in their genes. They steal in Romania, they steal in America. Besides, they're too dark.' A quarter or a third of all the babies in the orphanage were Gypsies. A physician later told me that the real reason we shouldn't take a Gypsy baby was because Gypsy women had poor prenatal care and they only abandoned their babies if they were sickly or handicapped.

"So, we went from crib to crib to crib—400 of them. It was all a blur to me. No. It wasn't a blur. Each child was distinct. But, I didn't understand what I was seeing. Each child had no meaning to me.

"After we had toured the whole orphanage Floriana brought me back to the first ward we had visited. As we had gone through the orphanage the staff had kept telling me that the little blond boy was the best boy in the orphanage. The French, the Germans, and the Italians had all wanted him. But, he had been unavailable because his papers had not yet come through. In order to adopt a child from an orphanage in Romania the child had to be orphaned or abandoned. If the child was abandoned, and had no parental contact for a full year, then the orphanage could go to court and take custody of the child. Then the baby was 'available' because the child 'had papers.' We later found out that the 'little blond boy' was the child of a 14 year old girl from a prominent family in Arad. The girl had breast fed the baby for 17 days and had then walked out of the hospital. She had never come back. The baby had been transferred to the orphanage after a couple of months. At the end of a year, the papers had been filed. The boy was now 14 months old and was 'available.'

"A year and a half later I learned that several months earlier Alexandru had gone to Bucharest to see his aunt Floriana. He had told her that he knew of a wonderful little boy in the orphanage in Arad. And, did she know of anyone to adopt him. Yes, she said, a wonderful couple in Chicago! But, he warned, they had to come and choose the baby as soon as the papers came through. That was because a number of German couples were dying to adopt 'the *blondeh*'—the blonde boy.

"So, as I said, we returned to the first room we had visited. I walked over and picked up the little blond boy. He had a pudgy little face. He was very pretty. Gheorghe took a picture of the baby and me, I was told. I didn't notice. Later, people who saw the picture of us staring into each others eyes would proclaim, 'Bonding! Bonding!' But, as I said, I didn't even recall that moment. Anyway, I do recall that as I looked at him he did seem sweet. His name was Viorel Leontin. Floriana asked, 'What do you think?' I panicked. I stammered, 'I . . . I . . . I don't know.' I wasn't ready to make a decision, yet; so I said, 'Medical records! Yes, medical records. Let's look at the medical records!' She gave me a look as if to say, 'Hey, dummy. I've done this for 20 years. Don't you think I know what I'm talking about?' Ignoring her look I spouted, 'Yes! Let's look at the medical records!' So we retreated to the director's office and we spent a great deal of time going through the boy's medical records. Floriana examined the charts for height, weight, and other characteristics. For every measure her finger slid across the paper and shot up, up, up. She looked at one indicator after another and said, '*Op! Op! Op! Alles goot!*' She also told me that he had had an AIDS test and that it had been negative. Although all his records were good I asked time and again, 'What about this?' 'What about that?' I asked question, after question, after question. But, each time she would say, 'Yes, yes. *Alles is goot.*' This went on for two hours."

"Two hours?"

"Yes, two hours. I was a little . . . nuts.' Now, when people call me for advice about adoption I say, 'This is the most important decision of your life. You can get rid of your car, you can get rid of your house, you can even get rid of your spouse, but, you can never get rid of your kids.' So, after two hours I finally asked the *big* question. I said, 'Are you *enthusiastic* about this boy?' '*Ya!*' she exclaimed. So, I said, 'Okay.' And, that was it. I had a son!"

"That was it?"

"Well, not quite. We then drove over to city hall to do the paperwork. We parked in back and went in a side door. Alexandru pointed to the left and said, 'This is run by the mayor.' He then pointed to the right and said, 'This is run by me.' We walked down the hall and went into his office. He pulled out the file for Viorel Leontin, my son! He began to write, and then he wrote more, and more, and more. Everything there is hand written. The typewriters are big clunky things from the 1950s. And, there's no computers, faxes, cell phones, or photocopiers. So, I sat there as he wrote. Every once in a while I would sign something. This went on for a long time. So, finally, I said, 'Well, is this a good time to call Susie and tell her the news?' 'Sure.' While the paperwork continued I went to another office to try to call home. We tried, and tried, and tried. But, we couldn't get a long distance line. It's very hard to call out of a Communist country. And, it's very hard to call into a Communist country. That's because the telephone systems are so archaic. After awhile Alexandru reappeared and said, 'Let's finish the paperwork. Then we'll go to the post office in downtown Arad to call.' That's because the post office runs the telephones in most European countries. We went back to his office. We finished the paperwork at about five o'clock. And, I had a son! I shook everyone's hand and we left the office.

"As we walked down the hall Floriana turned to me and said, 'And, tomorrow we go back for the little girl.' I was stunned. Finally I said, 'Sure. Okay, Sure.' We continued walking.

"We drove the few blocks to the post office. We went in and filled out a slip. We gave it to the clerk, along with a couple packs of Kent cigarettes. Because we had given him a good bribe we were told it would be about an hour, and not the usual six hours, to complete the call. So, we sat there for an hour. Finally, it was time for us to call. However, Romania is eight hours ahead of Chicago; so it was already too late to catch Susie before she left for work. And, I didn't know the number of her school. So, we called Floriana's daughter, Elena. I told her the good news and I asked her to call Susie at work. She said, 'But I don't have enough information. You have to tell me what the boy looks like.' I thought for a moment and then I said, 'He looks like a little blonde linebacker.'

"After the call we went next door for a pizza. They brought us this terrible cardboard tasting . . . stuff. And, my orange juice was nothing more than some powder in a glass of water; and, it tasted extremely medicinal. I had one bite of the pizza and one sip of the orange juice. We quickly left.

"We then drove to Alexandru's house. It was on the edge of the city. Since he was the city attorney of Arad I assumed that he lived in a large house. However, he lived on the fifth floor of a large apartment building. It was a relative nice building, by Romanian standards. But, there was no elevator. So, we had to drag my bags up five flights of stairs. He lived in a smallish apartment with bright, abstract designs on the wall. They looked modern but were actually traditional Romanian folk designs. The house was furnished with heavy, old-fashioned wooden furniture. And, there were large wooden book cases with glass fronts that were full of books. Just like my *baube's* house. And, the plumbing was a bit better than Floriana's.

"Alexandru's mother-in-law, Floriana's sister, was visiting that day. She had been a nurse, but was now retired. She was a jovial woman with a ruddy complexion and orange-red hair. Alexandru's wife, a short woman with brown hair. was making dinner. Since it wasn't going to be ready for an hour Alexandru took. me to the market to pick up a few things. In particular, he needed to indulge his American guest's odd desire for Pepsi.*

"We drove to the market. The market was located in a square and had many stalls. Since it was late in the afternoon only a few of them were occupied. Those that were open were run by Gypsies who were selling flowers or vegetables. I decided it was time to take some 'local color' photos. So I walked from stall to stall taking pictures of 'colorful Gypsies' with their 'colorful vegetables' and 'colorful flowers.'

"Suddenly, I came upon a stall with a red-haired Gypsy baby. She was *beautiful*. She had a round face; the face of a cherub from heaven. She looked as if she had just flown off the wall of a cathedral. She wore traditional Gypsy clothing, a babushka, and three skirts. I turned to my translator and in a very determined voice I said, 'I want to buy this baby!' He laughed. But, he wouldn't translate. So, I said, again. 'I want to buy this baby!' He laughed again. Just then the mother walked up. She, too, was redheaded. She was rather gaunt, but if I took her home and fattened her up, I thought, she'd look just fine. So, I turned to my translator and said, 'I want to buy this baby and her mother. Then I'll have everything a man can ask for, three children and a mistress.' He laughed, again, but wouldn't translate. The husband walked up. He was a very typical looking Gypsy with dark skin and a full black beard.

"Just then, a Gypsy boy came up to me and said, '*Francez?*'** I said, 'No, American.' He said, 'Click, click. *Fotografie?*' I said, '*Da*,' yes. So I took the

---

* pronounced: Pep-tze
** pronounced: Fran-say (French)

boy's picture and then I turned back to the red-haired baby. The parents also indicated that they wanted a photograph taken. I agreed. The father immediately grabbed a carton of Kent cigarettes and laid it in the baby's lap. The implication was that he was as proud of the cigarettes as he was of his baby. However, he then had a change of heart. So he yanked the carton out of her lap and put it behind her. I then took photos of the baby, the family, and the Kents. I took a few more photos of couples who came up and asked, '*Fotografie*?' But, as more and more people came up to me for pictures I thought I was starting to be taken advantage of. So begged off. I took the little boy's address, and I told them that I would send him all of the pictures. As we walked away Gheorghe said, 'Don't sent them directly to him because then they'll have your address; and, you might get some visitors in America you may not be too crazy about. So, sent them to Alexandru and he will give it to them.' I agreed. I turned to him once more and said, 'I still want to buy that mother and her baby.' He shook his head and walked on.

"We got back into the Dacha and drove down a large thoroughfare. Both sides of the street were lined with row after row of large public housing projects, just like in Bucharest. These apartment blocks were dreary, with balcony after balcony holding drying laundry. We turned down a side street and pulled up in front of Alexandru's apartment building. His building was a block back from the main street. In front of his building were peasant houses that fronted the main street. In their backyards were vegetable gardens, chickens, and endlessly barking dogs.

"Alexandru got out of the car and took off the windshield wipers and the antenna. I thought that was odd. So I said to him, 'Why are you doing that?' He said, 'Because they steal them.' 'Who?' 'The Gypsies.'

"We went upstairs. Dinner was ready. The meals I had eaten in Romania had all been . . . poor. They had consisted of vegetables and cold chicken or stringy beef. But, at Alexandru's I had a wonderful dinner. It was the best dinner I had in Romania. It consisted of chicken soup with noodles, vegetables, and boiled chicken. It was just like my *baube* used to make when I was a kid. I ate and ate and ate. It was delightful. After dinner we sat and chatted. Later, I took some silly pictures of them wearing funny hats and holding barbells. It was fun. They treated me as if I were family. Of course, I had come well recommended. So, we chatted away. He then showed me his family pictures. Then I showed him a picture of my wife. I told him that my wife's grandmother had come from Romania. She was from Galatz. When he saw her picture he yelped, 'Moldova! Moldova!' It was as if he were yelling 'Scarsdale!' 'Scarsdale!' It was . . . endearing.

"During the evening I also frequently told him I would be happy to take his sons, who were eight and ten years old, with me to become rich 'advocates,' lawyers, in America. He laughed but he didn't accept my offer.

"While we talked the television played. This was the first chance I had had to see Romanian television. I was told that there was only one station. It had been only two or three hours a day before the revolution. Most of it had consisted of programs showing 'Ceausescu receiving the adulation of children,' or 'Ceausescu laying flowers on a monument,' or 'Ceausescu inspecting a chicken farm.' Now, most of the programs consisted of people sitting in front of cardboard sets talking about politics. The news programs were no better. The anchors sat there woodenly reading from badly written scripts. There were also badly done news clips.

"Between programs there would be long periods, five or ten minutes at a stretch, of flowers. The camera would just sit there trained on flowers. If you could imagine the worst 1950s TV shows in America, this was worse. But, once in a while, they would have an American or European movie. We saw one at Floriana's house, in English, with Romanian subtitles. I don't recall what it was, but it was in English. We also saw some music videos. Once a Tina Turner video exploded onto the screen. It was fun! But, mostly, it was just dreary.

"During that evening Alexandru once asked, 'What do you do in your spare time?' I could see this was 'the key question.' So, I said, 'I love to read and to watch the news.' But, then I had to explain that there was a great deal of news on television in America. I told him I loved to read the *New York Times* and find out what was happening to the revolution in this country or the famine in that country. And, I loved to do my research. My wife, on the other hand, was usually worn out from teaching by the time she got home. So, she liked to sit and watch her soap operas in the evening on the video. He looked perplexed. 'What are soap operas?' he asked. I then had to spend a half hour explaining how Proctor & Gamble, a long time ago, created programs where everybody slept with everybody else in order to sell soap.

"As the evening progressed, he also mentioned, in passing, that his legal fee would be $500, or a $1,000 if we were able to get a second child. I told him that I didn't have that much cash with me and I asked him if I could give it to him when I returned. He said that was fine. Now I hear that Romanian lawyers take five or even ten times that much for adoptions. They now know American prices.

"Later, I went to one of Alexandru's relative's houses to sleep. When I got to the room I rummaged around my suitcase. I dug out my stash of Hershey Kisses. They were my one link to Western civilization. So, with my chocolate Kisses and a good book I drifted off to sleep."

Chapter 9

The Little Olive-Skinned Girl

"The next morning Alexandru and Gheorghe picked me up. We drove back to the orphanage. On the way, Alexandru told me that there weren't many nice baby girls in the orphanage. But, we could go and look. So, I said, 'I'm not in a hurry, what if we go to Timisoara? It's only 25 miles away. Maybe they have nice babies there. Or, we could fly around to other towns in Romania.' No, Alexandru told me. He had called the orphanage in Timisoara and there were no nice babies left there. He suggested that we try the orphanage in Arad and see if we could come up with a nice girl. If not, when I came back to pick up Viorel we could find a girl. I said, okay. So, we went back to the orphanage in Arad and toured it, again. We looked at all 400 kids, again. It took about two hours. Floriana had decided that it would be nice to have a little girl about a year younger than Viorel. It's interesting how Floriana's 'common sense' changed my life. Incidentally, one day I mentioned in class that my kids were 10-1/2 months apart. One of the adult women in the class said, 'Oh, that's cruel. Why did you do that to your wife?' I shrugged. 'It was God's will,' I replied.

"So, after touring the entire orphanage we ended up in one ward with four little girls. The staff told us that these were the nicest little girls in the orphanage. There were two little sisters, 4 months and 14 months old, a little fair-skinned girl with dark hair, and a little 4 month old olive-skinned girl with cute features. However, there were no papers for the fair-skinned girl, so she wasn't available. There was an incomplete set of papers for the olive-skinned girl. And, Alexandru thought he could get the mother to sign for the two sisters. I shrugged, 'Well, I guess I'll take the two sisters.' The staff gasped. I turned to Gheorghe, 'What did I say?' 'You'd give up the little blonde boy, the best boy in the orphanage, for the two sisters?' 'No! *Unu, doi, trei*,' I said counting off my fingers, 'I'll take all three!' The staff exploded in laughter. 'Now what did I say?' 'They say you're nuts! You're nuts if you think they're going to give you three babies. And, you'd be nuts if you took three babies. Two!' So I said,

'I guess we'll take the little olive-skinned girl.' I was told her name was Consuela* Maria. I took a picture of her in the crib. But, before I could even touch her, Alexandru grabbed my arm. 'Hurry, hurry. It's getting late, and we have to go see her parents.' He then dragged me out of the orphanage. I never even touched her.

"We reached the car and drove off towards her parent's village. As we drove through the city we passed block after block of dreary housing projects. As we drove along I asked, 'Do you need gas?' Alexandru said, 'There are no gas stations this way. We'll get gas later.' In fact, he told me that Arad, which had a 100,000 people, had only four gas stations. Things had been quite different before World War II. In fact, Romania had been a huge producer of gas and oil. However, after Ceausescu had decided that he wanted to export everything, the gas disappeared.

"As we got near to the edge of town the buildings became more traditional. They were small two- and three-story houses. This was an older section of town, but a nicer section. Alexandru told me that this area had been inhabited by ethnic Germans. But, over the last few years most of them had left. They had either immigrated to West Germany or to the United States. Now this area was fairly empty. Later, I read that there had been a large German population in Romania for many centuries. However, since World War I the numbers had fallen. By World War II, there were 800,000 Germans left in Romania. But, many were killed, imprisoned, deported, or vanished during World War II. By 1989, there were 240,000 Germans left. Today, there are only 120,000 (Humphrey, 1993a). Alexandru also said that there had been many Jewish merchants and professionals in the cities of Romania before the war. But, now they too were almost all gone. They had been killed by the Nazis or had immigrated to Israel.

"We continued out of town and joined the main highway to Hungary. However, the 'main highway to Hungary' was merely a blacktop road with one lane in each direction. We sped along the road for 25 miles. One mile before the Hungarian border we came to a turnoff. We turned left down a gravel road. Eventually, the road became dirt. I assumed that in winter or bad weather the village was inaccessible, except by tractor.

"The village was an old, traditional Romanian village. We drove past many small wooden peasant cottages as we searched for Consuela's parent's house. When we found it, it was abandoned. Alexandru spoke to the neighbors and was told that the family had abandoned the house because they couldn't afford to pay the rent. This meant that they were poor, even by Romanian peasant standards. However, they now lived only a few blocks away. So, we drove there and pulled up in front. There were three little boys playing in the dirt yard. These were Consuela's brothers. One was a stocky young boy, about 2-

---

* pronounced: Con-sue-ella

1/2 years old. However, the two older boys, who were six and eight, were very skinny. And, they had the same features as Consuela. The fourth brother wasn't home. However, a year and a half later I was stunned when I learned that I had been wrong. The oldest 'brother' I had seen was actually a girl. And, the fourth brother was a girl, also. I was amazed. The oldest child was so emaciated that it's still hard to believe that she was a girl.

"The children were cute, but they were very poor. Their clothes were ragged, and they were very dirty. There was a scruffy black and white dog sitting in the corner of their yard. Alexandru walked up to them and asked where their mother was working. Meanwhile, I reached into my suitcase and I took out some Hershey bars. I walked over to them and said, '*Ciocolata*?'* Their eyes widened and they nodded. So, I handed them some candy. Their wary expressions soon turned to big smiles. I was happy to see them smile. But, I had mixed feelings. I felt like the ugly American who goes to the village in Viet Nam. He gives chocolate bars to the mother and the kids and then takes away the baby. I knew that this wasn't like that, but that's what it felt like.

"The children told Alexandru that their mother was working on the nearby collective farm. So, we drove over. On the way, Alexandru explained that this woman originally had four children, three of whom we had just seen. She then had a fifth child, but it had died. She then became pregnant with a sixth child, but she couldn't feed it. So, she put the baby in the orphanage. This is no surprise since Romanian peasants make $200 a year. In fact, Romanian doctors make only $30 a month."

"Really?"

"Yes, that's even less than Polish doctors make. They make $50 a month. Anyway, so we drove over to the collective farm. As we pulled up the people looked at us like we were from the moon. We were alien, from 'the city.' We parked near the barn and Alexandru asked for the mother. They went inside and called her out.

"A woman came out of the barn. She looked 70 years old. I imagine that she was probably 30 or 35. But, if you spent 20 years shoveling manure in the sun, you'd look old too. She wore a World War I overcoat and babushka. She looked tired. I looked at her intently. She was about 5' 2" with a squarish, yet petite, body. She had a pretty face. And, she had nice breasts. I thought, if we cleaned her up and sent her to America, how would she fit in? Just fine, I concluded. But, I didn't like the tone of those words—too smug, too arrogant, too rich. But, what I meant was: Will my daughter fit in? Will she be pretty? Will she be *happy*? I hoped so.

"Alexandru got out of the car, walked over, and began to talk to her in Romanian. Floriana, Gheorghe, and I got out and leaned on the side of the car. Gheorghe whispered, 'You wore a white shirt and a tie. That's a nice touch.' I

---

* pronounced: chio-co-lata

stood there and watched as Alexandru and the woman talked for about twenty minutes. Four times during the conversation Alexandru raised his arm, pressed his fingers to his thumb, like a French chef, motioned towards me, and said, 'Pro-fes-sor, Un-i-ver-si-tate, A-mer-i-ca!' This last word rolled off his tongue and hung in the air to indicate that the baby would be going to 'the land of milk and honey.' At the end of the conversation she said to him, in Romanian, 'The French, the Germans, and the Italians all wanted my baby. I always said, no. But, to you, I say, maybe. I'll see you at your office on Monday.' He thanked her and walked back to us. He told us what she had said. I thought she would never appear at the office.

"We climbed into the car and started back towards Arad. I was exhausted. Although everyone was chatting away, my head drooped and I fell asleep. As we drove past the peasant huts and the rolling hills I slept. This often happened to me in Romania. That was because of the eight-hour time difference. Each day Floriana told me to go to bed at midnight. But, my body said it was 4:00 p.m. So, I'd often stay up half the night reading. Then, at 8:00 a.m., they would wake me up. But, to my body, it was midnight. So, most of the time I was in Romania I was half asleep.

"That night Alexandru wanted to take Gheorghe and me out to dinner. So we went to the best restaurant in Arad. We drove over, parked, and walked up. But, all that was left of the restaurant was four walls and a large hole in the ground. Alexandru was embarrassed. We then went to another nice restaurant. That too was closed. Then a third one. It was closed, also. Finally, we went to one of the main hotels in Arad. As we walked to the entrance Alexandru told us to be careful. That was because there were some unsavory black marketeers hanging around the front entrance. They were easy to spot. They were slick looking guys in black leather jackets. Romanians called them 'sharks.' Under the old regime they had been informers for the Securitate. Now, they were 'independent businessmen.' Their main job was changing money for tourists, which was illegal. However, 'everyone' did it. Alexandru explained that the official rate of exchange was 20 *lei* to a dollar. But, on the black market you could get three, four, or even five times as much. If you changed money with someone you knew, you'd get a modest rate of return. However, if you were willing to take a chance, and deal with sharks, then you'd get more. But, sometimes, they'd cheat you and you'd get nothing. And, he emphasized that tourists should never change money with anyone because they might be the police. Then you'd end up in jail.

"So, we walked past the sharks on to a plaza in front of the hotel. An open-air café was set up on the plaza. Most of the people at the tables looked like college students. They appeared to be talking about the great philosophical issues of the day. Like most students do. We walked past them and went inside. Near the entrance was the hotel's restaurant. We were seated and we ordered. I don't recall much about the food, but I do recall this. At one of the tables were two men and a woman. They ordered drink, after drink, after drink. Suddenly, the woman jumped up, raised her arms, and began an unsteady Greek dance. As she careened around the tables she threw money to the spectators. One of the band members jumped off the stage and began grabbing up the money, as if he had somehow earned it. This went on for about twenty minutes. She twirled around and around and around. Several times she danced into the kitchen. Each time we thought the exhibition was over, but she always emerged. As she danced, her big breasts bounced, and bounced, and bounced. The longer this went on, the greater the lust in the eyes of the men in the restaurant. Word of this spectacle began to spread to those on the plaza. People began to crowd into the restaurant to watch. Finally, the woman danced over to her table and passed out. At first this diversion had been amusing. Later, it was just pathetic. Alexandru shook his head. 'She must be Yugoslav,' he solemnly concluded.

"After the entertainment we went home and I went to sleep. The next day was Sunday and we didn't have anything to do. So, as a treat, Alexandru drove us to Timisoara, 25 miles away. This was where the revolution had started. As we drove towards the center of town I could see this was a bigger city than Arad. The boulevards were wider, the city was brighter, and less oppressive than Arad. Also, Timisoara was a university town, which perhaps explained why the revolution had started there. Arad had had a university, but, Ceausescu had closed it.

"We drove to the center of town and parked near the main square. As we walked to the square we saw a large crowd of people ahead of us. We entered the square near the Opera House. On the balcony to our left a chorus was singing. Alexandru whispered to me that this was a memorial service for those who had been killed in the revolution. I looked across the square and there were thousands of people. Some were solemn, some were joyous, some just stood motionless and cried. We began to walk around the square. We saw hearts made of flowers that had been laid down on the pavement. They had been placed there by parents whose children had been shot in the revolution. I was touched. I thought, here I am, this . . . 'this guy from Chicago' and I am part of 'history.' Wars and revolutions were always things you saw on a little box. You saw it because a camera crew followed the Croats fighting the Serbs, or the Afghans fighting the Soviets. But *this* time, *I* was actually there, in Timisoara, witnessing the grief and joy of the survivors of the revolution. I was sorry that I had never become a foreign correspondent. I probably would have loved it.

"When the chorus had finished singing a color guard of Romanian soldiers emerged from the opera house and slowly marched across the square. They moved towards the large medieval church at the other end of the square. The church had three green conical towers on it. The soldiers stopped in front of a clustering of traditional crosses near the steps of the church. Dozens of thin amber candles burned among the crosses. As the soldiers stood silently several people made speeches.

"When the ceremony ended, the restaurants on the square were opened. I was told that they had been kept closed during the ceremony in order to avoid anyone getting drunk and disrupting the proceedings. So, when the speeches were over we went into a restaurant on the square. This was the best restaurant in Timisoara. It was dark and cavernous inside. In Romania the summers are hot. And, the lights are rarely turned on in shops or restaurants because it makes them even hotter. Besides, it's too expensive. The restaurant's heavy cloth shades were pulled down and the drapes undulated across the windows. It was very smoky. The look of the restaurant was very old world. It had large, sculpted wooden columns. And, heavy drapes were hung between the columns. We sat down and they handed us menus. Gheorghe turned to me and said, 'Cow or pig?' 'Cow.' And we ordered. A little later they brought us some cold, greasy, stringy beef. The food was bad and I was sleepy. The restaurant was very smoky, and I hate smoke. I looked up and I saw the light filter in around the edges of the shades. The, suddenly I had . . . a revelation."

"A revelation?"

"Yes, a revelation! Like Paul of Tarsus on the road to Damascus."

"Is that a nice thing for a Jewish boy to say?"

"Well, I don't know. But, that's what I had. I was tired, sleepy, and hungry. I was cranky. And I was a *tourista*. But, suddenly, I realized what was going on. I understood through the haze. I was in, 'The Balkans,' 'The Dark and Mysterious Balkans!' A place where people huddled in the shadows hatching petty conspiracies. A place where individuals carved out a tiny niche of personal freedom against their oppressors. But, mostly, it was a place for suffering. The essence of Romanian history was once explained to me: 'When you've been down on your belly for four hundred years—getting it up the ass— it's hard to stand up and have any dignity.'

"After that moment I became what I should have been all along, an ethnographer, a social scientist, instead of just a cranky tourist. So, from then on I began to appreciate the country.

"We finished our meal and we wandered around the town. We came upon a beautiful medieval square. It resembled a square I had seen in Venice. A square that was inland, away from the water and the tourists. Although the buildings were in disrepair, it gave you a sense of what the town had been like 200 or 300 years ago. Later, we wandered past a house where a plaque had recently been installed. It had a picture mounted on it. The picture was of a professor who had been killed during the revolution. A few blocks away we walked past a modern house. In fact, it was the only modern house I can recall seeing in the entire country. After a time we returned to the car. As we drove back towards Arad I fell asleep.

"The next morning Alexandru and Floriana picked me up. We drove to a house and parked. They went inside and I waited in the car. I watched the poor people of this medieval city as they hurried her and there. I realized that my good luck, in being an American, and their bad luck, in being Romanians, was simply a matter of chance. And, if things had worked out differently I would have spent my life in Kovno. I hadn't earned my freedom, my prosperity. I was not a better person than these poor folks, I was just luckier (see Rawls, 1971; see also Kymlicka, 1990; Rasmusssen, 1990; Franklin, 1990).

"After several minutes Alexandru and Floriana came out and we drove off. We pulled up next to Arad's City Hall. And, much to my surprise there was Consuela's mother and father. They were dressed in old coats. She wore a babushka. He was very skinny. I remember staring at him as Consuela and the other children all had his delicate features. Also, the grandmother was there. And, so was another woman. She was in her late twenties or early thirties. She wore a blue jean skirt, a blue jean jacket, and had white, punky hair. I asked who she was; and I was told she was Consuela's aunt. I was shocked, astonished, by the difference between the two sisters. Consuela's mother was 'a peasant.' The other sister told me she was 'a city girl.' She looked as if she were walking down the street in Niles, Illinois. And, I thought that if my daughter looked like that, I'd be delighted.

"After we greeted the family Floriana and Alexandru went around the corner to talk to them. Meanwhile, I was told to wait in the car. My translator was late so I didn't know what was going on. After twenty minutes Floriana came back. She said, 'It's *kaput*.' I sighed. I was sad. We had lost the little girl. But, Alexandru had told me that if this didn't work out we could look for another girl when we returned to pick up Viorel. But, still, I was sad.

"To my surprise, Floriana then turned and walked back to the family. A few minutes later my translator arrived. I said to him, 'Gheorghe, it fell through. Find out what went wrong.' He disappeared around the corner. He was gone for twenty minutes. Finally, he returned and said, 'Yes, it's *kaput*; it's finished; she signed.' And, then I said, with a rising and falling voice, 'Oh, you mean *kaput*, not *Kaput*.' I was delighted!

"Alexandru, Gheorghe, the mother, and I then walked over to the City Hall to sign the adoption papers. Gheorghe, the mother, and I stayed in the hall while Alexandru bought stamps for the documents. I felt awkward waiting for him since Consuela's mother and I couldn't speak to each other. In the meantime I watched the comings and goings in the City Hall. I noticed that there were lots of 'guys' there, guys in slick suits, glad-handing each other, makin' deals. I realized that these were the lawyers. And, lawyers everywhere in the world were the same.

"After about twenty minutes Alexandru returned. He led us into a room with a young woman in a bright, modern red dress. She was given the documents. She turned to the mother and asked her many questions in Romanian. The mother said, '*Da. Da. Da.*'—'Yes, Yes. Yes.' Then she turned to me and said, in English, 'Do you wish to adopt this baby?' I thought to myself, 'Here I am. I'm free, I'm independent, I go where I want, I do what I want. Do I *really* want to do this?'—Forgetting that I had one baby, already—and, I demurely replied, 'Yes.' The woman in the red dress signed and stamped the documents. And I had a baby girl!

"We then walked back to the rest of the family. We shook hands and I took a few pictures. I couldn't think of anything to say to them. So, I finally said, 'I will love her baby very much.' It seemed so trite, but it was true. Then, off-handedly, the 'city sister' said, 'We have a cousin in *Ca-li-fornia*. So, if there are any problems, you can just give him a call.' I thanked her, shook everyone's hand, and left.

"We then drove back to the orphanage to do some final paperwork. After that I was going to fly home. Once I had left, Alexandru was going to submit the papers to the government. It would take about three months to work their way through the bureaucracy. Then Susie and I would fly back to get our babies. Some people, however, spent weeks 'waiting for papers' in Bucharest. That was impossible for us, and, rather silly.

"On the way to the orphanage Floriana and Alexandru chatted. Several times during their conversation she repeated '*Noroc*! *Noroc*!' I said to Gheorghe, 'What does that mean?' 'Lucky! She thinks you're *very* lucky.' 'So do I. I am very, very lucky.' We drove up to the orphanage and went in. We finished the last few pieces of the paperwork. Before I left I said to the director, 'Are you *sure* that these are *really* my babies, *no matter what*?' She said, 'Oh yes, yes; they're yours, don't worry.' I said, 'You won't give them to anybody else while we're gone?' 'Oh no, no, no. But, your home study was not complete and we're missing some papers. You *must* get me these papers. And, soon, in two weeks.' The reason for this haste was because the president of the country, Iliescu, had to sign them."

"The president of the country had to sign the adoption papers?"

"Yes. That is because the government was still operating under the old system—where adoption papers, and every other piece of paper, had to be signed by the president. That was the way Ceausescu was able to maintain absolute control over the country. The papers might take a month or more to work their way up to him. And, time was a concern because the presidential election was coming up in three months. So we *had* to have all the papers back to them in two weeks. As we left I asked once more, 'Are they *really* my children?' 'Yes, they really are your children', the orphanage director assured me.

"As we got into the car I said to her, 'We would like to help you when we come back. Is there anything we can bring you from America?' 'Yes, there are two things we could use. One is liquid vitamins, and the other is powdered milk. You can't get them in this country, even if you had the money. They simply don't exist.' 'Okay. I will bring them', I said. I shook the director's hand and we left.

"We then drove to the airport. I thanked Alexandru profusely and said that we'd see him soon. Floriana, Gheorghe, and I then boarded the plane and flew back to Bucharest. Throughout the flight, Floriana had kept leaning over to me saying, '*Noroc*! *Noroc*!' I nodded in agreement.

"After the plane landed we walked back to the terminal. Suddenly, I remembered that I had left my camera under the seat, the camera with my babies' pictures in it. We hurried back to the plane. As we approached the plane a cleaning woman ran off. We looked under my seat, but the camera was gone. Gheorghe was incensed. He demanded to see the police. But they couldn't be found. He complained, endlessly, about the theft to the military officer in charge of the now empty terminal. The officer just shrugged. Gheorghe finally demanded to leave a note on the airport manager's desk about the camera and the mysterious cleaning lady. All of this took an hour or two. And I could barely keep my eyes open. Finally, he asked if I was upset about the camera. 'I just lost the pictures of the kids, not the kids themselves,' I answered. So, finally, after he wrote the note to the airport manager, we left. Soon after we returned to Floriana's the airport policeman called and said the camera had been 'found.' So, we drove back and picked it up. I now had pictures to show Susie.

"When we got back to Floriana's, the second time, we attempted to call Susie. We tried for several hours to get a line, but we had no luck. Then suddenly, the phone rang. It was Susie! While we had been trying to call her, she had called us, at four in the morning, Chicago time. I hadn't talked to her in almost a week. So I told her the story about 'the little olive-skinned girl.' As I talked I gave her no hint how the story was going to turn out. I concluded the story by saying, 'It's *kaput*, it's finished, she sighed. So, we now have two children.' There was a long pause. Then Susie whispered, 'Oh, wow.' That was all. After a moment I began to jabber. I said, 'Now listen, I've been thinking about names. Since we're going to name them after our parents, how about Jerrold Sanford and Bari Elizabeth?' To paraphrase her response, she said, "They're awful. We'll discuss this when you get home.' I said, 'Yes dear,' and hung up.

"We had one more day until the plane left. So, the next day we did a little touring. We drove to University Square. The square is enclosed by the University of Bucharest, the National Theater, and the Intercontinental Hotel. It was here that 13 demonstrators had been killed during the revolution. Commemorating the deaths was a large cross on an island in the middle of the square. Many smaller crosses surrounded it. And, there were many tall thin amber candles burning all around the crosses. Across from the island was a wall on which poems and song lyrics had been written. There were also many candles and flowers along that wall.

"We then went by the University Library. During the revolution Securitate snipers had been firing from there. Eventually, some incendiary shells were fired in and the library, with many rare medieval manuscripts inside, burned to the ground. Everything in the library was lost. We also drove to several famous art galleries. However, they were all closed because of damage during the revolution. We also drove over to the Museum of the Communist Party. But it was now . . . *kaput*.

"The next morning Ion, Gheorghe, his parents, and I squeezed into the car and headed for the airport. All week long Gheorghe and I had talked about him going back to the *universitate* to get his degree. He wasn't enthused. But, when I suggested that he come to America he became interested. Finally, I said that he could come to my junior college and live with me. He agreed. So, on the way to the airport he announced to his parents that he had decided that he was going back to go to the *universitate*. They were happy and began to applaud. And, then he added, '*Universitate* in America!' They gasped. And then he concluded, '*Universitate* Junior College in America!' They began to cheer. Now, I had thought that he could come her, work halftime and go to school halftime. But, I found out that you can't work on a student visa. And, as his 'sponsor,' I would have had to put up a $40,000 bond for his four years. So, unfortunately, this plan became *kaput*.

"When we arrived at the airport, Ion told the soldiers at the gate that I was an 'important American official.' They let us pass and we pulled up to the terminal. I said my good-byes and told them I'd be back, soon. I boarded the plane and I flew to New York. I waited for several hours in New York and finally got a flight back to Chicago, The plane was crowded, overbooked, and a lot of people were milling around looking for their seats. The stewardess began to say, 'Just sit down anywhere while we count.' Meanwhile, in the back of the plane, near my seat, was an elderly Romanian peasant couple. They were lost; and, they didn't speak a word of English. I thought I would try to help them. But, before I could get to them they were separated. The husband was whisked off to the front of the plane. Meanwhile, the wife was seated in the back near me. Both were near tears. So I worked my way to the front of the plane and motioned for the husband to follow me. I brought him to the back and sat him next to his wife. They seemed relieved, and happy. I turned to them and said, '*Romanesc*?* 'Romanian?' Their faces lit up. They nodded. I pointed to them and I said, '*Bucuresti*, New York, Chicago?'** They nodded again. I pointed to myself and said, 'Bucuresti, Arad, Bucharest, New York, Chicago!' They smiled broadly. They then leaned back in their seats and began to look out the window. They watched the ground crew scurry about. They were mesmerized. Finally, the plane took off. The stewardess soon came around with drinks. I turned to them and said, '*Ceai, apa,* Pepsi?' 'Tea, water, Pepsi?' They looked dumbfounded. They actually had a choice. But, they didn't answer. So, I said, 'Pepsi?' They nodded, and we got them each a Pepsi. They seemed delighted.

---

* pronounced: Ro-ma-neshk
** pronounced: Chee-kah-go

They sipped their Pepsi's and resumed looking out the window. About half way home we flew over a town in Indiana. They looked down and said, 'Chicago?' I said, 'No, no.' But, there wasn't much more I could say. I had packed my Romanian-English dictionary in my luggage. I could have kicked myself.

"When it came time for dinner the stewardess came over and asked me what we should do. I leaned over to them and said, '*Carne, pui*?' 'Meat, chicken?' They said, '*Carne*.' Then I said, '*Lapte, apa*, Pepsi?' 'Milk, water, Pepsi?' They, again, looked bewildered. I said, 'Pepsi?' They said, '*Da*, Pepsi.' The meal arrived and they ate it. When they finished they took out a few crumpled *lei* to pay for the meal. They probably had twenty or thirty cents worth. I pushed it back into their hands and shook my head. They were dumbfounded. But, since I couldn't explain about free meals on airplanes, that ended our conversation. However, I thought they deserved a little desert. So, I took out two packs of Juicy Fruit gum that I had squirreled away for myself. I said, 'Gummie?' They nodded. They took the packs of gum. They took out two pieces for themselves and tried to give the rest back to me. I said, 'No, no.' They smiled and thanked me. Later the stewardess came up to me and said, 'Congratulations. We should hire you.' I said, 'I've used up my five Romanian words. There's not much more I can say to them beyond '*lapte, apa*, Pepsi.'

"During the flight I happen to sit next to a woman who was coming home from Turkey. She had been a Peace Corps volunteer in southeast Turkey twenty years earlier. This was an area bordering Syria on the Mediterranean coast. She said that what had once been a small town had grown into a big commercial center. She told me about her experiences there, and I told her how I had just adopted two babies from Romania. Our conversation was very pleasant. As we neared Chicago she asked me what I was going to do with the elderly couple when the plane landed. They had shown me their little telephone book the first time I had said, Chicago; and, they had pointed to a name and a phone number. I planned to call that number and I hoped someone answered. If no one did, then I assumed that I would adopt them, for a few days. When the plane landed I walked them out of the jetway. We were met by a large group of people who rushed up and hugged the elderly couple. It was their grandchildren and great grandchildren. We told them what had happened and they thanked us. And, they congratulated me on my new babies. We chatted for a few minutes, shook hands, and I said good-bye.

"As I came off the plane Susie met me. So, after we left the elderly couple and their relatives Susie said, 'Tell me everything.' I repeated the entire story about my week in Romania. She said in a sprightly voice, 'Let's go and get the pictures developed.' But, I said wearily, 'Susie, it's ten o'clock at night. I have to go to work tomorrow. There's no place we can get the photographs developed, anyway. Remember, this is the suburbs, not the big city. Tomorrow morning I'll do it. I'll drop it off on the way to work at the one-hour place. And, I'll pick it up on the way home.' 'No, no,' she insisted. She had to see the photos, *now*! I had been up for almost 24 hours. So, I said, 'Tomorrow, but, now I *have* to go to sleep.' Still she insisted on seeing the pictures, and I insisted on going to sleep. But, since there was no way to develop the pictures, I won. We drove home and I quickly went to sleep. The next morning I brought the pictures in and that afternoon I picked them up. When she came home from school she grabbed the pictures. For a long time she just stared. She was transfixed. She was looking at . . . *her babies*."

Chapter 10

"Your Babies Are Waiting"

"That first day back I called our caseworker. I told her that we had to have the home study finished in a week. But, she said that she had a bad cold so she put us off until the following week. The next week she came to our home to do the last of the four interviews. By then I had finished collecting all the required documents. This included a document that certified that our dogs had rabies shots."

"Really?"

"Yes. So, we had our last interview. I had thought that a home study would have been a probing, *intense* exploration of our lives and psyches. But, instead, it was mostly just a lot of routine personal questions. For example, she asked: 'Do you have any brothers or sisters?' 'What are they like?' 'How do you get along with them?' 'How did you do in college?' 'Why did you choose this major?' 'Why did you choose that job?' 'How do you like your job?' 'How do you like your wife?' 'How do you like your puppies?' And, so on. It seemed to me that there were an awful lot of softballs thrown. However, my wife and I had been married for almost twenty years. I had had the same job for twenty years. Susie had the same job for ten or twelve years. Therefore, there weren't any complications. There were no divorces, there were no extra kids floating around, there were no mistresses. It probably was a simple family study. But, it took a week longer to do than we had anticipated. So, two weeks after I got back, the family study was completed.

"We then brought the family study to Raymond and Elena for translation. We had thought that they could quickly translate everything into Romanian and then we'd quickly send it off. But, they were too busy to do the translations immediately. So, we attached a note in Romanian that said, 'Romanian translation to follow.' We then went to the post office. They guaranteed that our documents would reach Bucharest in five days. They assumed it would take two more days to reach Arad. So we sent them. We sent them certified, air mail, special delivery, whatever. And, off they went. Five days to Bucharest, and two days to Arad. We waited. About ten days after we mailed the original documents, the translations were finished. So, we put them in the mail and we waited.

"Every few days I had to call the American Embassy in Bucharest to get an answer for one question or another. Each call was a chore. First, since they were eight hours ahead of us I had to call at 1:00 a.m., our time, in the hope of catching someone at their desk at 9:00 a.m., their time. Second, you had to actually get through. This was difficult. You would begin by dialing 011, which put you on the international network. Then you dialed 400 for Bucharest; and, finally, 104040 for the American Embassy. However, you almost always got a recording saying that there were no available circuits. One night, after two hours, I finally got through to the embassy. Almost no one was at the Embassy that day. There was only a secretary to answer the phone. She couldn't answer my questions, but, she could read me the list of the documents I needed for the adoption. I said all right. She said I needed an approved I-600A orange form, which becomes a Visa #37 Cable, the adopting parents' birth certificates, the adopting parents' marriage certificate, the adopting parents' tax return, a home study, the adopting parents' medical certificates, the adopting parents' police clearance, and a certified decree of adoption from a local court. At the end of our conversation I asked her why no one was at the embassy that day. I think she said, 'It's a holiday. It's Flag Day.'

"One day we called the international adoption coordinator for the Illinois Department of Children and Family Services. She had already signed off on our family study, but we had a quick question to ask her. Her reply to our question was to tell us that we couldn't adopt the two kids we had chosen because they had parents. We got a little . . . hysterical. I pulled out the manual on international adoption that the State Department had sent us. I reread the section on the case law for international adoption. It said that you could adopt an orphan. And, an orphan is a child who has no parents. And, you know the child has no parents because an orphanage has legal custody of that child. In other words, it was a legal fiction. And, the international adoption coordinator for the State of Illinois hadn't read the manual. So, we were relieved. This was just another brief aggravation in an endless series of aggravations.

"We also needed a letter from the doctor that Susie was okay after a recent operation. One doctor wrote, more or less, 'She's all right; and, she doesn't drool.' Another doctor wrote us a better letter. We took that one with us.

"Then *The Great Naming Trauma* began. We wanted to name the kids after our parents, all four of whom were gone. My wife had already rejected Jerrold Sanford and Bari Elizabeth. They were 'stupid' she said. Bari, like bury her alive? She just couldn't stand it. After much discussion we were getting nowhere. Suddenly, she said, 'Well, how about naming our daughter, 'Ariel?' 'Ariel!' I exclaimed, 'That's wonderful!' I had loved the name ever since I had read it in a high school Shakespeare class. And, besides it was French! Did I mention my soul was French?"

"Yes. Repeatedly. *Please*, go on."

"Okay. Since we had given my daughter a French name, I thought that we might as well give my son a French name. So I said, 'How about Jacques? Jacques and Ariel, now that would be wonderful!' But, my wife said, 'That's also stupid. Besides, all his friends will call him *Jacques Strap*. It's dumb.' So, I went to our French teacher and had her give me a list of French names. Armed with my list I confronted Susie. 'How about Alain? Edouard? Francois? Henri? Jean? Pierre? Rene? Yves?' She vetoed everyone. The discussion went on for weeks. Finally, she said, 'I'm Russian and Romanian, you're Lithuanian and Hungarian. So, where's all this French stuff coming from?' So I explained, 'My *soul* is French.' She wasn't impressed. As time wore on I became desperate. 'How about Jean-Paul? Jean-Luc? Jean-Claude?' She didn't go for those, either. So, after a great deal of discussion we finally settled on Joel Benjamin. Joel for Jack and Benjamin for Bernice. And, we chose Ariel Elena for our daughter. Elena for Esther. I then told my sisters the names we had chosen. One of them said, 'I understand three of the names. But where does Ariel come from?' 'Isn't it obvious?' I said. Ar-r-r-iel, Har-r-r-old!'

"While we waited for the papers to arrive in Romania we had many other tasks to complete. First came the house. When we had purchased our house it was unfinished. So, we decided it was now time to finish it before the kids arrived. We had a narrow little deck on the back of the house. We hired a carpenter to enlarge it. But, the deck took a long time to finish. So, the carpenter was at our house every day for weeks. Also, the house had never been painted properly. The previous owner's son had taken the cheapest brand of paint he could find and slopped it on. In fact, he had painted up to the drapes, but not behind them. So it was time to paint the house. That was 'a production.' Also, we needed to carpet two hallways and the bedrooms. We did that, too. And, that, too was a major project.

"One day I was looking through the neighborhood paper and I saw swing sets. Yes, swing sets! My children *needed* a swing set. So, I began to look around. In fact, I drove all over the area looking at different swing sets. I spent days and days on this. Finally, I found just the right one. It had a two level house. It had a ramp going up to the second floor and a slide coming down. It had four swings on one side and a tire on the other. It was perfect. It was as if there was a large sign on it saying: 'For overindulgent older parents.'

"Also, I *needed* a video camera. So, I sat down with *Consumer Reports*, *Consumer* magazine, *Video Guide*, video this, and video that. I went from store to store looking for the 'right' camera at the best price. Again, after weeks of searching, I found a very nice video camera.

"We also had to get an International Driver's License for each of us, in case of emergency. That took an afternoon. Afterwards I stopped at a local hotdog stand for a quick dinner. The restaurant was full of fathers and their children. I don't remember seeing any mothers. I almost went up to each one of them and proclaimed: 'I'm going to be a daddy, too!'

"During all this running around I decided to relax and see a couple of movies. So one afternoon I went over to the video store. I was looking around and I found a video entitled, 'How to take care of your newborn.' It was in the public service section so they didn't even charge me for it. I brought it home, and we played it. It showed you how to bathe a baby, how to carry a baby, and how to change the baby. We had no idea how to change a baby. So, this was a very useful little video.

"By this time we realized that we needed to find a pediatrician. We called several friends and they all recommended the same doctor. We met with the doctor, a nice, grandfatherly gentleman. To summarize the meeting we asked, like imbeciles, 'How do you take care of a baby?' And, he said, 'Feed it, change it, and give it lots of love.' Like I said, we felt like imbeciles.

"During this time we would call the Immigration Service to check on the progress of our paperwork. The same woman always answered the phone. Let's call her, 'Miss Shimultaskus.' And, whenever I called her she'd answer the phone and slowly say 'Im-mi-gra-tion, Miss Shim-ul-tas-kus.' You could actually *feel* the weight of the world on her shoulders; and, the weight was just too much to bear. In spite of this she was able to transfer us over to the immigration officer that handled our case. We were later told that our immigration officer was very good because she actually talked to people! The average immigration officer *never* talked to people. So, we would call her every week or two and ask about our FBI fingerprint clearance. She'd say, 'Don't worry. Plenty of time. No rush. Plenty of time.' And, we waited. Weeks went by. Later, I read a report by the Government Accounting Office on international adoptions. It said the procedures for international adoption were 'reasonable' but 'inefficiently administered.' That was because there were problems with bad fingerprints, lost files, ignorance of the law, lack of courtesy, and inaccessibility of INS officers (Johnson, 1993). In fact, when I called the INS on a regular line I could *never* speak to a real person. All I would get was one recording after another; and, then the phone would click off. Only when I used the 'secret number' that my caseworker had given me could I reach an immigration officer.

"While we waited for the papers to arrive in Bucharest my wife's anxiety grew and grew. Disbelief began to set in. She thought that some rich German couple would arrive at the orphanage one day and say, 'Those are cute babies. I want to buy them.' They'd give the orphanage a million dollars and they'd take our babies home. Susie began to think she'd never get her babies. However, I thought it would happen, if we could just get through all the bureaucratic baloney that needed to get done.

"Then, on April 27, 1990, a *20/20* show on Romanian babies was broadcast. We had taped it, but we didn't get a chance to watch it until midnight. The first story was about Toby and Alona Scott, a couple from California who had been waiting for three years to get their baby out of Romania. That was because all adoptions had been frozen after Ceausescu had been caught selling babies. Because of this, there were 250 children who were legally adopted, but couldn't leave the country. However, when Ceausescu was overthrown these babies were immediately released. The Scott's then flew to Bucharest. When the parents arrived to pick the baby up she didn't know who they were. That was because 'mommy' and 'daddy' were six-inch-tall figures in a photograph. In spite of this, they grabbed the baby and hugged and kissed her. They then flew home to the United States with her. When they got off the plane the mother said, 'This is California! Walk on it.'

"They had a second story about a couple from Michigan, Carol and Bill Stevens. They flew to Bucharest in January, right after the revolution. They toured the orphanages. They found three babies to adopt. One of them was a little boy, two or three years old, who looked exactly like the father. The father was Italian, I think, and the boy was dark, with dark hair. He looked like his natural child. They were crazy about the boy. They also found a younger boy and a baby girl to adopt. But, the Romanian government said that they could only have two. So, they decided to take the dark-haired boy and the girl. After they had made their decision the husband flew home. Meanwhile, the wife stayed on in Bucharest to do the paperwork. While she waited, she had the babies tested for AIDS. The test results indicated that the boys were HIV positive. And, United States immigration laws forbid anyone who has AIDS or is HIV positive from entering the country. So, they had to leave them. She came home with only the baby girl. We cried.

"After the program ended my wife went a little crazy. It was one in the morning, a German couple was buying her babies, and our papers hadn't arrived after five-and-a-half weeks! We felt that we had to get another set of papers in the mail, immediately. So we started by calling airlines. We found out that American Airlines had a flight leaving for Bucharest that morning. So, we were going to drive to O'Hare and hand carry a set of the papers to the airline. That way they would be in Romania within 24 hours. Then we planned on sending a second set with an air freight company. However, we found out that most air freight companies didn't go to Eastern Europe. Eventually we found one that did go to Romania. And, then we were going to go to the post office that morning and send a third set. We believed that at least one package would eventually get there. However, at 2:30 in the morning the phone rang. It was Elena. She said her mother had called and the papers had just arrived in Arad. Surprisingly, both the Romanian and English versions of the papers had arrived in Arad on the same day, although they had been mailed ten days apart. Suddenly, I understood what had happened. All foreign mail probably went to the secret police, who didn't exist anymore. The initial set was in English. It had a little note in Romanian attached saying, 'Romanian version to follow.' Since they probably didn't want to struggle through the English version they put it on a shelf and waited until the Romanian translation arrived. When the second package arrived they put that on the shelf until they had some spare time. Then they pulled out the Romanian version and read it. 'Oh, this is nothing,' they probably concluded, and sent them both on their way. So, finally, after five-and-a-half weeks, the papers had arrived.

"Because our papers were a month late, everything was delayed. However, about a month after the first call we received a second call from Elena. It was 2:00 a.m. She said that her mother had just phoned from Bucharest. She had told her that the papers had finally worked their way up to the president, and he had just signed them. However, the local court in Arad needed some time to process them. So everything would be ready by late June. And we should plan on leaving for Bucharest on Friday, June 22. This was perfect timing since that happened to be the last day of Susie's semester. Elena concluded the call by saying, 'Your babies are waiting.'

"After that I was convinced that we would get the kids. Even my wife's disbelief began to fade. I could tell that because she would come home each day with $100 worth of clothes or toys for the kids. One day we went out and bought two whole rooms of furniture for them.

"As the day approached for us to return to Romania we began to gather things to take with us. I went to a local warehouse outlet and bought a case of powdered milk. I also bought a case of liquid vitamins. I then picked up nylons, razor blades, chocolates, and many cartons of Kent cigarettes. We also bought clothes for our new children. We really didn't know what sizes they would need, so we bought a little bit of everything. We also picked up a case of disposable diapers. And, we filled a suitcase full of toys. We felt that we needed car seats for the kids on the airplane. Tarom didn't provide them so they said we could take ours along without charge. But, that meant that we had to *shlep* these two clunky car seats with us all the way to Romania and back. But, we felt it was important for the kids' safety, so we did it. Also, my wife ordered two stroller-backpacks. They could be used as a backpack for carrying the kids and they also unfolded into small strollers. They were red, white, and blue. I thought they were very yuppyish.

"The night before our flight we were still collecting things. We had so much 'stuff'—clothes, diapers, powdered milk, vitamins, and so forth, that we spent the entire night packing. We ended up with eleven boxes and suitcases. All our bags wouldn't fit into a taxi so we had to call a limousine. When the limousine driver arrived he said, 'I can't fit all this in.' We ignored him and stuffed everything into the limousine. Then we squeezed ourselves in and we drove off. So, on June 22, 1990, we flew to Bucharest to get our babies."

Chapter 11

My Babies!

"When we arrived in Romania it was summer, and it was 100° F every day. Each day we had to get up at eight in the morning in order to get our bureaucratic chores done by noon. That was because it simply got too hot to do anything in the afternoon. Also, their time was eight hours different. So, just like my first trip, they would tell us to go to bed at midnight, but it was 4:00 p.m. in our bodies. So, we'd be up all night. And, then, just as we started to fall asleep, they would wake us up. A further complication was that there were no screens on any of the windows. We had a lot of insects visiting us during our stay. One set of frequent visitors were '*furnica*,' ants. We stayed at Floriana's in Bucharest. And, when we told her about the furnica she just tossed some white powder on the bedroom floor. The ants quickly disappeared. However, each time I got out of bed I had to walk through the powder.

"Also, every morning when I got up I had mosquito bites all over my legs. Since I was covered with a thin blanket at night I eventually realized that it must have been bedbugs that bit me every night. So, by the time we flew home I must have had 50, 60, a 100 bites on my legs. Also, there was no air-conditioning. In fact, the only place in the whole country, as far as I know, that had air-conditioning was the American Embassy. But, more on that later. A more serious problem was that I got diarrhea every two or three days. It wasn't pleasant. I took a lot of Imodium. My wife, who keeps kosher, mostly ate vegetables or cheese. So, she didn't have the problem.

"We arrived in Bucharest on Saturday, June 23. We had nothing to do on Sunday. So, Ion, our driver, drove us up to a resort area not too far from Bucharest. The resort had a ski lift there. However, there was a long, long line to take it up to the top. We were tired, and sleepy, and we didn't want to wait. I was ready to leave. But, Ion was a good fixer. He went in the exit and found the ski lift operator. He asked him if we could avoid the line and go on the ski lift right away; that is, if he gave him a pack of cigarettes, which, incidentally, he didn't have. Without hesitation the ski lift operator agreed. So, we went up the mountain, I bought a pack of cigarettes, we came down from the mountain, and I gave it to the ski lift operator. So, we saved an hour.

"Also, we had a new translator on this trip. Gheorghe was busy. So, instead of him we had another friend of Floriana's names Nicu. While Gheorghe was young, artsy, and fun, Nicu was mature, worldly, serious, and extremely interesting. Nicu was tall, slim, gray-haired, and about 60. He was a retired engineer who had spent most of his career in the trade ministry. Later, he had run a computer center at a factory. And, he too was a great fixer, as we later found out. He became a friend, just as many of our other helpers did in Romania. They all treated us just like family.

"To continue. On Monday we had a bureaucratic chore to complete in Bucharest before we could pick up our babies. So, on Tuesday morning Susie, Floriana, and I flew to Arad. Alexandru met us at the airport and drove us to the orphanage. We knocked on the door and we were shown into the director's office. Susie was immediately dispatched to the ward to pick up the babies. Meanwhile, I waited with my new video camera for their entrance. After several minutes the babies were brought in. Susie held Joel, and Floriana held Ariel. Both kids were attired in their Oshkosh jeans. They already looked American. Susie and Floriana held them, played with them, and showed them off. The babies were wonderful. And, they were *our* babies. After several minutes of this I was ordered to put down my video camera and to take one of my new babies. I went over and hugged and kissed them both endlessly. Later, we gave the orphanage director the cases of powdered milk and liquid vitamins. And, all the staff who had helped us were given gifts of cigarettes, nylons, cosmetics, coffee, gum, and candy.

"The kids were then returned to the ward so we could do all the paperwork. The first thing we were shown were the new birth certificates. They said 'Viorel Leontin Klein' and 'Consuela Maria Klein,' So, now, officially, they were our children. The court had issued the new birth certificates when they had approved the adoptions. But, although the children were ours, we still had to secure their release from the orphanage. So, we started the paperwork. One of the orphanage's translators spent an hour handwriting all the release forms. When she finally finished I handed her $10. 'Thank you for your trouble,' I said. Her eyes opened wide and she said, 'Do you know how much money this is?' How could I tell her that I spend that much on dinner in America without blinking an eye. But, since her salary was probable $15 a month, it was a lot of money for her. We then went up to the ward.

"The ward was dreary. Drearier than I remembered. The walls were dark and hadn't been painted in years. The cribs, which were painted 'institutional white,' had been chipped and repainted over and over again. Physically, the ward reminded me of pictures of United States orphanages from the 1930s, or even the 1890s. And, then there were the kids. Some of the children just lay there, motionless, and stared at the ceiling. They didn't cry. No one responded when they did. Others rocked back and forth on their hands and knees. They usually had a glazed look in their eyes. The 'good ones,' those that had the drive to insist on human interaction, stood up and held out their little hands. Their faces pleaded, 'Please, touch me.' Those were the ones that would be adopted.

"We picked up our kids and kissed and hugged them some more. Floriana, Alexandru, and the staff also wanted to hold them. So, we passed them around the room. Meanwhile, I played with some of the nearby children.

"Each child had one beat-up toy tied to their crib. The orphanage director told us that the toys attached to Joel and Ariel's cribs would probably comfort them. She told us to take them along and leave two other toys in their place. I mentioned to the director that I noticed that there were fewer babies than before. She said that over the last few months 100 of the 400 babies had been adopted. That is, the 'nice babies' had been adopted.

"While we were on the ward we met a Romanian-Canadian businessman. He was there with a film crew from Romanian television. He asked me to tell them my story. A few months later he sent me a copy of the tape. I was stunned to see my children. They looked *awful*. They didn't look the way I had remembered them. Physically, Joel didn't look too bad. Most of the time he looked blank. But, occasionally he would smile. Ariel, on the other hand, looked dreadful. She had no muscle tone in her entire body. She was totally limp. And, she had no expression at all. When we got her home she was interested in the television. So, we sat her in a car seat in front of the TV. She would sit there, not moving. However, her eyes would dart back and forth as she followed the action on the screen. She sat there for six months. She couldn't lift her head, sit up, or crawl. She couldn't do anything. The doctor recommended that we do some special exercises with her and she began to improve. Later, relatives of ours told us that they had thought, 'I hope she'll be normal.'"

"And, now she's fine?"

"Yes. But, there's more. When I saw her at the orphanage in June I said, with astonishment, 'What happened? She isn't olive-skinned anymore.' 'She's a *blondeh*,' Floriana proclaimed. 'What?' 'Oh, don't worry,' she reassured me. 'She's fine, now.' So, then, I understood. Ari had 'something' that made her yellow. But, I didn't understand or appreciate that at the time. I just thought she looked Greek or Italian. Was I stupid. I just didn't understand. She was four months old and sick. I remember the staff saying on the first visit, 'He's good, she's bad. She cries all the time.' So, they didn't bother with her, and she lay there, untouched, for seven months. And, when we picked her up we saw that she had a bald spot on the back of her head. That's child neglect in America. You go to jail for that. But, in Romania a lot of the kids are neglected. If she had stayed in the orphan-age she probably would have gotten worse and worse. At three they would have probably sent her to an irrecoverable orphanage. And, she probably would have died. All because she was sick."

"Sad. But, you got very sick, too. Didn't you?"

"Yes. The day after I returned home I got the 'flu.' It went on all summer. I would get up at nine and by eleven o'clock I was sweating, shaking, hot, and cold. I would say to Susie, 'I don't feel well. I'm going to lay down and be sick.' She would then put her hands on her hips and say, 'You don't even want to help with the kids!' 'No, I'd say, 'I just want to be sick.' Finally, in August, when it was time to go back to school, I went to the doctor. 'What's wrong with me?' I asked. 'You have hepatitis.' 'Hepatitis? How do you get hepatitis?' 'From going to Eastern Europe.' That was cute, but not enough information. So I said, 'How do you get this?' 'From contaminated food and water.' 'Oh.' However, I needed to know more. So, I stopped by the college's library and looked up hepatitis in a medical dictionary. It said that hepatitis comes from contaminated food and water, contaminated with fecal matter."

"Oh."

"The doctor had given me a test for Hepatitis B, the most serious type, the type that can cause liver failure and death. But, it was negative. So, I probably had Hepatitis A or C, the milder forms. These have endless 'flu-like symptoms' (see Heeg and Coleman, 1992; Driscoll, 1992; Butler, 1992). Later tests for Hepatitis A and C proved negative, also. So I probably had a virus with 'hepatitis-like' symptoms. One more thing. A year later, *National Geographic* ran an article on pollution in Eastern Europe. On a map it said 'Romania's largest city, Bucharest, has no sewage treatment plant' (Thompson, 1991: 45). 'Aha!' I thought. But, when I asked Raymond about this he said, 'There's nothing to worry about. The sewage from Bucharest goes right into the Danube. Bucharest gets its water from up north. It's clean. Nothing to worry about.'

"To get back to Arad. We spent only that one day in Arad. Late in the afternoon Alexandru drove us to the airport. We thanked him and gave him his $1,000 fee. We waved good-bye as he drove off. We then went into the waiting room. The terminal looked as if it hadn't changed since 1930. The entrance to the coffee shop didn't even have a door, just an old curtain—and I expected Rick, from *Casablanca*, to walk through it. So, we sat down next to a large potted plant and waited for our flight. The kids cried a little, but mostly, they were quiet. As we sat there people would come up to us and say, in English, 'Thank you for saving these babies.' But, I would say, 'No, no, you don't understand. We did this for *us*, not for them.' They usually ignored my response, and thanked us, again. Finally, the plane was ready to leave. It was an old two-engine commuter plane. The flight took about 45 minutes. Joel was fascinated with the noise, the vibration, and the sights. And he particularly loved the landing with the big whoosh of the engines and the plane bouncing along the runway. After we left the airport we drove back to Floriana's house. On the ride back to her house Joel looked out the window of the car as if it was a television screen. He was fascinated by all the sights, sounds, and movements.

"When we had picked up the kids at the orphanage they were both sick. We were told that they had '*bronchita*,' bronchitis, and '*rickette*,' rickets. Although Floriana was a doctor, she was now retired. So, when we got back to her house she called one of her friends to come over and treat the kids. And then to check on them every night a new doctor would come to the house. Each prescribed a different medicine. Soon we had numerous medicines for their *bronchita* and *rickette*. In fact, we had a different medicine for every orifice of their body. We had green medicine for their mouth, purple medicine for their nose, and orange medicine for their tushy. Eventually, the doctors searched around and located 'a new wonder drug' that had just gotten to Romania. It was called, Amoxicillin. It was so new that the labels were still in the original German. Though this 'new wonder drug' has been available for years in this country. So, each night another doctor would come and prescribe another medicine. They were always nice, helpful . . . and insisted that we pay them in dollars. We quickly learned the routine. They would come to the house and examine the kids. They would write out a prescription. Then they would sit around for an hour or two and chat. They were all very pleasant. They would charge us $20 for the visit. For us that was a bargain. But, since they made $30 a month, it was a bonanza for them. Then they would go to the black market and they would sell the dollars for *lei*. They would get three to five times as much. So they'd get two or three months salary by simply coming over and taking care of our babies. And, we were happy to have them.

"Incidentally, in 1992 a study was published on the health of adopted Romanian babies. It found that only 15 percent were healthy and develop-mentally normal. This was in spite of the fact that these babies were assumed to be the most 'attractive and vibrant' children in the orphanages. About half of them had evidence of a past or present Hepatitis B infection. And, one-third had intestinal parasites. All were negative for HIV. Also common was to have a short stature due to emotional deprivation or 'prolonged psychological harassment. And, their weight-for-height was poor. Only 10 percent of the children over one year old were considered to be developmentally normal. The study concluded that 'Romanian adoptees are an extraordinarily high-risk pediatric group as a consequence of decades of government-sanctioned child neglect and abuse' (Johnson, et. al., 1992; see also Hostetter, et. al., 1991; Stephenson, et. al., 1992; Nydon, 1984).

"Now, to return to my children. We were told in very stern tones that all these medicines had to be given every four hours, no matter what. So every four hours, even in the middle of the night, Floriana woke us and the kids for us to give them their medicines. We asked her if all these medications were really necessary. Yes, she assured us. But, she said, the very best medicine was to go to the Black Sea for two weeks every summer. Also, whenever we had to drive somewhere all the windows in the car had to be rolled up. That was so the kids wouldn't 'catch a draft' although it was 100° F out. I soon began to feel that perhaps this was more like 'folk medicine' than 'real medicine.'

"Incidentally, when we returned to Floriana's with the kids that first night we were unsure about the sleeping arrangements. We finally decided that Ari would sleep in a little bed at the foot of our bed. Since she couldn't even turn over, we felt that she was safe. Joel, who was active, slept between us. Also, we brought an entire suitcase full of toys. Ari had very little interest in anything. Joel, however, did like two things we had brought. One was a balloon that we tied to his big toe and the other were boxes inside of boxes. He played with the boxes endlessly."

Chapter 12

The Odyssey

"On Wednesday morning, the day after we returned from Arad, our bureaucratic odyssey began. Susie and I, without the kids, were driven to the American Embassy. It was in an old mansion. It had a high gate around it with Romanian police officer at the entrance. There was a block-long line of Romanians waiting to get in. They had been there all night. But, since we were Americans, we were allowed to walk directly to the gate. We showed the Romanian police officer our passports and he waved us right in. We went through security on the ground floor and then up the stairs to the reception area. We were told to see 'Nina Malexandru.' She would be handling our case. We waited. Finally, our name was called. We went up to a little window, like at an old-fashioned bank. Ms. Malexandru spoke perfect English, although I assumed she was Romanian. She handed us a packet of papers and told us to fill them out. Her attitude reeked of disdain and disinterest. I had always assumed that the US State Department was a class act. And, in this particular situation, I thought they would be delighted to help us. In fact, I had expected the American counselor officer to stride up to us, stick out his right hand and say, 'Bill Bennet, Ogden, Utah. *Glad* to see ya.' But, in effect, they said, 'Have a seat, take a number. We don't care.' Afterwards my wife and I argued about Ms. Malexandru's attitude. Susie would say, 'I think she was incredibly cold.' Then I would say, 'No, I think she was incredibly indifferent.' But, the general attitude of the embassy staff was, 'Why are you pestering us with this petty personal problem, we're busy people. We have a country to run.' Later, Raymond said that Nina Malexandru was probably Securitate—a spy; who else would speak perfect English in Romania? And, that's why she couldn't have cared less about our adoption.

"So, we sat down and began to work on the packet. The cover sheet was titled: 'Requirements for Adopting Parents Concerning Issuance Documentation of the Adopted Child's Entry Visa.' It said we needed: an approved I600A orange form from the INS or approval by cable. This was called a Visa #37 Cable. Then we had to fill out an I-600 blue form. We needed an adoption decree for each child—original, certified, and an English translation. We also needed each child's new court-issued birth certificate bearing the same name as that on the child's passport—original, certified, and English translation. A relinquishment statement for each child and a medical exam for each child by the Titan Polyclinic in Bucharest was also required. And, two photos of each child, in semi-profile, showing the right ear were needed.

"We shrugged, sat down, and filled out the papers. What the INS had told us was that the first half of the case file was filled out in the United States and then cabled to Bucharest. That was the Visa #37 Cable. Then the second half was to be completed in Bucharest. We finished the forms and we paid a $300 fee. Ms. Malexandru then officially informed us that we had an approved I-600A orange form. We then had to fill out the I600 blue form. Once we finished that, an hour or two later, we returned to Ms. Malexandru. We were told our first task was to have two photographs taken of each child. But, they could *only* be in a semi-profile showing the right ear. And, this could *only* be done at one photo studio, in the entire country. 'Well, where is it?' I asked. 'It's near the university,' she said. 'But, where?' I asked. She dismissed me with a wave of the hand. 'Your driver will know.' I collected my papers and we left.

"We met Nicu, Ion, and Floriana outside. They had been waiting several hours for us. We told them that we needed to have the children's pictures taken at a particular photo studio 'near the university.' To my surprise, they knew which studio I was referring to. So, we drove back to Floriana's and picked up the kids. I had assumed that since this was 'the only photo studio in the country' that could do this for the embassy it must be some 'fancy shmansy' high tech studio. But, in fact, it was just the opposite. It was, honest to god, Matthew Brady! They had a big, black box camera with glass plates that slid in and out! We sat our kids down in front of the camera. They were sick and it was a 100° F. Then they said the children must remain motionless for seven minutes! Under the circumstances, our children were unable to remain motionless for seven seconds. Soon, they began to cry. Then they began to scream. We quickly snatched them up and left. Nicu then told us that he was an amateur photographer and that he would be willing, and able, to take the pictures; and the embassy would never know the difference. I thanked him. So, we went home and put the kids to bed. The next day he arrived with his cameras. He took the pictures and they turned out fine. And, he was right, the American Embassy never knew the difference.

"Our next task was to get the kids their medical exams. We were told by Ms. Malexandru that there was only one doctor in the entire country who was 'approved.' Floriana, because she was a doctor, knew someone, who knew someone, who knew this doctor. With the help of a half dozen packs of cigarettes Floriana was able to arrange an appointment for us for that Friday.

"On Friday morning, we got up, dressed the kids, and drove to the clinic. I expected the doctor to be a Germanic professor with a high, white starched collar. I assumed the doctor was a great scholar who would be doing the Americans a favor. And, I expected 'the clinic' to be a classy place. But, in fact, the doctor was just a typical Romanian doctor. That is, a middle-aged woman, who didn't even speak English. And, 'the clinic' was just Cook County Hospital. We went into the waiting room and sat down. When our name was called, we were ushered in past a long line of Romanian peasants who were waiting outside for a chance to see the doctor. As we were whisked past the Romanians our difference from them was striking. The women wore old clothes and babushkas. We, however, had our bright, new clothes and our red, white, and blue backpack strollers.

"When we entered the doctor's office the kids were coughing and wheezing. She tapped them on the chest and she tapped them on the knees. She looked into their ears and she looked at their eyes. She spent about 15 minutes checking over each child. To be charitable, the exam seemed, cursory. She then signed the bottom of the form and checked the box that said, 'apparently healthy.' That was it. I was surprised. So I said, 'What about blood tests? And, what about all the other things that need to be checked on this form?' She said, 'It is not necessary, not for babies. For grown-ups you do all this. You do the syphilis test, the blood test, and all this; but, for children, you don't need to bother.' So, I said, 'Are you sure?' She said, 'Oh, yes. I do this for the American Embassy every day. Don't worry, this is just fine.' I shrugged. We put our children back into their red, white, and blue backpack strollers and went down to the car. We drove the kids back to Floriana's and then Susie and I returned to the embassy.

"We presented the complete medical forms to Ms. Malexandru. She flew into a rage. She screamed, 'This is not acceptable! The forms are all blank, *nothing* was done!' I calmly, yet firmly, said, 'I did what you told me to do. I took *your* forms to *your* doctor. I told her to examine my children. That's all I know. I am not a doctor.' She snatched the forms from me and stormed away. She then grabbed the phone and made a call. I assumed she called the doctor. She screamed and yelled into the phone for a *long* time. Then she put the phone down and returned to us. 'They're okay,' she said meekly.

"Later, when we returned to Floriana's house, I realized that I had given Ms. Malexandru some extra papers. And, if they were lost, we'd have to start the entire process again. The next day, in a panic, we drove to the embassy and retrieved my papers. Later, I made a similar mistake with some other important papers. At that point I realized that I was suffering from 'High anxiety.' I also was suffering from my diarrhea, sleeplessness, and bedbug bites. I was surprised how quickly I had become an anxiety-ridden wreck.

"Late one afternoon we took the kids to the zoo. By the time we got there, at five or six o'clock, the zoo was already closed. But, of course, this was Bucharest. So, we gave the gatekeeper a couple of packs of cigarettes and he let us right in. We strolled around for an hour. We showed them the lions, tigers, and elephants. But, they didn't respond. They didn't appreciate, or probably even understand, what they were seeing. In fact, during the first six months we had them home I would crawl around on the floor, roar, and then 'eat them' like a lion. They had no idea what I was doing.

"After a week in Bucharest life began to get routine. Each morning we would get up and go off to another office to file more papers. While we were gone, 'Nanna,' a friend of Floriana's, would watch the kids. Nanna had been a childcare worker at Orphanage No. 1 with Floriana for twenty years. She was wonderful; and, so was her husband, 'Dada.' He would get in line at 5:00 a.m. to get milk for my babies. Then, he'd come again in the afternoon with some more milk.

"Although Nanna took good care of the kids, Ari just laid there. Joel, although 17 months old, was unable to walk. But, after several days with Nanna and Dada, he started walking by holding on to their fingers. When we saw this we were delighted. We applauded. Then one day Joel opened a window, by himself! I felt he was so clever! Just like a scientist! We were very proud.

"After we finished collecting all our documents for Nina Malexandru we began the second half of our odyssey. We now had to deal with the Romanian government. So, we drove to the Romanian Passport Office. It was located in a huge, Stalinist building. We entered and found ourselves in a tiny, dimly lit entryway. Blocking our way was a uniformed officer hunched over a desk. On his desk was an old-fashioned gooseneck lamp which threw a dirty light across his ledger. There were benches on either side of the room. A dozen people sat there quietly, in the dusk, waiting for 'The State' to dispense its favors. Behind the official was a long, dimly lit corridor with an endless line of offices. The walls of the entryway were made of huge stones. The room felt like a cell. And I felt I knew how prisoners felt waiting for the fall of the truncheon on their neck.

Or, perhaps, how Jews felt before being interrogated by the Gestapo. For me that room was a physical manifestation of fascism, of 'The State.' Did you see David Mamet's film, *Homicide*?"

"No."

"In the beginning of the film an FBI SWAT team is about to assault an apartment. The FBI agents wear black outfits and black stocking caps. They look like terrorists. Members of the team carry shields which are worn on the edges. Both the shields and the agents look shabby. One of the agents counts off on his fingers before they burst through the door. You can almost hear the metallic click of his fingers. This was a manifestation of the cold, efficient, mechanical state. In Romania it was the terrorist state."

"I thought this was supposed to be a love story?"

"So, to go on. So we sat in this tiny, dark room for a long time. Occasionally an official would come out, whisper something to someone on one of the benches, and they'd disappear together down the hall. Finally, an official came over whispered to us. We walked to his office and sat down. We gave him a few packages of cigarettes. He said that he'd really like to help us but there was a clerical error on one of the birth certificates. That is, both birth certificates had the same birth date. Therefore, he couldn't process the passport applications. He told us that we would have to return to the office that had issued them. Once the mistake was corrected he could then immediately issue the passports. We thanked him and left. We then drove to the health department office that had issued the certificates. It was in a nondescript Bucharest neighborhood. The building was V-shaped, and the entrance was at the corner. We walked up but found that the door was locked. We knocked and they opened the door. They let us step into a small three-by-five entryway; but, they wouldn't let us into the building, itself. They then took our papers and disappeared. Susie, Floriana, and Nicu waited in the hallway. Ion and I went back to the car. We sat there quite awhile, perhaps an hour. Ion finally said, 'This is ridiculous. Give me some cigarettes.' I gave him four packs of Kents and he disappeared into the entrance. A little later he came out and said, 'It's taken care of. It will be fifteen more minutes.' A few minutes later they brought out the corrected certificates.

"We then had to return to the passport office with the new certificates. But, I also had to cash some traveler's checks. So, Ion dropped Nicu and me off at the bank in downtown Bucharest. Meanwhile, Susie, Ion, and Floriana went back to the fascist passport office.

"We had gone to this particular bank because it was the only bank, in the entire country, where you can cash foreign traveler's checks and get dollars. And, there is only one teller at the one bank who gives out the dollars.

"I entered the bank at 1:00 p.m. The bank, which was the size of Niles Savings in Niles, Illinois, had hundreds of people waiting in line to get dollars. No, I'm saying this wrong. A line implies an ordered, and perhaps even polite, human gathering. However, here there was simply a mass of hundreds of people pressing up to this one teller's cage. Before you could get in this 'line' you had to make your way around the edge of the crowd and go to one of the other tellers. You gave her your passport and your traveler's checks, and then you filled out a little form. She then explained to you that the bank would take 7.5 percent of the money for doing you this favor. If you agreed, they then pulled a huge ledger off the shelf and recorded the information by hand. There were no computers, everything was done by hand. Once the information was recorded you moved away from that window and insinuated yourself into the crowd. And, you waited. It was 100° F that afternoon, and the bank had no air-conditioning. As I stood there other people's sweating bodies rubbed up against mine. And, the crowd slowly undulated like a belly dancer in slow motion. As the other members of the crowd rubbed and pushed and pushed and rubbed the experience was sensual, almost sexual.

"An hour after I arrived a fella' worked his way over to me. He asked, 'Do you speak English?' 'Yes', I said. 'Where are you from?' I asked. I thought he was going to say, 'I'm from New Jersey.' But, instead he said that he was from New Zealand. Then he told me that he was here to look for babies. 'Oh, how nice,' I said. But, I didn't tell him why I was there. So, we began to chat. While I was in Arad the lawyer had asked me to find someone 'nice' for the two sisters I hadn't adopted. I had thought of a couple in Chicago that I knew who wanted Romanian babies. Throughout my half hour conversation with the New Zealander I couldn't decide whether to tell him about the babies in Arad. Finally, I decided I couldn't be selfish. Who knew if the couple in Chicago would even want these babies? So I said, 'I happen to be here to adopt two babies. And, I know of two more babies in Arad.' As I said that I saw the ears of another couple perk up. They pushed their way over to me and said, 'Are you here to adopt babies?' 'Yes.' 'So are we. We've come from England.' So, then I repeated the information about the babies in Arad. There was a Romanian translator nearby who also pushed her way over to me. She said, 'I'm looking for babies for an English couple. Can you help?' So I gave her the information on the babies, too. We then passed the time chatting about other topics. Finally, after three hours, my name came up. I forced my way past the embassy officials from Guinea, Ghana, Mali, Chad, and Niger. I pushed my way up to the window. The teller, who had a large bushy moustache, put aside his ham sandwich and cigarette and handed me my money. I left the bank at 4:00 p.m.

"The next day was Sunday. Nanna watched the kids and we drove to a town called Sinai,* about a hundred miles north of Bucharest. As we drove through the countryside Nicu, Floriana, and Ion taught Susie a Romanian lullaby. I was so sleepy that I was incapable of even memorizing an eight-line lullaby. I dozed off as we drove north. About half way there we drove through Ploesti.** It was an oil producing center and it had been heavily bombed by the Americans during World War II. Nicu remembered living there as a child and having the bombs 'fall on my head.' He said that the people of Ploesti hated Americans for what they had done to them during the war. However, in the rest of the country they liked Americans. After a long ride we arrived at Sinai. We parked at the foot of a large hill. We walked up a long curving roadway. There were many other tourists. After several long minutes we arrived at a lovely nineteenth century castle. It was called the *Peles*, the palace. It was painted white with exposed wooden boards. It looked like an immense English cottage adorned with spires and turrets. It had been built about fifty years ago and Ceausescu had claimed it as his own. He had forbidden any visitors to enter the Peles, except himself. And, this he did only once a year. After the revolution it was opened to the public. However, on that day the public was barred because there was a tour of 'important foreign officials.' But, Nicu, with our cigarettes, had a little chat with the man at the gate. He explained that we were 'important

---

* pronounced: Si-nie-ah
** pronounced: Ploy-esh-tee

American officials' and we needed to see the Peles. So, we were allowed in; much to the chagrin of all the Romanians trying to gain entrance.

"We passed through the gate and walked up to the building. We entered it through a small anteroom. We were told that we had to take off our shoes. So we removed them and we put on little slippers. We were then allowed to enter. We glided into a hallway with a richly lacquered floor. We then passed into a large central ball with a second floor balcony. All the dark brown wood in the room glistened. There were massive medieval chairs around the edges of the hall. And, there were large tapestries covering the walls. We marched up and down the grand staircases, we snaked our way up narrow, circular stairways, and we wandered through the armory with its medieval suits of armor. We spent two hours in the Peles. It had seemed like only a few minutes. The Peles had been dazzling. It was a crime that Ceausescu had kept this all to himself.

"We left the Peles and started down the hill. A great many tourists were still streaming up. I could tell they were tourists because they had video cameras. No Romanian could ever afford a video camera. I then looked to my left and saw an elderly peasant couple cutting the grass with scythes on the Peles grounds. The woman was dressed in an old, bulky overcoat and wore a babushka. She and the other worker, her husband I assumed, swung their scythes back and forth. They then gathered up the grass and tied it into bundles. Susie looked at me. Her look said, 'If our grandparents hadn't gotten out of here that could have been us.'

"On the drive back from Sinai we stopped at a clustering of cars parked on the side of the road. This was an open-air market. Nicu explained that these were Yugoslavs who had come across the border to sell their wares. The traders were doing a brisk business. It was not hard to understand why since there was nothing to buy in Romania.

"Later we stopped at a restaurant. In the United States, it would have been called, 'a roadhouse.' But, in Romania it was simply a beat up little restaurant on a rural lane. We pulled up and walked in. I remember the walls were cream colored. There were several Romanian couples inside. I looked at the waitress. She was quite attractive. She had nice breasts—not too large. If she had grown up in the United States she probably would have done to college. She might have become an administrative assistant, a neurosurgeon, or a lineman for the county. At that moment I wanted to snatch her up and carry her off to America. So she could 'fulfill her potential.' But, I didn't. And, I assume she's still a waitress serving bad food in a Romanian restaurant with dirty cream-colored walls.

"On another day we visited Snagoff, a popular resort near Bucharest. Snagoff had a pretty lake with hotels and restaurants on the shore. It was nice, but it looked as if the resort had been frozen in 1890. There were a lot of foreign tourists there. But there were few Romanians because they couldn't afford the prices. We got a table overlooking the lake and had lunch. It was very pleasant.

And, as a treat Nicu ordered an entire case of Pepsi. But, like many things in Romania, it just didn't taste right. In fact, on my earlier visit there hadn't been any Pepsi in the entire country. I had asked Nicu the reason for this. He had explained that Castro had failed to ship a boatload of sugar to Romania. So, 'there's no Pepsi in Bucharest.' Yes! There's no Pepsi in Bucharest.

"When I returned I read there was another shortage in Romania. There weren't enough lightbulbs. This led some Romanians to spend their spare time stealing lightbulbs from hotels. Other Romanians stole lightbulbs for profit. In Romania they were worth ten cents each. However, in Hungary and Yugoslavia they could be sold for a dollar each (Engelberg, 1991a).

"During lunch we were told 'the famous Snagoff story.' The story went like this: Nicolai and Elena Ceausescu had a summer home in Snagoff. One day Elena was awakened by a cock crowing. She was annoyed. So, she had all the cocks in Snagoff killed. On another day a barking dog awakened her. Again, she was annoyed. So, she had all the dogs in Snagoff killed. She slept soundly after that.

"The next day we had to stop by the Tarom office to check on our tickets. We drove to their office in downtown Bucharest. When we walked in I was struck by the appearance of the office. All the walls were padded. It looked as if the office had been a restaurant and they had simply pulled all the seats out, left the padding on the walls, and made it the ticket office. So, the office looked as if it had been decorated in 'Bad Italian Restaurant.' Also, their 'main desk' was simply an old table with a large, rotating metal ticket holder. The ticket holder had slots for dozens and dozens of tickets. However, there were only a few tickets in it. The 'information center' for Tarom, The National Airline of Romania, was a woman sitting at a folding table answering the phone. Behind her was an old, black theatrical drape strung across the back of the room on a wire. I assumed that behind the drape was Tarom's 'operations center.' This was probably the nerve center of the airline. When our turn came we did our business and left.

"Afterwards we had some spare time. So we went to the main Romanian Orthodox Church in Bucharest. It was an old Byzantine church. When we arrived a service was in progress. We stood at the door and peered in. It was very dark inside. But, through the smoke of the sacramental candles we could see the Byzantine look of the church. There were many medieval tapestries draped on the wall. The gold cups glittered in the candlelight. We stood there for a long time peering in. But, we didn't enter because the church was packed with worshippers. However, the thing that struck me the most was not the church. Instead, it was an old woman outside the door who was begging. The church, though dark and smoky, glittered with gold. The woman, however, sat on a tattered old blanket. She extended a small bowl towards each parishioner that entered. She looked wretched. As I watched her from a distance I suddenly recalled a long forgotten memory. I remembered that when I was a kid I took the CTA El train to downtown Chicago. And there used to be men on the El who tried to sell you little plastic animal puzzles for a dollar each. I often bought them. I did this not because I wanted the puzzles. Instead, I bought them because I pitied the men. And, here, again, there was the same feeling of pity. I gave her some money and we left.

"After we left the church we drove towards the center of Bucharest. We passed the law school. Nearby was a very old church. It was one of the few churches in Bucharest that Ceausescu had not torn down. In fact, Ceausescu had torn down one quarter of the entire city to build a grand palace called the 'House of the People.' As a result, there were very few churches left. This church was one of the oldest. It was striking. It was small and vertical. It was painted green with white uprights. It had traditional bell towers and looked medieval.

"Later, we drove to the House of the People. We followed a Gypsy wagon for a block or two. It was stuffed with people in typical Gypsy garb. In a travelogue the scene would have been called 'picturesque.' But it wasn't. There were two old, worn-out horses pulling the wagon. A third one followed behind. And, a scrawny dog ran along side. Except for an accident of birth I could have been one of those people.

"A little later we arrived at the palace. It was an immense, squat, twelve-story building. It sat on a hill overlooking blocks and blocks of barren land. I later learned that it had almost 4 million square feet of floor space and was larger than the Pentagon. It had 2,500 rooms, including a 240-foot-deep bomb shelter. Its construction had displaced 40,000 people. And it had employed 100,000 workers to construct it. It had cost $1 billion dollars. That was 20 percent of Romania's entire national budget. The design has been described as 'Stalinist *kitsch*.'

"We parked and walked up the hill. As I entered the building I could see it was magnificent. The main staircase was made of solid marble. It was reported that during the construction of the building it had been ripped out six times because Ceausescu hadn't liked the way it had looked. The grand ballrooms were the most magnificent rooms in the building. Each was two stories tall. And all the wall panels and doors reached to the ceilings. Each ballroom had an immense chandelier. These chandeliers were, literally, yards across. There was an outdoor balcony on one side of the building. I walked out and saw a broad boulevard that stretched into the mist. Ceausescu had built the boulevard to be six-and-a-half feet wider than the Champs Elysees. Lining the boulevard were large, luxury apartment buildings meant for the Securitate. The boulevard had originally been named, 'The Victory of Socialism Boulevard.' However, after the revolution it was given a new, antiseptic, anatomical name, "The New Artery Boulevard" (Revzin, 1990; Tagliabue, 1991; Catchpole, 1992; Waxman, 1990; "Palace For Romanian Lawmakers," 1993).

"When we returned to Floriana's, I went to bed. Susie sat and chatted with Nicu for three hours. After I woke up I felt refreshed. We then ate dinner. After everyone had gone to bed I decided I needed to start learning Romanian. So, I took out my teach-yourself-Romanian book and began to memorize the vocabulary. I began with words that were special to me: *noroc*, lucky; *adopta*, adopt; *dragoste*, affection; and *furnica*, ant. Then I turned to the letter A: assist, *ajuta*; assistant, *ajator*; atrocious, *atroce*; and, so on.

"After three hours of work I had gotten to the middle of the B's: bedtime, *ora de culcare*, bee; *albina*; and beg, *ruga*. But soon my eyes closed and my head dropped onto the dining room table. I woke up a little later and found Zadek, the cat, sitting on the table next to me. Zadek, or Zadecku, as he was often called, always wanted to be rubbed. I usually obliged him. Sometimes, however, he was totally uninterested in me. That was when he had to meet his 'needs.' He would then zoom out the door or jump out of an open window. But, those times were few. Mostly, he laid on the table next to me while I rubbed him. Sadly, Zadeku is now gone.

"After my 'A-B Night,' I was awakened at 8:00 a.m. That morning we had to overcome our last great obstacle, the Justice Ministry's Translation Office. We had to have our documents translated and stamped by them as our embassy accepted only documents translated by them and bearing their official stamp. And, even if we had taken the papers to a Professor of English at the University, it wouldn't have sufficed. That was because, like everything else in Romania, the American Embassy required 'the official stamp.'

"I gathered all our documents and Nicu took them down to the translation office. He arrived at 9:00 a.m, Friday morning. He found that there was a six-hour wait just to drop the documents into a tray. Then it would be four to six weeks for the documents to be translated. However, Nicu knew that we had airline tickets to leave in a week. So he went to a back stairway, and found his way down to the typing pool. He then bribed some of the secretaries, and found out where the English translator's office was located. He went to the translator and said, 'These people need these papers right away, do you think you can help?' He then gave her twelve or thirteen packs of cigarettes. That was probably worth a month's salary. And, on the black market, it was worth three to five month's salary. She then said, 'Well, we're rather busy now, how about Monday afternoon? And, I'll do it over the weekend, myself. Is that alright?' 'Well, alright,' he said. So, on Monday afternoon he returned and he picked up our papers. A few days after we got home there was a front-page article in *USA Today* about a woman who was attempting to adopt a baby from Romania. She had been at the Intercontinental Hotel in Bucharest for two months 'waiting for papers.' She was spending $109 a night, and had run up thousands of dollars in bills. Her problem was that she just didn't have a good fixer (Neuman, 1990; for other adoptive parents personal experiences see Bohlen, 1990i; Quinn, 1990; Riniker, 1991; Waller, 1991; Wisby, 1991; Harder, 1990; Raymond, 1990;

Rummler, 1991; "Romanian 'Orphans' Find Homes," 1991; Jordan, 1990; Dunphy, 1990; Love, 1991; Little, 1993; Sammons, 1992; Talaly, 1994; Porter, 1993; Campanella, 1993; Graves, 1993; Aitken, 1993; Fleming, 1994).

"During that weekend we went sight-seeing in Bucharest. We drove by University Square, where many students had been shot during the revolution. I got out of the car and walked past some Gypsies selling flowers. Nicu said, 'There are two kinds of Gypsies: those that are nomadic and those that are urban. Many urban Gypsies, like these, are petty merchants; they sell flowers. In fact, under Ceausescu the only form of capitalism allowed in the entire country was this type of flower selling. In spite of this, the lives of Gypsies in Romania are hard. And, many Romanians, even liberals, hate them. Now that they're free, I think many will leave' (see Ingram, 1992a; Protzman, 1992; Cordrescu, 1992; "Germany Deports 100 Romanians," 1992; Binder, 1993a; Kamm, 1993; Kinzer, 1992; "Gypsies and Germans, Wronged," 1992; "Romanian Gypsies Are Skeptical About Germany's Financial Help," 1992).

"I picked up my video camera and began to film a large, traditional wooden cross in the center of the square. It was draped with flowers and encircled by thin amber candles. There was another memorial on a nearby street corner. On the wall of the building behind the memorial were painted songs and poems commemorating the revolution. While I was filming a young Romanian man came up to me and asked, 'What do you think of the revolution? What do you think of Romania, now? The Communists are still in charge.' There wasn't much I could say that he would appreciate. I could have told him that politics, like economics, was entrepreneurial. If he wanted change He had to go out and do it himself. He would have to organize a group of people. Then he had to print petitions and literature and get his group to gather signatures for those petitions. Once this was accomplished he would have to call a large meeting to endorse a candidate. His group would then have to fan out throughout Bucharest in order to hand out literature and to knock on doors. This then had to be repeated in every city, town, and village in the country. And, he had to accomplish all this with no money, no media exposure, and frequent government harassment. As I said, I just don't think that my speech would have meant much to him. So, instead I spouted some platitudes about organizing and working hard. It all sounded rather hollow. After a few minutes of vacuous chatter I smiled, shook his hand, and walked off. I'm sure he was just as unsatisfied by our conversation as I was.

"We then drove around the city. Not far from the downtown we drove past a little street that looked just like Paris. I asked our new driver, Petru, who didn't speak English very well, to pull over. He didn't understand me and drove on. But, even for that moment, I could see that a hundred years ago Bucharest was, the Paris of the East. We then drove to another part of the city which was lined by charming old villas. I was told that Mrs. Ceausescu had wanted to tear this section of the city down so she could enlarge one of her many palaces. But she had been overthrown before that had occurred.

"We then drove over to the main synagogue in downtown Bucharest. I had expected to drive up to a grand building on a broad boulevard. Instead, I found the synagogue to be an old, small, three-story yellow brick building on a narrow side street. We drove past some street construction and parked. In order to get to the building we had to climb over piles of sand and gravel and then circumvent a wide hole in the pavement.

"We opened the gate and entered the small courtyard in front of the *shul*. The building was closed that afternoon. However, we had read that there were going to be services over the weekend. There were posters on billboards with photos of 'famous American artists' who were going to be singing that weekend. We had never heard of any of them.

"That night, as a treat, we went to the only Chinese restaurant in the entire country. The restaurant was in a hotel. As we made our way through the lobby we passed a throng of German tourists. The Romanians we were with had never eaten at this restaurant because it was very expensive. But, this night, like every night in Bucharest, it was our treat. We arrived at about 7:00 p.m., and we got the last table in the restaurant. The waiter handed us the menus. There was page after page of dishes to order. I was astounded. Food was in short supply in Bucharest. This restaurant seemed exceptional. When the waiter came over to us I said, 'Do you have all these dishes?' 'Oh, no,' he said. 'You can only order what is starred. That is what we have available.' About half the items on the menu were starred. I was still impressed. So I said, 'Can we order any of these dishes?' 'Well, no. Actually, we only have five things; and, they all have shrimp in them.' We laughed. And, since Susie kept kosher, we left. We eventually found another restaurant and had dinner.

"The next day we went to a large park in Bucharest. The park had a small carnival, a circular walk lined with the busts of famous Romanian poets, and a large garden. However, the garden was unkempt. We were told that since the revolution the park employees had lost interest in maintaining the garden. Later, we went to a very large park in the center of Bucharest. It had a lovely lake. We walked along it for over an hour. After our walk we went shopping.

"We drove to the finest department store in Bucharest. The entire area surrounding it was rubble. We parked in front of a crumbling concrete dock. However, the building no longer existed. We were just a hundred feet from the entrance to the department store. I couldn't understand why we were able to park so close to the entrance until we got inside. We walked up the marble steps and entered the store. I was immediately struck by how dark it was inside. It was like a tomb. I glanced around and saw that the shelves were bare. As I walked across the marble floor a small cloud of dust arose. Apparently, no one ever walked across this floor. The clerks, with no customers, chatted, shuffled around aimlessly, or stared off into space. I remember thinking to myself that this is what the first department store to open after the nuclear holocaust will look like.

"We went upstairs. I think there were seven floors. Starting at the second floor there was a wide oval in the center of the building where the escalators were to be placed. However, they had never been installed. So, there was a long, curving glass rail which was abruptly interrupted by pieces of plywood that had been thrown up. Spray painted on each of them it said, DANGER.

"Nicu explained that Ceausescu had built this store as a show place. The day before he came to open it an endless line of trucks had delivered merchandise. But, the day after the opening the trucks reappeared and took almost all of the merchandise away. We wandered over to the electronics department. It had two or three boom boxes, a few radios, and a hill of flashlights. In the women's clothing department were some coats and a few expensive women's dresses. In the men's department there were twenty or thirty checkered suits. Although almost all the shelves were bare, there was a mountain of socks. They even towered over the hill of flashlights.

"After the 'finest department store in Romania' we went to a second department store. This was a huge store with thousands of people bustling about. And, there were even things to buy. But, most of the people weren't interested in what was available. For those few things they did want to buy, like shoes, there were long lines. However, this 'nice' department store, by Romanian standards, reminded me of the basement of Goldblatts.

"We then went across the street to a toy store and bought a few wooden toys. They were a tiny fraction of the cost they would have been in the United States. We then walked a few blocks to a shop that sold traditional peasant clothing for tourists. Most of the clothes were made of white cotton with elaborate red stitching. We bought a few things for the kids. We then walked back to the car and drove to a record store. The store looked as if it had been the set for a grade B 1950s beach movie. It was quite large, but mostly empty. It had a tile floor. And, dust was everywhere. The displays hadn't been changed since 1962. And, most of the bins were empty. However, I found numerous Elvis records. In fact, everywhere you went you heard Elvis. They had just discovered him."

"You mean, *re*-discovered him."

"No, they had jus discovered him, for the first time."

"Jeez."

"We then drove by an immense Stalinist building with two huge towers. It had been built in the 1950s. It was probably the most depressing building in the entire city. There was a long carved stone mural in front of the building showing some great battle scene. I assume it was the fight of the people for 'socialist freedom.'

"Then we drove to Gheorghe's house for dinner. We hadn't seen too much of him during our second visit. However, we had seen his mother and father, Nanna and Dada, every day since they were babysitting. They made us an elaborate meal, but I didn't find the food very appealing. Otherwise, the evening was very pleasant. The father was a retired engineer and he had attached a primitive VCR to his TV. He put in a cassette. It didn't play very well and it wasn't in English but it was . . . diverting. Then we turned on the television. We saw the new government being sworn in. Gheorghe explained to me that these men were mostly technocrats and not Communists, although President Iliescu was a former Communist. However, he also explained that people did not become high-level bureaucrats unless they were connected, somehow, to the Communist Party.

"After watching TV at Gheorghe's house I realized that Romanian television hadn't changed since my first visit. There were still long periods of time when they merely broadcast pictures of flowers. There was also a lot of folk music. And there was some news. That night we also saw some Bulgarian television because Dada had set up a special antenna for his television. However, Bulgarian TV was even worse than Romanian television, although that's hard to believe. Bulgarian programming consisted mostly of happy peasants folk dancing. That is, showing grainy 1950s film, of happy peasants folk dancing. It was as if we were watching a *Saturday Night Live* skit entitled, 'Bad Bulgarian Television.'

"On Monday morning we drove to a new cemetery which was being constructed to honor those that had been killed in the revolution. It was on a busy commercial strip. A trolley clattered up and down the street. In the cemetery there were hundreds of white headstones. Most had pictures on them. Almost all of the photos were of young university students. Many of the graves also had wooden plaques with poems on them. The poems all spoke about the fight of these students for freedom; and, the lives they would never lead. One grave was even adorned with a surfboard.

"That afternoon it was 100°, as usual. So on the way home from the cemetery we stopped at a café. We ordered some juice and ice cream. But, I didn't know that in Romania they had only one kind of ice cream, Nescafe ice cream. It was dreadful.

"We returned to Floriana's house early in the afternoon. Nicu was there with the translations of all our documents. We were delighted. This meant we were almost finished. Although Susie was happy she couldn't keep her eyes open and soon fell asleep. Nicu and I sat down in the dining room and began to chat, as we had done many times before. He said that he had been a trade official for the Romanian government. He told me about the various countries in Eastern Europe that he had been to. He began with Bulgaria. He said, 'Well, the Bulgarians are a dull, Slavic people. They are humorless and slow; as opposed to the fiery, Latin Romanians.'

"How do the Bulgarian and Romanian governments get along?' They were both Communists, he explained, so they had to get along. But, in fact, years ago, Bulgaria seized two provinces from Romania on the Black Sea coast; and, the Romanians have never forgiven them. He said Hungary was nice. Budapest, the capital, had had an old world flavor to it. There had been many pretty older buildings there. But during the 1956 revolution much of the capital had been destroyed. It had been rebuilt with Communist 'apartment blocks'. Now, it was merely drab. However, he felt that the Hungarian people were very sophisticated and he was quite impressed with them. He thought Prague was also quite nice. It was hilly and smaller than Bucharest. Poland, however, was flat and uninteresting. Warsaw had been destroyed during World War II and had been rebuilt in a drab Communist style. Yugoslavia, however, he thought was wonderful. There were places on the coast he had visited where you could drive up from the tropical, Mediterranean coast into a mountain climate in just a few miles.

"I then asked him if Yugoslavia was a coherent country. He said no. The north had been part of the Hapsburg Empire, but the south had been part of the Turkish Empire. The north, Slovenia and Croatia, were Catholic, and closely tied to Austria and Germany. The south, however, was Eastern Orthodox and Moslem. Also, incomes in the north were five times higher than in the south. The north was industrial and prosperous, whereas, the south was poor.

"Later, I wrote a paper on Yugoslavia. I learned that during World War II the country had been controlled by the Nazis and Croatian fascists. The Serbs, who were Communist 'Partisans', fought them. During the war, 1.4 million Yugoslavs died. The Nazis had killed four hundred thousand and the other million had died in fighting between the Croats and the Serbs. So, the war then going on in Yugoslav was the Serbs getting even for World War II. The conflict had simply been frozen for 50 years by the Communist regime.

"Nicu also told me that he had made several visits to Russia over the years. He thought the people were very friendly, but very poor. 'They've been through a lot,' he said. He said that on his first trip to Moscow, in the mid-1960s, he went in to a butcher shop. Instead of meat he found 'a Cheops of fish'—a pyramid of cans of fish that rose to the heavens.

"I then asked him about Western Europe. He said that Switzerland was very pretty. It was a very nice place 'for retired people.' I asked him what he thought of the Germans. He said, 'They're a sturdy, orderly people. If you get to know them they're friendly. If you spend a couple weeks with a German they'll invite you into their home and into their family. They're a very warm people.' 'And the French?' 'The French are cold. You could drink with a Frenchman for a year and he'd never invite you to meet his family. They are very aloof.'

"We then talked about the Romanian economy. Nicu explained that the Romanian people didn't understand freedom. They thought freedom meant the freedom not to work. In the six months since the revolution economic production had gone down 50 percent; and, it had been an extremely poor country to begin with.

"When I got home I did some research and found some startling information. For example, under Ceausescu agricultural production was poor. However, everyone was afraid to tell him the truth. So, agricultural yields were inflated by 600 percent. Also, Romania had a lower proportion of students in universities than almost any other country in Europe. Also, it had fewer television sets, per capita, than Burkina Faso, Kenya, or Zaire. Forty percent of all its scientific, industrial, and transportation equipment was worn out. Furthermore, Ceausescu had built his economy on a rigid Stalinist scheme that had strongly emphasized heavy industry. As a result of this much of the economy was concentrated in a few giant, and inefficient, industrial plants. For example, the country had three times as much oil refining capacity as it needed. Also, many factories operated at below 50 percent capacity. And, in fact, one aluminum factory used more electricity than the entire population of Romania (Brogan, 1990).

"Later, I ran across the United Nation's 'Human Development Report for 1992.' The report had a 'human development index' which combined indicators such as national income, life expectancy, and educational attainment. In its ranking of industrialized countries Romania ranked last. And, in an overall ranking of all 162 countries in the world, Romania was number 60. That was between Brazil and Cuba. For example, Romania's life expectancy was the lowest of all industrialized countries, 70.8 years. Japan was the best at 78.6 years. The United States was 75.9. Also, Romania's average years of schooling was only about 60 percent of the United States level, 7.8 versus 12.3 years. And, maternal mortality was more than 100 times worse than the best industrialized country."

"What?"

"Yes. Romania had 210 maternal deaths per 100,000 live births in 1988. Iceland had two. We had 13."

"Wow."

"Then I checked the 1993 report. Romania was still dead last for the industrialized countries. But, since there were now 173 countries in the world this made its overall ranking fall to 77. It was now ranked just above Albania. It was even behind Azerbaijan and Turkmenistan.

"In the 1994 report it was again at the bottom of the industrialized countries except for Albania. Overall, it was 72 out of 173 countries. It now ranked between Syria and Azerbaijan, which was then at war with Armenia. Romania's life expectancy had fallen to 69.9 years and its maternal death rate was still poor. One criteria in the index was 'years lost to premature death'. Romania's was the highest in the industrialized world at 19 years. The best in the index was Switzerland at 8 years; and, the United States was about average for the West at 11 years. Also, in total spending on education as a percentage of the gross domestic product Romania was last for the industrialized countries. Similarly, health care spending was last at 3.9 percent of the GDP for industrialized countries. The United States was highest at 13.3 percent. Romania's GNP per capita in 1991 was $1,400. The United States was $22,340; and, we were only number seven in the world. And, lastly, in 1991 Romania's GNP was $31 billion whereas the United States GNP was $5,677 billion ("United Nations Development Programme," 1994; see also Crosette, 1994)."

"Depressing."

"Yes. But to go on with Nicu's story. He told me that Ceausescu had created an economic disaster long before the revolution. For example, one day Ceausescu decided that Romania should not owe any money to anyone. He believed that if he was debt free no other country could force him to do anything he didn't want to do. So he decided to pay off the countries entire foreign debt, quickly. To do this he began to export everything the country produced. There had been a great deal of oil produced in the country. Almost all of that was exported. Also, they exported most of their natural gas. So, in the winter, people had heat for only two hours a day. There wasn't enough food, either. People were forced to wait in line for hours to get what meager supplies were available. Ceausescu also decided that Romania should be self sufficient in chemicals. So, he refused to allow the importation of chemicals. Some of these were chemicals which were crucial for the production of pharmaceuticals. As a result of this policy many pharmaceutical plants simply closed down and pharmacy shelves were empty.

"Nicu then went on to tell me a little about his personal life. He said that when he was young he had been married and divorced. At work he knew a woman who was a friend. Eventually they fell in love, married, and had a baby. His son was now at the university studying to be an engineer. He talked glowingly about his son. He said his son was athletic and he frequently went hiking with him. As an indirect way of giving me some grandfatherly advice he told me how he couldn't wait for each stage of his son's life to unfold as he grew up.

"After telling me about his personal life he suddenly stopped talking. Then he said, 'Did you know I went to jail?' 'No. For what?' 'For nothing. . . .' His voice trailed off. 'What do you mean?' 'When I worked for the Trade Ministry my boss was the son of the former president. Some high level government officials in the new regime wanted to get him. So, they cooked up a scandal and had him arrested. But, I was involved because I had cosigned all the trade documents. So, I became a fall guy; and I was arrested, too. I had friends in the Trade Ministry who went to the Securitate. They told them that I was totally innocent. The Securitate said that they knew that, but they didn't care. And, they said that if I made trouble during the trial I would be in jail for a very long time. But, if I kept my mouth shut I would be out in two or three years. So, I kept quiet, and I went to jail. I sat there, bored, for a year. The jailers didn't treat me badly, but I had nothing to do. Finally, they gave me some books and paper and I kept myself busy. Eventually, I was released. It was impossible for me to go back to the Trade Ministry. So, instead, I went to work in a factory. Since I was an engineer I was put in charge of the computer center. I spent ten years building it up. I was like my child. But, after a decade I decided it was time to retire; and, I did.'

"On another afternoon I told Nicu about America. At one point I explained to him about buying a house. That is, banks and mortgages. In spite of my explanation he thought I was rich. A few days after we returned home a letter of his arrived. He suggested that I send him $100,000, in cash, and that he would open up an adoption agency. It would be like a hotel where pregnant women could come until their babies were born. Then the babies could be given up for adoption. He then explained, in very great detail, how we could take the foreign currency we received and manipulate it in Romania in order to make a great deal of money. I thought the letter was hilarious. But, Susie concluded he was deadly serious. So, I wrote to him and said that I was $99,000 short and that I had to turn down his offer. But I learned something important from his letter. Here we have this sophisticated, worldly engineer. A man who had traveled all over the world. A man who was much more sophisticated and worldly than the average Romanian. And apparently he didn't understand money. It was really a shock.

"Now, back to my story. One afternoon Nicu's wife called. She said she had just returned from the Tarom office where she had gone to confirm our airline reservations. Now, in America, 'confirming an airline reservation' simply meant calling and asking if everything was all right. In Romania, however, it was a project. It meant going down to the Tarom office and waiting in line for five and a half hours. Nicu said that this was not an unreasonable length of time. In fact, he said, she had done quite well in getting to the front of the line that quickly. When she reached the clerk she showed them our passports and asked for our tickets. The clerk told her that she could have the tickets for George and Susan Klein. But, since she didn't have the visas or passports for the children, the clerk couldn't give her their tickets. So, Nicu took copies of the kids passports, visas, and birth certificates with him that evening to give to his wife.

"The next day she went back to the office and waited in line for another five and a half hours. When she reached the front of the line she handed the clerk all the kid's documents. The woman said, 'Oh, no. I'm sorry. I can't give you the children's tickets. You see, the tickets are for Joel and Ariel Klein. However, the passports, the visas, the birth certificates all say Viorel and Consuela Klein. So, when the *real* Mr. Klein comes for his tickets they'll be gone. And, then I'll be fired.' But, Nicu's wife knew what was really going on. So, she said, 'Well, I'll see your supervisor after lunch.' Nicu had anticipated this kind of problem, so he had asked me to give him $5 the night before. With the $5 his wife then bought five packs of cigarettes. She then returned to the clerk. She gave her the cigarettes and said, 'I've come back for the tickets for the children.' The woman said, 'Well, on second thought, I guess you can have them.'

"We were now ready to return to the American Embassy to get the kids entry visa's. And, again, we would have to face the dreaded Nina Malexandru. We arrived at the embassy at 9:00 a.m. We brought with us the original adoption decrees, certified copies, and English translations. We also had the children's new birth certificates, certified copies, and English translations. We also had, in English and Romanian, the relinquishment statement from Ariel's parents and relinquishment statements for both children from the orphanage. We had, in English and Romanian, the medical reports. We also had our two required photographs for each child. Each in semi-profile with the right ear showing, as the embassy had required. And, we had the children's Romanian passports and visas, with the old Communist symbol emblazoned on each.

"The US State Department regulations required that children who were being adopted be seen by a consular official. So, although both of the kids were sick, we dragged them with us to the embassy. After we parked, we put them in our backpack strollers and walked to the American Embassy.

"We went up to the embassy gate, showed our American passports, and the police officer whisked us in. Meanwhile, hundreds of Romanians, who had waited all night, waited in line. We then entered the Embassy. To the right, about ten feet in front of the door was a Marine guard. He sat in a booth behind thick bulletproof glass. I said to him, 'Where's the bathroom?' He didn't hear me. So, I shouted at him, 'Where's the bathroom?' He screamed something from behind the bulletproof glass. I had no idea what he was saying. After several of these exchanges I realized that the bathrooms were right next to the front entrance. So I gave Joel to Susie and I went to the bathroom. I then retrieved my son and we then walked up a few steps to the landing. There some security men searched us and allowed us to go up to the second floor waiting room. As we walked in one of the consular officers barked, 'Wait a minute! I want to see those babies!' I thought, 'Oh God, more grief!' Then she said sweetly, 'They're so cute! Everybody, come here and look at these cute babies.' I sighed. When she and the staff finished clucking over our babies she told us that we could take them home. We carried them out to Floriana and Nicu and they took them home.

"We then went back in to see Nina Malexandru. We gave her all our papers. She looked through them with disdain and said, 'Have a seat.' So, we sat down and waited for our kid's visa applications to be processed. We waited for a half hour, an hour, an hour and a half, two hours. Although it was a long wait, it wasn't a bad wait. That's because it was 100° outside and the Embassy had air-conditioning. However, eventually, I got bored. I began to look around. Since I'm a criminologist, and I know something about terrorism, I said, 'Susie, have you noticed that the bathrooms are right next to the front door?' 'So?' 'That's so a bomb left in the bathroom will blow out and not in.' 'Oh.' I then said, 'Have you noticed the doors to the waiting area are all heavily padded?' 'So?' 'It's probably because there's steel plates under the padding. So, if a bomb goes off in the waiting room the staff won't be killed.' For half an hour I pointed out what looked like counterterrorism precautions. My wife grew increasing anxious as I talked. Finally, she said, 'Why don't you shut up. Maybe they're listening.' I shrugged and shut my mouth.

"Finally, about noon, Nina called us and said, 'The papers will be ready after lunch. Come back at 1:30.' We hesitated. We hated to leave the air-conditioning. But, Nicu and Ion had returned and were waiting outside. So we left.

"We had decided to give Susie a treat. Since she kept kosher she had spent the entire two weeks in Bucharest eating vegetables, cheese, fruits, and fish. So, we decided to go to the only kosher restaurant in Bucharest. It was at the Jewish Community Center. The Center was in an old building, on a drab street, in a decrepit neighborhood. We drove over and parked. The Center, by no accident, was across the street from a police barracks. As we walked towards the entrance we saw that it was guarded by a policeman. As we approached the building the glum looking officer demanded our passports. He scowled at us. He asked what we wanted. We said that we wanted to go for lunch at the Jewish Community Center. He turned to Nicu and Ion and said, 'Why do you want to eat here? You can't even read the menu.' They told him that they were our friends and that they wanted to eat with us. He shrugged and let us pass.

"When we entered the building we saw that 'the restaurant' was merely a large room with tables. I put on a yarmulke and we went in. An elderly rabbi with a long white beard immediately complained that Nicu and Ion didn't have their heads covered. So they put on yarmulkes, too. We were then allowed to sit down. A waiter, who spoke English, took our order. Soon they brought us soup, a little salad, and a little meat. Surprisingly, it was pretty good. As we ate I looked around the room and saw that the average age of the twenty or thirty people having lunch was 70 or 80. It seemed rather obvious that these were the people who had refused to immigrate to Israel; these were the people waiting to die. Before World War II there had been as many as a million Jews in Romania. Half of them had been killed during the war. Of those that remained almost all of them had immigrated to Israel. Now, there were only seventeen thousand Jews left in the entire country. Fifty percent were over 60 years old and less than 10 percent were under 20. Thirteen hundred of them emigrated each year and thirteen hundred died. So, soon, there wouldn't be any Jews left in Romania.

"It was common knowledge that the immigration to Israel had been so massive because Ceausescu had sold Romania's Jews to Israel" (Szulc, 1991; Hundley, 1995b).

"He sold them to Israel?"

"Yes, just like he had sold the babies to Western Europe for $30,000 each. Romania has become a country of hustlers. And the best hustler in all Romania was probably the Chief Rabbi of Romania, Rabbi Rosen. He died recently. He had been in his eighties. But, first, a little history. In September 1940, General Ion Antonescu took control of the government. He filled his government with members of the fascist Iron Guard. In 1940 through the secret Hitler-Stalin Pact, Transylvania was transferred to Hungary. Its 150,000 Jews were murdered. In June 1941, Romanian and German troops invaded Russia and 'liberated' the former Romanian province of Bessarabia. They soon began deporting, and later murdering, its 200,000 Jews. Antonescu agreed to deport Romania's remaining Jews, but he changed his mind. This may have been due to Allied pressure as the war neared its end. So about half of Romania's Jews survived the war.

"After the war, the Communists took power. The Jews, like everyone else, suffered. However, in the late 1950s a Jewish businessman from Britain named Henry Jacober built an automated chicken farm in Romania. In exchange for his help he received exit visas for five hundred Romanian Jews. Gheorghe Gheorghiu-Dej, the dictator, liked the farm and ordered that five more be built. As Jacober imported more and more equipment the number of exit visa's granted to Jews increased. By 1964, the Ministry of the Interior, which ran the farms, became the biggest meat producer in Romania. By then the number of visas for Jews was entirely dependent on the amount of eggs and chickens that were exported to the West. When Ceausescu came to power he stopped issuing exit visas to Jews. Later, he reinstated the program. But, this time Jews could be 'exported,' but only for a price. A visa cost between $2,000 and $50,000 per person. In a few exceptional cases it was $250,000. Ethnic Germans were also allowed to leave Romania after cash payments from West Germany. This money was said to be put in a secret account for Ceausescu. Eventually it was reported to have been $400 million. Ceausescu's favorite slogan was, 'Oil, Jews, and Germans are our most important export commodities.'

"In 1948 Rabbi Rosen became the Chief Rabbi. He had been expected to follow the Communist Party line on religion, that is, atheism. Instead, he spoke up for the Jewish community. He also traveled widely and became a goodwill ambassador for Romania. As his international stature grew, so did his influence in Romania. When Ceausescu came to power he helped strike a deal with Rabbi Rosen. Jews could only be granted exit visas for hard currency, that is, usually suitcases full of hard currency. Meanwhile, the American Jewish Joint Distribution Committee, 'The Joint' donated millions of dollars to support the remaining Jewish community of Romania. Today, the JDC spends over $4 million a year in Romania. This is far more than in any other Eastern European country. They fund old-age homes, clinics, and other social services. They even funded the kosher restaurant we ate at in Bucharest. Some feel Rabbi Rosen was an apologist for Ceausescu. Others saw him as having cleverly manipulated Ceausescu in order to save Romania's remaining Jews. His legacy can be appreciated by some recent comments I read. In one interview Rabbi

Rosen said 'Ceausescu was my enemy, he tried to kill me. . . . If there was one man in Romania who fought him, it was I. It is a stupid lie that I collaborated with him.' However, he also said that Ceausescu was 'not as bad' as he was painted. 'I have known worse men,' the Rabbi commented, 'worse Communists.' He concluded: 'If I had the possibility to save Jews by shaking hands with Hitler, I would have done so' (Brogan, 1990; Hoffman, 1992; Tugend, 1992a, 1992b; Pacepa, 1987; see also Kamm, 1991a; Price, 1993; Sacharow, 1990; Goldberg, 1993; Pilon, 1992: 5, 57, 66; Bernstein, 1994; "Rabbi Moses Rosen, 81, Leader of Romanian Jews," 1994).

"Go on with your story."

"After lunch we returned to the embassy. We were told it would be a 'little longer.' Finally, at about 2:30, a consular officer came out and handed us the visas. Each 'visa' was an envelope with a few lines of typing and the child's picture attached. Our documents were inside the envelopes. The six lines of typing and the attachment of our children's pictures had taken five-and-a-half hours. Before we left, however, I wanted to make sure there were no problems. So I said to the counselor officer: 'The Immigration Service told us that sometimes the visa is incomplete or incorrect and the visa holders must return to the country of origin. I don't want to come back here. Is there any possibility that something will be wrong?' She assured us that the visas were fine. We thanked her and left. We went back to Floriana's. We arrived about three o'clock, and we immediately came down with diarrhea, from the lunch at the Jewish Community Center.

"The night before we left for home we had to settle our financial affairs. Since Floriana, and everyone else, were doing us a favor, a very big favor, all the gas, meals, and other expenses were our treat. However, it would have been impractical for us to be constantly changing dollars into lei. So, Floriana paid for everything. And, now it was time to reimburse her. She sat down and added up everything on her list. When she finished she announced, '10,000.' 'Ten thousand dollars?' I said. I thought that seemed a bit steep, but then, we had run around a lot. 'No', she replied, '10,000 *lei*, $500.' 'Oh.'

"I then paid our translator, the couple who watched the kids, and Nicu, our fixer and confidant. I slipped some extra money into Floriana's pocket as a gift. And, then offhandedly I said to Ion, our driver, 'Here, this is what I owe you.' He suddenly grew angry. 'I didn't do this for money!' he barked. I then realized that I had blundered. So I said, 'I mean this is a gift.' He smiled and took the money. We all hugged and said good-bye.

"After everyone left Floriana came over to us. 'Could you do me a little favor?' 'Sure, what?' 'Could I have one of your paper diapers?' 'Sure, why?' 'So, I can show everyone how wasteful Americans are.' 'Sure.' We then went to bed.

"The next morning Ion drove us to Otopeni Airport. Floriana, Nicu, Nanna, Dada, and Gheorghe all came along. We stood in line for a bit and chatted.

When it was time to go we kissed and hugged everyone. We all began to cry. Nanna then said, 'Don't you want me to keep the little girl for a year. It will be so hard with two.' It was sweet of her to offer. But, we couldn't say, 'Are you crazy?' So we thanked her and said we would take both of them home. Again, we kissed and hugged everyone. We put our babies into our backpacks and we dragged our suitcases up to the customs officer. We handed him some cigarettes and said, 'This if for you.' We then pointed to our bags and said, 'Just diapers.' He waved us through.

"We went upstairs to the waiting room and sat there. We played with the kids while we waited for the flight to board. When they called the flight we had to go downstairs. We had so many bags that we had to have some of the airport janitors help us take them down the stairs. And, of course, we gave each of them a pack of cigarettes. Our passports and tickets were then checked. Once we were cleared we walked to the airplane. We sat in the front part of the plane, in the no smoking section. We took out the car seats we had been dragging around and we strapped the kids into them. We then put on our seat belts and waited for takeoff. The stewardess asked everyone to move to the back of the plane, for balance. However, she told us that Susie and the babies could stay where they were seated. So, I moved to the back of the plane and we took off. Immediately, our children began to scream. We thought some milk would quiet them down. So Susie took out a can of Sanalac. When she opened it, it exploded. Half of the cabin was covered with Sanalac. And, our kids kept screaming. In fact, they screamed for the next hour and a half.

"From Bucharest we flew to Vienna. We changed crews and half the people on the airplane got off. I believe some of the people who wanted to go to America got off, just to get away from our kids. Soon, however, some Romanian American women began to play with the kids. They walked Joel up and down the aisle and they played with Ari. The kids finally quieted down. We soon took off for Chicago.

"'How long will it be?' I asked. 'Seventeen hours.' I slumped. 'Give me a Pepsi,' I said. She said, 'No Pepsi, orange.' I grudgingly took the first of many bottles of orange pop on my endless 17-hour flight back to Chicago. During the flight the kids napped, played, and were passed around the cabin. They behaved okay. On the other hand, I was not okay. I don't sleep well on airplanes. So I was up almost the entire flight. Also, my legs itched terribly from all the bedbug bites. I must have had a hundred or more. Also, I was very tired. So, I spent the entire flight gulping orange pop, swallowing aspirin, scratching, and suffering from the crew smoking in the no smoking section. Finally, after an endless 17 hours, we landed in Chicago.

"We took the kids in our arms and carried them down the steps. The new international terminal was still under construction. So we had to take a bus with our bags and our babies to the old terminal. The bus lurched back and forth as we headed for the terminal. When we arrived at the terminal we dragged ourselves, our babies, and our luggage over to Immigration. We got in the line that said, 'US Citizens.' We made our way to the front of the line in about ten or fifteen minutes. When we reached the immigration officer, who was a rather severe-looking man who was standing on a little box, he pointed to the Romanian passports. He said, 'Oh, no. You've got to go to Immigrant Processing.' Suddenly, I understood what our numerous trips, documents, and stamps had been about. We had been so anxious during our two weeks in Bucharest that we hadn't thought about what we were doing. But at that moment, I understood. The children had been adopted by us through a Romanian court. When the judge had signed the papers in Arad they had become our children. But, we had to secure exit visas from the Romanian government in order to take them out of the country. Then we had to secure an entry visa from the American government to let us bring them in to this country. That is because they were, 'Aliens.' If we had wanted to stay in Bucharest with our children, forever, then we wouldn't have had to go through all of the nonsense. But, since we wanted to get them out, we had had to slog through both governmental bureaucracies.

"We walked over to Immigrant Processing. We handed our papers to a guy with a blue suit and a plastic badge. He disappeared behind a closed door. We sat down across from some women wearing saris and some men wearing checkered suits. We waited there for about an hour. Finally, 'the guy' came out and said, 'All done. Go right through this gate. Lights will go off and armed men will rush at you with their guns drawn. Ignore them.' Then go to the baggage area. But, your bags are probably stolen by now. Have a nice day.'"

"You made that up."

"Yes."

"Go on."

"We went to the baggage claim area and we collected our bags. Since it was an hour after the flight had arrived I wasn't sure that our bags really would be there. But, to my surprise, they were. But, we had so many bags and boxes we couldn't handle them. So a security man helped us to the waiting room. We had called ahead and had told everyone when we were coming. But, we had apparently told them the wrong day. So, the only person there, from all our friends and relatives, was Elena. Raymond had been there earlier, but he had left to go to work. So, only Elena was there, and she had to go to work, too. So, we all kissed and hugged, showed off our babies, and sent her off to work. We ordered a limousine and piled all our suitcases, strollers, and babies in and headed home.

"As we drove toward the house euphoria began to break through my exhaustion. Twenty minutes later we were home. We were all exhausted. Susie and the kids went to sleep. I had been up for thirty hours, but I *had* to eat a hamburger. I took a long, hot shower. And, for the first time in two weeks I felt clean. I then drove to my favorite 'Imitation 1950s Greasy Spoon'. The food was passable. But, the hot fudge sundae was wonderful. As I drove home I blasted the air-conditioner. My stomach was full and my babies were home. I was . . . fulfilled."

"Fulfilled?"

"Yes, fulfilled."

Chapter 13

"Everything Vill Be Just Fine"

"The next morning we got up and took the kids to our pediatrician. We told him about the kid's illnesses and the medications prescribed for them in Bucharest. He then thoroughly examined them. Afterwards he said, 'Now, show me all the medicines they gave you.' We pulled out a blue plastic lunch box filled with all our medications. Half of them had leaked, so the contents of the box was a soggy mess. We showed him the green medicine for the mouth, and the purple medicine for the nose, and the orange medicine for the tush. And we showed him the Amoxicillin. He said, 'Well, the Amoxicillin is fine.' But, he said with the wave of his hand, 'Throw all the rest of this out.' He pushed the box away with disdain. We tossed the bottles into the garbage. Then I said, 'But what about the *rickette*, the rickets?' he said, 'I see no indication of rickets.' Then I said, 'But, what about the *bronchita*, the bronchitis?' He said, 'I see no indication of bronchitis. They have upper respiratory infections.' 'They have colds?' 'Yes. And, in a week or two they'll be just fine.' I was relieved, and a bit astonished. As we got ready to leave he said, and I'm adding the accent, 'Don't *vorry*, take it easy, everything *vill* be just fine.' And, it was."

Chapter 14

Afterward

On April 27, 1990, *20/20* broadcast a program on Romanian babies entitled "Nobody's Children." The program, plus a number of other reports on Romanian orphans, produced a strong public reaction. Many couples began to inquire about adopting Romanian children. As other couples were beginning the process of adoption we were ending ours. I had flown to Romania in March 1990 and selected our children. In late June, we returned to pick them up. We spent two weeks in Romania and returned in early July.

Under the Ceausescu regime only 17 children had been adopted by Americans from Romania from 1982 to 1989. However, in 1990 that number increased to 90. Many French, German, and Italian couples also had adopted Romanian babies in 1990. Most of these children came from institutions.

On October 5, 1990, *20/20* broadcast another report on Romanian babies. This program, entitled, "Shame of a Nation," was horrifying. It focused on the 'irrecoverable' children who had been left to die in Auschwitz-like orphanages. These children, many of whom appeared to be starving, lay in their cribs covered in excrement and flies. Young girls, half-naked with their heads shaved, were locked in giant cages. There they screamed and splashed in urine and excrement. In such orphanages it was reported that 40 percent of the children died each year. The report concluded that this was 'genocide by neglect.'

This program created a flood of couples who flew to Romania to adopt. Ironically, most of these couples were not interested in adopting children from these institutions. Instead, they wanted to adopt normal, healthy new-borns. This led many couples to scour the countryside for young children to adopt. Incredibly, many of these people came without any contacts and without being able to speak the language. They found babies by making contacts in hotel lobbies with 'baby brokers.' These brokers were often petty criminals ('sharks'). With hundreds of couples desperate to find babies competition between them often became fierce. The sharks used this knowledge to charge exorbitant fees and bully the couples. The profits for arranging these adoptions were usually a few thousand dollars. For Romanians these fees were astronomical. However, for Americans and Western Europeans these costs were a bargain. So, many couples were quite willing to be exploited, as long as they got a baby.

Soon rumors of baby buying began to filter out of Romania. *60 Minutes* sent a film crew there in 1991. They produced a segment entitled, "Children For Sale." In that story it was reported that "Romanian babies were now the hottest item on the Romanian black market." The cost of a child was reported to be from $3,500 to $7,000. Much of this, the sharks claimed, was needed for bribes. However, prices varied greatly. One family was willing to sell a four year old for $500; other families were asking $25,00 for a newborn. Couples desperate to adopt often paid thousands of dollars to adopt a child. Here "buying and selling" was "the heart of the process." The reporter concluded that capitalism had finally come to Romania, but this was capitalism that had gone haywire.

In March 1991, Kathleen Hunt, an American journalist who spoke Romanian, published an article in the *New York Times* Sunday magazine entitled, "The Romanian Baby Bazaar." She reported that she had found a 'nightmare world of hustlers.' A world where impoverished Gypsy women, that she called 'baby machines,' sold their children. The consul at the American Embassy in Bucharest estimated that half of all the children adopted in Romania did not come from institutions. And, the consul could not recall the adoption of even one severely handicapped child. Of the 50 couples that the reporter had followed many were not what she had expected. Almost half of them already had biological children. And, many of the couples, who were born-again Christians, were uncomfortable with the constant demands for bribes, falsified documents, and direct cash payments for babies. However, since many of them were unable to gain entrée to the orphanages because of corrupt officials, they were forced to turn elsewhere. One American found himself 'driving around villages, basically asking what's the price per pound for babies.'

Lee Aitkin, another American journalist, flew to Romania on a whim to adopt a Romanian baby in 1992. However, she found that she was 'caught up in a grotesque scenario, the corrupt final days of the Romanian adoption bazaar.' She found that an air of frantic competition had gripped Westerners in Bucharest as they desperately searched for babies. She reported that children were adopted from maternity hospitals, Gypsy huts, tenements, and even the back seats of cars. And, Gypsy families were following foreigners down the street offering their babies for sale. She saw a little girl being sold on the street for $1,200 and a VCR. She also saw an American woman brokering babies out of a hotel suite for $6,000 each. She found that the couples that were involved in this trade considered themselves to be good Samaritans. To these couples Romania was a 'doomed and gruesome country' where people were so poor that a child would be better off anywhere else. She concluded that "the atmosphere felt less like a rescue mission than a gold rush; people with means mining a precious resource, white babies, from a country too poor to resist the exploitation.'

Afterward

Finally, the adoption scandal broke in Romania. Romanian television broadcast a lurid report showing three Gypsy children being sold to undercover journalists. Three days later, Prime Minister Petre Roman ordered the formation of a National Adoption Committee. This was to be headed by Dr. Alexandra Zugravescu, a pediatrician. Zugravescu ordered a freeze on all new adoptions. She also ordered a census of all orphanages and the creation of a master list of all available children in those institutions. Eventually, new legislation forbad all private adoptions; and the rules gave priority to Romanians in all future adoptions. When the ban was lifted foreigners were only able to go through a few officially licensed agencies to adopt Romanian babies. No child was available until it was offered to Romanian couples for six months. And, no agency received more than a few children a year (Hunt, 1991; Lawson, 1991; Neeley, 1991).

After the scandal broke many couples had to admit that they had adopted children of questionable legality. However, because of staff shortages at the American Embassy almost all of these adoptions were approved. However, just before adoptions were closed the parents of many non-orphan children that had been adopted in Romania were denied entry visas into the United States. These parents demonstrated outside the United State's embassy for several weeks. Eventually, 250 of these children were allowed to enter the United States under a "parole status" because they had been adopted by or had bonded with their American parents (Johnson, 1993: 46-47).

In the end, 2,552 children were adopted from Romania in 1991. This was about 28 percent of all the international adoptions in the world for that year. However, in 1992 that number fell to 145 and then to 88 in 1993. The great Romanian baby bazaar was over (see Glasser, 1992; Gottesman, 1992; Singer, 1993; Charalambous, 1994; "Britons in Baby-Smuggling Case Go Free," 1994; Ingram, 1993a, 1993b).

Part II
The Analysis

Chapter 15

Introduction: The Adoption Story

In July 1990, I flew home from Romania with my two adopted babies. During the flight I thought to myself: This was an interesting experience, why don't I write a book about it? So, I grabbed a napkin and began taking notes. Over the next few months I wrote notes on the backs of envelopes and scraps of paper. Whenever a memory came to me, I wrote it down. I then arranged all my paper into piles and organized each one. I thought I could produce my manuscript quickly by dictating it into a tape recorder. However, my dictating took endless hours. It took many evenings, weekends and endless months to type the text. On my first reading of the manuscript I realized that 'talking' and 'literature' had little to do with each other. After six years of revisions I completed my book.

The original manuscript that I wrote included everything interesting that occurred in my life in 1989 and 1990. That is, the adoption of my kids, the deaths of my father, my uncle, and my mother-in-law, and the removal of my wife's benign brain tumor. All these events were extremely interesting to me. However, in discussing 'the adoption book' with my wife she kept asking: "But, what do these other things have to do with *adoption*?" My answer was, "nothing;" however, it all was *interesting*. Eventually, I came to realize that we were both right. The medical portions of the story were interesting, but they were irrelevant to the adoption story. So I dropped them from the manuscript. However, there was another reason that caused me to eliminate them from the manuscript.

I had always thought that this material would lead to an analysis of topics within medical sociology (see Bird, 2000; Albrecht, 2000; Good and Good, 2000). For example, my mother-in-law had attended adult daycare. I had been unaware that such programs had even existed before she was diagnosed with Alzheimer's disease. I found that the need for such services was great but the supply was limited. Beyond that I had little to add (see Engstrom and Greene, 1992; Mitchell, 1999; McCurdy, 1998). The role of physicians interested me. However, it was not just their technical expertise, but how medicine, as a profession, sustained itself as a powerful interest group in society that I wished to explore. I was aware of some of this literature from an earlier research project on psychiatry (see Friedson, 1970a, 1970b, 1973). However, further reading left me uninspired (see Krause, 1996; Hafferty and McKinlay, 1993; Freddi and Bjorkman, 1989; Albrecht, 2000; Burrage and Torstendahl, 1990; Torstendahl and Burrage, 1990; Bird, 2000; Johnson, 1995). I was also interested in the expanding role of technology in medicine (see Bird, 2000; Nelkin, 1973; Koenig, 1988:486). Specifically, in fertility treatment (which we had undergone) (see Albrecht, 2000; Hope, 1998; Ashrof, 2000; Henderson, 2000), in death and dying (see Harvey, 1996, 1997; Kaufman, 2000; Lock and Honde, 1990; Callahan, 1993), and in neurosurgery (see Greenblatt, 1997). However, none of this literature inspired me with new ideas.

Once I had decided to narrow my manuscript to adoption my choice for analysis became 'obvious:' the sociology of adoption. I thought the 'subculture of adoption' was interesting; however, I felt I had covered it in the story (see Weir, 2003:137-143). However, the remainder of the sociology of adoption was not interesting to me either. Within the field I could have studied fertility rates, the legal status of abortion and birth control, social attitudes towards single and unwed motherhood, tolerance for mixed-race families in the United States, or the role of class in adoption in the United States (see Tessler, et.al., 1999:6-7). I also could have examined open adoption (Henney, 1998), transracial adoption (Simon, et.al., 1994; Tessler, et.al., 1999), the identity of adoptees (Grotevant, 1997; Westhues, 1998), American kinship and adoption (Wegar, 1997; Melosh, 2002), and the ethics and politics of international adoption (Rios-Kohm, 1998; Melosh, 2002). These topics, plus the entire sociological specialty of, marriage and the family, did not interest me.

However, what *did* interest me was the psychology of oppression after decades of Romanian Communism. Specifically, how the Communist Party, through the secret police, had created a population that was terrorized and paranoid. A population where trust between individuals had vanished. Where severe economic shortages had led to deprivation and passivity. In other words, a population that was powerless and atomized. Now, *that* was interesting.

Let me hastily add that my choice of a topic to analyze is not as idiosyncratic as it appears. So, let us put this into a more scientific perspective. There are three areas I could have analyzed. One was adoption. Although there is a sociological literature on adoption, I felt "saturated" by the time I had finished my manuscript. I did not feel I had any more to say about adoption. However, I did feel that the role of technology in medicine was a promising area of analysis. In fact, Giddens (1991) examines the idea that the human body is to be "worked upon." So, I read through the history of neurosurgery, the literature on death and dying, and the technology and sociology of fertility treatment. As I examined this literature several ideas came to mind but they were not significant additions to the field. However, when I began to explore the psychology of Communist oppression (in Adelman, 1984, for example) I immediately felt I had something to say. I also saw a connection between the terror of Communist oppression and that of the Nazis. I examined this literature (Delarue, 1964; Crankshaw, 1956; Aronson, 1969; Sofsky, 1993). However, this material primarily dealt with mass murder. Although it was quite interesting, it did not apply to the final stage of Communism in which terror had become primarily psychological. So, I left most of this material for my footnotes.

I also saw a connection to the criminal justice literature on policing. I examined the history of Communist policing (Shelley, 1996). I originally thought this was a 'hot topic.' However, as I wrote my analysis this material seemed less 'immediate.' However, Pacepa (1987), a Romanian secret police general who had defected to the United States, provided practical, and not just theoretical, descriptions of the workings of the Communist police system. I found his descriptions compelling and used them in my analysis. Also, Kideckal's (1993) superb ethnography of Romanian peasant life described the economic deprivation and atomization of Romanians.

As I poked through the sociology literature I saw a connection between my approach and the life history school of research (Laslett, 1999). I had already written sections on the 1989 revolution and the role of the Communist Party. Now, this life history material gave me an explicit framework for my analysis. Two topics emerged from this approach that were especially useful: context and levels. The revolution was the (historical) context of the story; and my analysis, from individual up to the center of Communist power, nicely fit under levels. However, I found much of the life history literature to be too 'touchy feely' (humanistic) for my taste (see Denzin, 1989, and Denzin and Lincoln, 2000, for example). So, I included a critique of this literature in my analysis.

I knew that this combination of personal exploration and theoretical insight was not just happenstance. In fact, it was typical of much research. And it is nicely explained by Glaser and Strauss (1967) as "grounded theory." In grounded theory, one moves back and forth between data and theory. Theory is 'grounded' in data and is constantly revised, as new data is applied to the (emerging) theoretical formulation. This cycle, of theory, data, and new theory ends when the researcher reaches "saturation." That is, when data no longer brings new insights (see also Strauss and Corbin, 1988; Miller, 2000:118, 120; Star, 1991:272-4; Klein, 2000).

So, let us begin with a review of the life history literature and then move on to context and levels—Communist oppression and the Romanian Revolution of 1989.

Chapter 16

Analytical Autobiography

This is an autobiography. An autobiography is usually thought of as simply 'a story.' However, a good autobiography is more than that. It is one type of personal document that social scientists use to analyze society. It is said that such documents are 'expressive' since they throw light on the feelings of individuals; however, they also allow one to analyze society. Social scientists also use life histories, dream reports, diaries, letters, and fiction to analyze society. The most commonly used of these is the life history. Such a history is a retrospective account of an individual's life. It is usually elicited by a researcher. An autobiography, however, is an individual's self-initiated description of his or her own life (Watson and Watson-Franke, 1985:2; Cole and Knowles, 2001:9-21).

This manuscript is such an autobiography. However, it is also a retelling of my experiences in a foreign culture at a unique historical moment (after the fall of Communism). In other words, it is not just a story; it is also *data*. However, what is culturally and historically significant, and what is merely personal, is not always obvious ("transparent"). Therefore, the data must be culled from the personal. Furthermore, once this data has been separated from the story it does not explain itself. That is, it must be interpreted or analyzed. That is why this is not a typical autobiography. Instead, it is an autobiography that is a *vehicle for the analysis of data*.

A life history or autobiography of this type is usually called an "interpretive ethnography." (Ethnography is a descriptive study of a culture or a group.) However, the original purpose of this manuscript was not to analyze a culture. Instead, the data that was collected was merely incidental to the telling of the story. Thus, I considered calling this manuscript an 'incidental ethnography.' However, this term seemed too ephemeral. Alternately, since the data was picked up accidentally in the course of the story. I thought of calling this an 'accidental ethnography.' However, I felt the data was too slight to be considered an ethnography at all. I also considered calling this manuscript as an 'interpretive autobiography' (see Gullestad, 1996: 3-7; Maines, 2001:206). However, "interpretation" is defined merely as explanation. This seemed a bit too vague. However, "analyze" is defined as separating something into its parts in order to study its structure (Ehrlich, 1980:465, 29; see also Schwandt, 2000: 191-4; Watson and Watson-Franke, 1985:5865). This seemed to be exactly what I was attempting to do. Therefore, I called this manuscript an 'analytical autobiography.'

Social scientists as well as the public view autobiography as a normal and natural form of story telling. However, some literary critics question if autobiography is a "legitimate genre." Bruner, for example, does not see autobiography in the usual way. Instead, he sees it as the "selective construction of the self." He argues that the "self-telling of narratives achieve[s] the power to structure perceptual experience, to organize memory, to segment and . . . build the very 'events' of a life. In the end, we become the autobiographical narratives by which we 'tell about' our lives" (1987:15).

Kundrup has gone even further. He has argued that the entire auto-biographical genre has become "exhausted." He makes three arguments to justify this point. First, he questions the ability of one's memory to discern events that are true to reality (the psychoanalytic critique). Second, he sees life as "constructed," that is, artificial and not true to reality (the structuralist critique). And, third, he sees daily life as superficial; and because of this, the "true self," and the larger social context, are missed in auto-biography (the sociological critique) (Gullestad, 1996:15, 1994; Eakin, 1992:190; Wolf, 1992:130).

Such arguments may be fashionable in literary circles, but that does not mean they are correct. First, an individual may not be aware of their unconscious wants, needs, and desires. However, an individual can be quite perceptive about their daily life experiences (the psychoanalytic argument). Secondly, even if one sees a life as "constructed" that does not mean it is artificial (the structuralist argument). And, thirdly, just because one goes about ones daily routine does not mean that an individual is nothing more than the sum of their roles (the sociological argument). Further, each individual has a unique personal identity. And, as one moves through life that identity changes. Therefore, personality or identity can be seen as a process and not just as a collection of static roles (see Sandstrom, Martini and Fine, 2003:115-120).

This autobiography will follow my experiences (my process) as I worked my way through my adoption. More importantly, by focusing on my personal experiences I will not simply examine abstract notions of culture or society. Instead, I will examine my experiences, and subjective reactions, in two different cultures (see Gullestad, 1996:18-19; Cohen, 1994).

One reason for this approach is that most social scientists have been too focused on abstract notions such as roles, social structure, or society (see: Holstein and Gubrium, 2004). Because of this they have slighted individual choice. A way to correct this is to mesh the personal with the social (Gullestad, 1996:20; Shelton, 1995; see also Giddens, 1991:5).

However, the notion of "personal choice" is a relatively new concept. For example, in the Middle Ages choice was very limited. For most people life was simply endless drudgery. And the only respite from this was to be in touch with God, or, at least, a "Greater Good." However, with the emergence of the Reformation this began to change. A new conception of morality began to emerge. This new idea was that morality sprang from a "voice within." This idea evolved into the notion that each individual was endowed with a moral sense or intuitive feeling of what was right and wrong (Taylor, 1991; see also Bjorklund, 1998). In order to become a true, full, and "authentic" human being one had to be "in touch" with these inner (moral) feelings. With this new form of inwardness modern individuals have come to think of themselves as beings with "inner depth" (Bjorklund, 1998). From this conception emerged new concepts of intimacy and privacy. In other words, in the Middle Ages life gained meaning through "transcendence" (with the divine). However, beginning in the eighteenth century life gained meaning through intimacy, immediacy, and the fulfillment of one's inner needs (Sennett, 1978).

This change was the product of the secularization of society. In the past religion had been the "holy center" of society. However, over time religion lost its sway. There are several reasons for this. First, science created an ever-expanding process of change. Second, an economic system emerged which focused on financial gain and individual achievement. Third, a secular state evolved which monopolized the legitimate use of force and was neutral, as were the public schools, in their stance towards religion (or differing creeds). Fourth, the notion of intimate, personal love between individuals and not just God, emerged. Fifth, secular law emerged. Such law was created and changed by humans at their own will. Inherent in the law was individual rights. And, one of these rights included the right to be a believer or nonbeliever (Hoibraaten, 1993:231-3).

As a result of these changes religion was no longer the center of society. It became just another institution in society. The indirect effect of this was that believers, as well as, nonbelievers could now explore questions of "ultimate meaning" (Hoibraaten, 1993).

Social scientists usually see this process as a transition from pre-modern to modern society. Pre-modern society is seen as dominated by tradition whereas modern society is viewed as having a wide range of choices. In our society such choices are often tied to passion. A choice the individual "had to" follow. Such choices involve risks and require education in order to achieve a successful outcome. So, freedom of choice can lead to achievement and satisfaction; or it can just as easily lead to failure and emptiness (Gullestad, 1996:22-24).

Autobiographies, or the chronicling of an individuals choices, have been studied by social scientists using two approaches. One type is the life passage or life cycle approach. These studies examine how a group socializes or enculturates children in order to make them members of society. That is, these studies emphasize the requirements of society. Researchers who take this perspective often use ethnographic methods. Here the researcher attempts to give the reader "direct access to reality." This style of research embodies the pursuit of naturalism. Authenticity is sought by invoking the speech of ordinary people (Shelton, 1995:86). Usually the researcher is portrayed as outside the situation that is being described. This allows "objective truth" to be captured. This naturalistic or documentary style approach gives an "aura of authenticity and immediacy" to the research (Mandelbaum, 1973: 177; Langness and Franke, 1965).

The other approach to autobiography is the life history study. This type emphasizes an individual's personal experiences and focuses on how they cope with society (Mandelbaum, 1973: 177; Langness and Franke, 1965). This style closely resembles the technique used in this manuscript. So let us examine it in detail.

The life history style melds an individual's experiences (their biography) and their reactions to those events (their subjective responses). Three approaches have been used in this type of research. The first is the "messy text" approach. The essence of this style is its "reflexivity." That is, manuscripts are written so that the writer exposes their own narrative techniques. The writer also emphasizes how reality is socially constructed. So, such writing is seen as a way of "forming reality." Such texts allow for multiple interpretations. They produce "situated" knowledge about people. That is, they stress the historical and social processes that shape the individual. The text recreates the social world in which an identity is formed. This style of research attempts to move from the local and the personal to the political and the global (Denzin, 1997:224-227).

A second type of life history study is Clifford Geertz's "thick description." This technique is based upon the premise that the social sciences are "not experimental science[s] in search of law, but interpretive one[s] in search of meaning." In other words, they are involved in "cultural analysis." Thick description analyzes a vertical "hierarchy of meaningful structures." These structures are the contexts in which events, behaviors, institutions, and processes can be described. Such a description focuses on "the flow of social discourse." The analysis of such discourse is microscopic. It involves "exceedingly extended acquaintances with extremely small matters." However, Geertz argues that to divorce such interpretations "from the whole vast business of the world—is to divorce it from its applications and to render it vacant" (1973:5, 7, 14, 20, 21, 18: see also Maines, 2001: 218, 242; Jenks, 2002: 172; Denzin and Lincoln, 2000:15).

Geertz does not see the social scientist as an objective observer who uncovers preexisting laws; instead, he sees the researcher as playing a "constructive role." He feels that to view social science analysis "as the conceptual manipulation of discovered facts . . . seem[s] rather lame." To employ such an approach "is to pretend a science that does not exist and imagine a reality that cannot be found. Cultural analysis is (or should be) guessing at meanings, assessing the guesses, and drawing explanatory conclusions from the better guesses." It should not be "discovering the Continent of Meaning and mapping out its bodiless landscape." For "where an interpretation comes from does not determine where it can be impelled to go. Small facts speak to large issues" (1973:20, 23; see also Bochner and Ellis, 1996:16).

The third approach is Carolyn Ellis' "evocative autoethnography." This technique is the writing of evocative literary and nonfiction stories. She argues that such stories add "blood and tissue" to the "abstract bones of theoretical discourse." She sees this style of writing social science as emotional, personal, reflexive, and therapeutic (1997: 117, 120; see also Shelton, 1995; Sparkes, 2002; Denzin, 1997:xiv). (A similar approach has been called "narrative ethnography"—see Tillman-Healy, 2002:339-40; Tedlock, 1991, 2000).

Ellis writes about the ebb and flow of personal relationships. She believes that writing social science should be an "intimate conversation about the intricacies of feeling, relating, and working;" it should not be about theoretical abstractions. She writes in the first person and makes herself the subject of her research. Unlike most social scientists she is not neutral and invisible. Instead, she discloses hidden details of her private life and their emotional content (1997:127; Crapanzano, 1980: ix; Denzin, 1997:253; see also Richardson, 2000).

Ellis argues that one must move away from describing reality in order to get the story "right." She portrays behavior so that the reader feels the emotional content of the story. In order to explain an event she often condenses a number of experiences into one "evocative composite." This "dramatic license" allows her to tell "a good story." She also reconstructs unrecorded conversations until they have the "ring of authenticity." She does not work at getting all the facts. Instead, she concentrates on "being true to the feelings." She also does not follow a chronological ordering of events. Instead she tells a story where meaning and interpretation are emphasized, and where the readers can feel what she felt. Thus, she writes social science as "creative nonfiction with scene setting, dialogue, and unfolding dramatic action." In the end, like all social scientists, Ellis writes a truthful account. But, her means of achieving this is through "systematic introspection." This allows her to add "*blood and tissue to the abstract bones of* [the] *theoretical discourse*" (1997:127-129, 120; emphasis in the original).

How does one react to Ellis' argument? There are two problems with Ellis' technique. And can interpretive autobiography solve these problems?

1. Fiction: Ellis is well intentioned, but her approach is wrong. Ellis melds several scenes into a composite. She reconstructs unrecorded conversations. She does not work at getting all the facts. Instead, she is "true to her feelings" (see also Angrossino, 1998:41, 2002:328; Gottschalk, 1998). This may be entertaining, but it is not true to life; it is not social science (see Atkinson, Coffey, and Delamont, 2003:64-69,181-186). However, in interpretive autobiography

everything is true. And, everything is included. No facts are left out. Both the vivid and the mundane are included.

2. Details: A second problem with Ellis' work is that by editing her material she leaves out a great deal of information. This is a crucial mistake because the details give us the information we need to make our own interpretation or analysis of the story. Howell makes this point by noting that the amount of detail given by early ethnographic researchers is "overpowering." Therefore, interpretation and "reinterpretations are made possible because of the very richness of [the] detail" (1994: 321). So, again, in analytical autobiography every detail was included in the monograph. This allows others to judge if the interpretations are correct.

There are six other problems with the life history approach. And analytical autobiography can help solve them.

1. The role of the researcher: Life history is usually the product of a researcher eliciting a life story. This makes the life history a "jointly constructed" effort. Thus, "the two together are collaborators, composing and constructing a story the teller can be pleased with" (Miller, 2000: 1213). Or, as Freeman has put it: "No comparison of life histories is possible without knowledge of the editor's [researcher's] perspectives and values that influenced the final form of history. Failure to assess or at least recognize the observers or editors role leads to an image of a life history that is distorted and incomplete" (1979: 393). In this analytical autobiography this problem is not relevant because all the data is included; and, there is no one between the data and the reader.

2. The self and the data: For the social scientist the magic word is data. In collecting this data one need not exclude the researchers role in the collection of that data. So, in many studies researchers include a few anecdotes; some even describe the research process in detail (Dwyer, 1982:2656). However, one cannot overdue this. Personal introspection may be entertaining, or it may even be analytical, but the monograph must be about the data.

On the other hand, the data is not absorbed like sunshine. One must work in order to collect it. Wolf notes that the research process is a "stunning roller coaster of self-doubt, boredom, excitement, disorientation, uncertainty, exhaustion, bullying, being bullied, cajoling, [and] being cajoled." In the course of all this the data is collected. Data which is recorded in "precious notebooks packed with disorganized thoughts, detailed observations of minutiae, descriptions of rituals, transcripts of conversations, diagrams, and detritus" (1992:127-8). Thus fieldwork, or autobiography, is based upon one's, personal experiences. And, including some material on one's own feelings is often appropriate, and may, in fact, be necessary (Bjorklund, 1998:145). Since analytical autobiography is a story the entire roller coaster ride is described. It is followed by the analysis.

3. Turnings (and Context): For most people, most of the time, life is ordinary. Only when something *interesting* happens is it usually worth telling a

story (Van Maanen, 1988). The most interesting moments in an individual's life is when major changes occur. Mandelbaum (1973) has called these "turnings" (see also Watson and Watson-Franke, 1985:10-16).* Turnings may also apply to societies; and, the fall of Communism was just such a turning (point) (see Sexton, 1981; Watson and Watson-Franke, 1985:15; Kaufman, 1986:24-5). So, this manuscript is about two dramatic events, one personal and the other societal. The personal experiences that occurred are described in the text. However, my knowledge of the overthrow of Communism in Romania was fragmentary and only gleaned from a distance. So, a description of Romania's revolution, which made my adoptions possible, is included here. This is necessary because Romania in the year 2000 can only be understood in the context of fifty years of Communism and its violent overthrow. So, my analysis begins with the Revolution of 1989.

4. Narrative and Analysis: Some analysis is scattered throughout the text. However, most of the analysis was left for a later section. This was not the original plan; this was simply the way the story worked out. Van Maanen explains why this happens: "Tellers of tales must keep the narrative rolling or risk losing continuity with the audience. The power of a story to spark interest and involvement is as much a function of staying close to the sequential, immediate, and tightly linked flow of events as it is a function of the substance of the tale itself." In other words, the audience is not asked to interpret or analyze the story. Instead, the "audience is asked to relive the tale" (1998:103).

5. Levels: From Microscopic to Global: Analytical autobiography is about both the experience and the data. However, these experiences are made into "facts" (given meaning) by selection and analysis (Rabinow, 1977:4, 152; Okely, 1992:2; Van Maanen, 1998:2; Miller, 2000; Watson and Watson-Franke, 1985: 58-65; Maines, 2001:221). The messy text and thick description approaches can be helpful here; that is because they give us direction in our examination of the data. By this we mean that these approaches, like analytical autobiography, involve the microscopic analysis of human behavior. They then expand outward from the biographical to the societal and then on to the global realm. Or, as Geertz has said: "Small facts speak to large issues" (1973: 23; see also Farberman, 1991: 481-4).

6. History: Marcus has argued that ethnographies have always been written in the context of historic change: the formation of state systems and the evolution of a world political economy. However, ethnographers have not usually described how individual cultures fit into larger systems. These larger systems have often been seen as merely "impinging" on these "little worlds"

---

* Denzin (1989) has used the term "epiphany" for a similar notion. However, this term seems too ephemeral to me (see also Cole and Knowles, 2001: 22-4, 119-120).

(1986:165-6). In order to rectify this problem history (turnings) has been included in our analysis.

In the following section we will present our analysis. We will begin the analysis with the historical context. That is the revolution and the repression that sparked it. So, the first part of this analysis describes the overthrow of Communism in December 1999. The second half of the analysis will attempt to understand the daily lives of Romanians, and why they chose to violently overthrow their government. In this analysis we will move from the individual level to the institutions that directly impinged upon the daily lives of the people. From there we will move up to the national system (the Communist Party). And, lastly, we will explore how global forces (Gorbachev's attempt to reform Soviet Communism) influenced the collapse of Romanian Communism. So, in the second portion of the analysis we will attempt to do a vertical analysis and expand beyond "my little world."

Chapter 17

Analysis: The Historical Context: The Revolution*

The revolution against the Ceausescu's began in the city of Timisoara** a city of about three hundred thousand people, on the western edge of Romania. That area, and nearby Transylvania, has a large minority of Hungarians. The 1.7 million Hungarians in Romania had been oppressed under Ceausescu. Hungarian schools were closed, the Hungarian language could not be spoken in Romanian schools, and Hungarian villages were slated for destruction. Ceausescu planned to demolish 8,000 of Romania's 13,000 villages and replace them with 500 "agro-industrial complexes." This was called "systemization." Many of these villages were Hungarian.

One of the leaders of the ethnic Hungarians was Rev. Laszlo Tokes.*** He was a Lutheran minister in Timisoara. Tokes had begun preaching about human rights. His bishop had ordered him transferred, but he refused. The Securitate,**** the secret police, then began to harass him. His plight had become well-known within Romania because *Radio Free Europe* and the *Voice of America* had broadcast his sermons. Because of this the area's 60,000 Hungarians defended him. Also, other minorities, such as the Germans, Serbs, and Gypsies, were supportive.

In December 1989 many people in Timisoara believed that Tokes was about to be arrested. The charge was reported to have been that he was hoarding oranges and lemons. Although this sounds absurd to Americans this was a serious offense in vitamin-starved Romania. Tokes' parishioners set up a 24-hour vigil around his house. On December 15 the government called in the police. When they moved towards his house a young man shouted, "Down with the dictator!" There were several seconds of stunned silence. Then everyone

---

* This section is drawn from numerous sources cited in the bibliography.
** pronounced Tee-mee-shwa-rah.
*** pronounced: Toe-kesh.
**** pronounced: Se-cur-i-tah-tey.

joined in. The crowd began to grow and eventually thousands of people poured into the streets. The police did nothing.

The next day large crowds again gathered. They began to chant "Down with Ceausescu!" "Good-bye to fear!" "Ceausescu will fall!" "Freedom!" "Dignity!" Again, the police and the Securitate held back.

The next day, Sunday, December 17, was an unusually warm, spring-like day. A large crowd moved into Opera Square, the central gathering place in Timisoara. The army was called out. Tanks and soldiers suddenly appeared. The demonstrators hoped that their very presence, their moral authority, as in other Eastern European countries, would cause the government to collapse. Soon people in the crowd began to urge the soldiers to join them. They shouted, "You are our brothers!" Eventually, one hundred thousand people gathered in the square. Throughout the day the mood was festive. But, in the early evening tensions began to rise. The demonstrators begged the young soldiers to join them. They chanted, "You tpo are Romanians!" Many of the young draftees appeared torn. However, none joined the demonstrators. A half hour later they were ordered to fire. Some refused and threw down their weapons. Those that did were then shot by Securitate officers. Some people had held their children in front of them so the troops would not fire. They fired anyway. Both the parents and the children were killed. Many died. The demonstrators fled. As they ran they tripped over bodies and slipped on the blood. Later, it was reported that Securitate officers went to the hospitals and collected the wounded. They were then taken to the morgue where they were shot. That night a storm washed the blood from the streets.

The first reports of the massacre, by Eastern European and Soviet reporters, stated that five to ten thousand people had been killed in Timisoara.

The next day, Monday, December 18, the sun was shining. In the morning a demonstration began in front of the medieval Cathedral in Opera Square. A woman waved a Romanian flag. Others sang, "Arise, Romanians! Arise!" Children lit candles for the dead. In the afternoon the soldiers returned. Again, they were ordered to fire. Some fired into the air. The others went over to the demonstrators. The remaining soldiers withdrew from the city. One diplomat later said: "They realized that they couldn't kill everyone in Timisoara."

There was an international outcry over the shootings. Strangely, at that very moment, Ceausescu decided to pay a state visit to Iran. On December 20, Ceausescu returned to Romania. He immediately called an emergency meeting of the party's Central Committee. He was furious. He vowed that reform would come to Romania "when pears grow on poplar trees." He ignored advice by Gorbachev to reduce the repression. He asserted that the troops had fired blanks in Timisoara. And, that shooting blanks was "like a rain shower." He ordered the use of live ammunition. But, he said the troops should fire over the heads of demonstrators. If that failed to disburse the crowds then the troops should shoot the demonstrators in the legs. He then berated his defense minister and security chief. He threatened others on the Central Committee with a firing squad. He screamed that the demonstrators were merely "a few hooligans."

At the finish of his tirade all twenty-five members of the Central Committee nodded in agreement. However, a few hours later the Defense Minister Vasile Milea was reported to have committed suicide. It was said that he could not bring himself to order his troops to fire on the demonstrators. But, his troops had already fired on the demonstrators. So, why did he kill himself? Everyone now assumes that he was executed on Ceausescu's order. Two days later the army again fired on demonstrators. However, after that, they went over to the revolution. But, to this day, the army, as well as many Romanians, deny the army ever fired on any demonstrators.

After the shooting in Opera Square factory workers in Timisoara went out on strike. The workers began shouting, "Ceausescu is guilty!" "Give us back our dead! Death! Death! Death!" They marched to the center of the city and many soldiers joined them. Young people began to flock to Timisoara. Workers occupied the factories and block committees organized themselves against Securitate attacks. By December 21, Timisoara had become a revolutionary commune. The city, however, was isolated. The phones had been cut off. And, special army and Securitate units were said to be headed for the city.

The news from Timisoara electrified Bucharest. However, there were no demonstrations. Ceausescu proclaimed "a gang of bandits, Hungarian spies, and traitors are creating civil disturbances in Timisoara." This pronouncement enraged many Romanians. But, still there were no demonstrations. However, Ceausescu then called a large demonstration of his own in front of the Central Committee Building. Such rallies had been routinely organized by the party throughout Ceausescu's reign. Thousands of party members would be ordered to report to the demonstration and to cheer their leader. But, this time the party members were joined by thousands of ordinary citizens. When Ceausescu called the Timisoara demonstrators "hooligans" a murmur began in the crowd. Then, a lamppost fell and the bulb shattered. A woman shrieked and people nearby thought she had been shot. Shouts of "Murder!" and "Give us back our dead!" began to be heard. Ceausescu was stunned. Just a month before he had been interrupted 106 times by applause at the Party Congress. He had been lauded as the "conductor," "the Maximum Leader," and "the genius of the Carpathians." Now, the TV screen went dead. And he fled.

Ten to fifteen thousand demonstrators then poured on to a nearby boulevard. They shouted, "Freedom!" and "Down with Ceausescu!" Tanks and troops herded them into University Square. In the melee that followed two demonstrators were crushed by a tank. When other demonstrators ran to help them they were shot down. At least 13 people were killed in the square that day. In spite of this, the demonstrators did not disperse.

Meanwhile, other members of the original crowd broke into the Central Committee Building. Ceausescu had had 30 volumes of his speeches published.

Thousands of these books were set afire. The demonstrators, tears of joy streaming down their faces, danced around the flames. Some of the demonstrators then began to march to the television and radio complex. Soldiers standing along the route did nothing. Two anticommunist poets, Mircea Dinescu and Ana Blandiana, were recognized by the crowd. They were hoisted up on their shoulders and carried to the station. The crowd entered the television and radio buildings and took control. Blandiana announced over the radio that the dictator had fallen. Dinescu appeared on television and said, "God has turned his face towards Romania again."

Meanwhile, as demonstrators surged through the Central Committee Building, several former Communist leaders suddenly appeared. They were the head of the new, and spontaneously created, National Salvation Front. They addressed the crowd and then they were taken to the television station in an armored vehicle. Meanwhile, at the Central Committee Building, anti-communist speeches went for another six hours.

By late that night, the crowds in the city had swollen to a million people. Many of them were students who had been "decree babies." That is, children who had been born because of Ceausescu's October 1966 decree banning abortions and requiring women to have four, and later five, children. As the crowd grew snipers suddenly began to fire. It was reported that Securitate troops had machine-gunned the crowds from helicopters, rooftops, and cars "Capone style." Many people were reported to have been killed. Many soldiers, who had joined the revolution, fired at the snipers. During the fighting the University of Bucharest's library caught on fire. Civil defense armories were looted and citizens formed armed "patriotic guard" units. They joined the soldiers in the three days of fighting that followed. The army and patriotic guard units quickly adopted a symbol for the revolution. It was the Romanian tricolor flag—red, blue, and yellow—with the Communist symbol cut out. This came to be known as "the flag with the hole in the middle."

As the battle raged the National Salvation Front took power. The Front was a broad coalition of anticommunists and former Communists who had fallen from Ceausescu's favor. Ion Iliescu, the Front's leader, issued an urgent proclamation on "Free Romanian Television" which called for the "quick liquidation of the terrorists."

The television station became the headquarters of the revolution. Scenes of the street fighting were constantly broadcast. They were interspersed with proclamations from the new leaders. Soon, the television station, itself, came under attack. The battle raged for some time, but, eventually, the terrorists were repulsed by army units loyal to the new government. There were many casualties, but Free Romanian Television was never driven off the air.

During those first few days the leaders of the National Salvation Front were constantly on the air. Ion Iliescu and Petre Roman, both former Communists, quickly emerged as the leading figures of the group. Also prominent was

Silviu Brucan, the former ambassador to the United States. Brucan had become a pariah to the previous administration when he and other dissidents had signed a 1989 letter complaining about human rights violations in Romania. Also present were Doina Cornea, a liberal critic of the Ceausescu regime, Mircea Dinescu and Ana Blandiana, the two dissident poets, and Rev. Laszlo Tokes, the pastor from Timisoara. All in all, the Front had almost a hundred members. However, the executive committee consisted exclusively of former Communists. There was Iliescu, Roman, and Brucan. There was also General Nicolae Militaru, the new armed forces commander, and General Victor Stanculescu, who had been Ceausescu's army liaison to the Securitate.

The Front used the television station as their political and military headquarters. This was not simply a matter of accident or convenience. That was because this was the first revolution broadcast on live television. Before the Iranian revolution Ayatollah Khomeni had spread his word through audiotapes played over the loudspeakers of mosques. After he took over television became his pulpit. In Romania, however, television was there from the beginning. It allowed a revolutionary morality play to be broadcast to the public. This was pivotal to the revolution; and, this was not lost on the revolutionaries. One Front member commented, "If television falls, the revolution falls. . . . That is for certain." Another added, "If we went off the air, it meant it was over." In the past, Romania's antiquated television equipment had been used to broadcast only two or three hours a day. And, this was mostly to show the people's adulation for the Ceausescus. But, now, the revolution in the street was live! People in the studio soon began to seize the microphone and shout, "We've won! We've won!" Others sang Christmas carols. This would have been impossible before the revolution. And, one anchorman apologized for lying to the public for years. Watching Free Romanian Television was like watching debates from the Continental Congress interspersed with live coverage of the storming of the Bastille.

Throughout the revolution the thirteen-story television station was repeatedly attacked by the Securitate. The apartment buildings across the street from it were pockmarked with bullet holes from the army's return fire. Otopeni, the international airport, was also the scene of heavy fighting. Its cafeteria was turned into a morgue. Baneasa, the domestic airport, was also repeatedly attacked by the Securitate. But, the army and patriotic guard units held on there, too.

Meanwhile, at the television station, General Stefan Gusa, the head of the army, announced that his troops had officially joined the revolution. General Vlad, the head of the Securitate, also incredulously appeared there, too. He urged his men to stop fighting and join the revolution. But, the fighting continued. By December 23, the fighting was going badly for the revolutionaries. It appeared that the Securitate knew everything the Front and the army were planning. Suspicion turned to General Vlad. That evening he was arrested.

Immediately, the situation began to improve. Soon after, Nicu Ceausescu, the 39-year-old son of the former dictator, was arrested. He had been head of the party in Sibiu, a city in north-central Romania. He was brought, bruised and beaten, before the television cameras. Nicu was only one of over forty relatives that Ceausescu had appointed to various government positions. There were another fifty to a hundred cronies in other top slots. One of the most important was held by Ceausescu's brother, Marin. He headed the trade delegation in Vienna. However, it was believed that his real job was to act as a conduit for the millions of dollars his brother sent to Swiss banks. He was soon found hanged. Eventually, Ceausescu's two sons, daughter, sister, and two remaining brothers were all arrested.

Meanwhile, the situation on the streets was still chaotic. Armed patriotic guards stopped and searched cars at numerous roadblocks throughout the city. They also joined army units in responding to sniper attacks. In spite of the gunfire, millions of people poured into the streets to celebrate the fall of the dictator.

The Securitate's base of operation was said to be tunnels underneath Bucharest. Hysterical witnesses reported snipers coming out of the subways or even popping out of fake gravestones to fire at mourners. There were other reports of thousands of Arab mercenaries fighting alongside the Securitate.

On December 24, Ion Iliescu announced that Nicolae Ceausescu, whom he called a "poisoned hyena," and his wife, Elena, had been arrested. After Ceausescu had fled the balcony of the Central Committee Building, he, his wife, and some aides had boarded a helicopter waiting for them on the building's roof. They had flown to Snagov, a nearby resort town, where the Ceausescus had one of their villas. They then headed back to Otopeni Airport in Bucharest. However, they were denied permission to land there. Instead, they landed on a highway outside of the city. The Ceausescus and the other passengers then got out. An argument ensued about where they should fly to next. Meanwhile, the pilot ran off and left them stranded.

The bodyguards then commandeered a car. They said, "We have two precious charges, He and She." They then drove to the town of Tirgoviste, northwest of Bucharest. There a group of patriotic guards captured them. They were taken to an army base and forced to ride around inside a tank so the Securitate could not locate them. The soldiers fed them stale bread. Elena complained, "They are feeding us bricks now!" Nicolae demanded a new suit. His request was refused.

The Ceausescus were eventually taken to Bucharest for a military trial. Looking old and tired they were stood behind a small desk. They were charged with genocide. Nicolae proclaimed, "This is nothing but a *coup d'etat*! A *coup d'etat* organized by a foreign power!" He was then asked, "Who gave the genocidal order in Timisoara?" He didn't respond. "Who ordered shooting the people in Bucharest? Who are the fanatics who keep shooting?" He replied: "I refuse to answer . . . no one was killed." At one point Ceausescu threw his fur hat on the table. He proclaimed, "I am Supreme Commander of the State, the leader of the party and I will accept only the judgment of the Peoples Congress."

The court quickly convicted them. The charges were: genocide, subversion of the state by ordering the massacre of unarmed civilians, destruction of communal property, subversion of the economy, attempted escape from the country, and having amassed more than one billion dollars in foreign banks. The Ceausescus responded with looks of disbelief. They then laughed. One of the prosecutors then asked, "Do you know who is holding you?" "Yes," answered Nicolae, "Securitate." "I was like a mother to you," Elena added plaintively. The sentence was then pronounced—death. The Ceausescus were led out into the courtyard. Three hundred soldiers volunteered to shoot them. But, in the end, two members of the court actually executed them. It was Christmas Day, 1999.

The entire trial was filmed. It was shown on Romanian television on December 26. The trial had been hurried, it was said, in order to prevent the Securitate from rescuing the Ceausescus and defeating the revolution. However, the playing of the film was delayed for a day. Why that had occurred is unclear. Also, when the film was originally shown the faces of all of the tribunal members were edited out. Only their voices remained. It was claimed that this was done in order to protect them from retaliation.

As the film played over and over again on Romanian television the faces of the Ceausescus were seen on the pavement—dead. A trickle of blood came from their heads. Was the trial hurried to save the revolution? Or, was it to prevent the Ceausescus from implicating most of the new government in their crimes? We will never know.

Soon people returned to the streets. They shouted, "Today is Christmas, the madman is gone." Formerly forbidden videotapes of Michael Jackson and Tina Turner appeared on television. Two days later came the first full-length film. It was Charlie Chaplin's 1940 classic, *The Great Dictator*. In that film Chaplin played the merciless dictator of a country called "Tomania."

The shooting stopped on December 26.

The National Salvation Front named Ion Iliescu as president. Iliescu was to head an interim government until elections were held in April 2000. Dumitru Mazilu, a diplomat, was to be vice president, and Petre Roman, a 43 year old professor, was named prime minister. As soon as the new interim government was named protesters began to complain that former Communists should not head, or even serve in, the new government. But, Ceausescu had never allowed any opposition to the Communist Party. There had been no Solidarity, no Vaclav Havel, no independent church; there had been only—Ceausescu. So, there was no alternative. Mircea Dinescu, the dissident poet observed: "We say in Romania that miracles last for three days. Like our revolution: after three days the professionals of power took over. The master was killed, his servants took over."

On December 27, the National Salvation Front went on television to announce its first decrees. Interspersed with these announcements was the film of the Ceausescus trial and execution—repeated over and over again. The decrees began by abandoning the "leading role" of the Communist Party in the country and the adoption of a pluralistic political system. The words "Socialist Republic" were removed from the name of the country. From then on, the nation was to be simply known as, "Romania." And, the Communist symbol was to be eliminated from the flag, as the revolutionaries had already done. A committee was formed to draft a new constitution. The new government agreed to respect minority and other human rights. The decrees also abolished the Securitate. However, 50,000 to 60,000 of its "regular troops" were absorbed into the army. And, the new government ended a rule that required that all typewriters to be registered with the police. Also, abortion was legalized. The "systemization program" of destroying villages was also ended. Romanians were no longer obligated to call each other comrade. The new government also made it illegal to refuse medical treatment to the elderly. This was a policy Ceausescu had used to keep his population young.

The new government also officially ended rationing. As a result of this chickens bound for Russia ended up on Romanian shelves. Oil and gas exports were cut. This allowed Romanians to have heat for more than two hours a day. Coffee, beef, pork, and chocolate began to appear on store shelves. They were also reports of fresh fruit. This led one woman to comment "I haven't seen coffee for . . . four years. . . . I heard there were bananas, but I myself haven't actually seen any."

On January 13, 2000, the government officially outlawed the Communist Party. However, the former Communists, who now ran the country, soon fell back into their old habits. When students demonstrated against the government President Iliescu called in 7,000 miners to "make order." They chanted, "Freedom and Silence" and "We don't think. We work," as they beat anyone who looked like a student or an intellectual. As the economy deteriorated and ethnic violence broke out President Iliescu moaned: "We truly confess not to know the zip code of paradise."

Three questions about the revolution have never been completely resolved. The first is: How many people were killed? It was initially reported that 5,000 to 12,000 people had died. It was also reported that 4,500 corpses were found in a mass grave. After the revolution, however, Dr. Milan Dressler, the coroner for Timisoara, revealed that the "mass grave" had been a pauper's cemetery. The coroner concluded that only 71 people had actually been killed during the revolution in Timisoara. However, some of the bodies of those killed in the revolution might have been taken to Bucharest. But, even if the numbers are somewhat higher, it certainly was not the five to twelve thousand that originally had been reported. However, many do not believe this. They believe that the Securitate must have covered up the massacre. And, they whisper that perhaps Dr. Dressler is Securitate, too.

Later it was common to read that sixty to eighty thousand Romanians had been killed in the revolution. However, on February 2, 1990, the government officially concluded that there had been only 682 dead and 1,200 wounded in the revolution (Cordrescu, 1991; Brogan, 1990). Also, it was common to see photos of Romanian soldiers, who lacked any combat experience, firing randomly in all directions at once. As a result of this, the government now admits that 90 percent of all the casualties were the result of friendly fire by soldiers or patriotic guards. In fact, there were probably never more than 100 Securitate "terrorists" (Micheletti, 1990).

Second, was this a real revolution or just a coup? A *Soldier of Fortune* article, in a section entitled "strange firefights," asked:

Beginning the evening of 22 December, what became of the famous 20,000 men of the Securitate? And among the diehards, why did none of them have RPG . . . rocket launchers to stop the army's tanks, as you always find in the street battles in Beirut? All they had were assault rifles, sniper rifles or . . . pistols. And in the army, why did no observer report deployment of light artillery . . . to meet the eventual counterattack of the motorized units of the Securitate? Other weapons always present in a *real* war that were missing in this case were mortars . . . and . . . antitank missiles. Could it be that the scenario had already been worked out the night before the *coup*?

Other questions: where was the navy with its 7,500 sailors . . . ? Where was the air force with its 32,000 men . . . equipped with . . . MiG[s] . . . and a fleet of combat helicopters? Same for the 15,000 frontier guards and the 250,000 men of the Patriotic Guard. To say nothing of the antiterrorist group based near Bucharest and the famous Directorate No. 5, assigned to protect Party dignitaries, all of whom took off.

In fact, it is reasonable to ask whether there was really any consistent opposition by the Securitate, or merely delaying actions fought by gangs of "desperadoes" trying to escape (Micheletti, 1990:51; see also Pacepa, 1987:211).

Although *Soldier of Fortune* magazine is perpetually paranoid, they do have a point. Also, why were there so many East Block reporters in Timisoara, an obscure Romanian town, on the very day of the "massacre?" In fact, Andrei Cordrescu, a Romanian emigree living in the United States, reports that the plot to overthrow Ceausescu was originally hatched in 1981 by Silviu Brucan, General Nicolae Militaru, and the leaders of the Securitate. However, the plot was put off when several generals were betrayed in 1984. Brucan and Militaru were not arrested because they were under the protection of the KGB. In fact, Elena Ceausescu used to show films of General Militaru having sex with his female KGB contact. Since the KGB controlled much of the Eastern European security services one could say that there was the "bad Securitate" that arrested some of the conspirators; but, there was also a "good Securitate" that protected other conspirators and eventually overthrew Ceausescu. One Romanian emigré explained it somewhat differently: "The people in the Securitate were some of the most educated and worldly people in Romania. They knew about the outside world—unlike most Romanians—and they knew how bad it was in Romania. So, they overthrew Ceausescu in order to improve things."

The third issue concerns the emergence of the National Salvation Front. The Front was supposed to have "spontaneously" emerged during the revolution. However, Silvia Brucan, a member of the NSF executive council, said on British television that he won a reluctant promise of support from senior Soviet officials for the revolution during a visit to Moscow in November 1989. Also, in a video made at the height of the fighting General Militaru said: "Why not [call it] the National Salvation Front? After all, it's been in existence for six months!" Also, Ion Iliescu, the leader of the NSF, and later the president of Romania, had gone to school in Moscow with Mikhail Gorbachev. So, one may conclude that the NSF rode the uprising in Timisoara to power (Reaves, 1990; Cordrescu, 1991; Stark and Bruszt, 1998:209n).

Chapter 18

Analysis Levels

Individuals & Institutions

The second part of the analysis must start at the individual level. However, in Romania governmental institutions were so intrusive that it is useful to discuss the individual and the institutional levels together. Then we will move up to the national and global levels to complete our analysis.

At the individual level the first group to examine are Romania's women and children. In October 1966, Ceausescu decreed that all women had to have four, and later five, children. The same year he banned all abortions. Live births doubled. However, illegal self-abortion and maternal deaths became common. As a result of this, maternal mortality was 100 times that of the best Western countries. Also, health care was inadequate. Infant mortality was ten times higher than in the best Western nations. Later, contraceptives were banned and monthly pregnancy exams were instituted by doctors called the "menstrual police." Also, single and childless couples were heavily taxed. And books on sex education became state secrets (Rothman, 1990; Burke, 1990; Reaves, 1990c; "United Nations Human Development Report," 1992:186; Cole and Nyden, 1990:475).

Since the average salary of a Romanian worker was $15 a month in 1990 large numbers of women could not afford to raise their children. Because of this children were abandoned and placed in orphanages. In the orphanages the children were divided into two categories, those that were normal and those with handicaps. The handicapped children were called "incorrigibles." The incorrigible children were sent to "irrecoverable orphanages." Here the children lived in cages with concrete floors. Their heads were shaved, and they were poorly fed. One-quarter to one-third of these children died each year. Also, low birthweight babies were classified as miscarriages and allowed to die

(Rothman, 1990; Bohlen, 1990i; Breslan, 1990; Churchill, 1991; see also David, 1988).*

In 1985 the first case of pediatric AIDS was reported. It is believed that the disease came from tainted blood from sailors in the Black Sea port of Castantsa.** "Microinfusions," that is, transfusions of small amounts of blood from each unit collected were given to "weak babies" to "perk them up." (The practice of giving adult blood to anemic children was ended decades ago in the West.) Ceausescu had decreed that AIDS did not exist in Romania; so the blood was not screened for the virus. As a result of this a relatively small number of tainted blood units infected many children. Between 1985 and 1994, almost 3,000 AIDS cases were detected among children. Also, almost all illnesses in the orphanages were treated with repeated injections of antibiotics. Reuse of needles was common. Any physician who deviated from such practices was investigated. Further, in the 1980s, the training of healthcare workers was discontinued as Ceausescu considered healthcare an "unproductive industry." (Rothman, 1990; Neeley, 1991; Lynch, 1990; Kenny, 1990; Bohlen, 1990g, 1990f; Battiata, 1990b; Kligman, 1998; 221-224). Thus, archaic and inappropriate medical practices, coupled with political control of medicine, led to thousands of maternal and childhood deaths.

In 1983 Ceausescu decided to increase his population from 23 to 33 million people. To accomplish this he created the Higher Council on Health. The council focused on "increasing natality" and curtailing "the interruption of pregnancy." The Council, through the Ministry of Health, began periodic examinations of women between the ages of 16 and 45. Early detection, recording, and surveillance of pregnancies was mandated. Later, local commissions were established to concentrate on "control and surveillance." This was to "enforce the political demographic." These commissions were made up of a physician, a prosecutor, and a police officer. These commissions met weekly and issued monthly reports. If the number of pregnancies was low, but the number of abortions was high, the area was considered "a zone at risk." If an area was designated as such a zone local police and prosecutors ferreted out physicians doing abortions (Kligman, 1998:95 9).

The Ministry of Health made physicians the "principle propagandists" for promoting births. In order to detect pregnancies urban women were given yearly, or even more frequent, medical examinations. If a woman was found to be pregnant she was closely monitored. Some physicians sought to find pregnan-

---

* For a description of equally dreadful conditions in Russian orphanages see a report by Human Rights Watch (Hunt, 1998). And, for an analysis of the astronomical death rates in Chinese orphanages see another report by Human Rights Watch (Munro and Rigby, 1996).

** pronounced: Cos-tanza

cies; other physicians avoided finding them so women could secretly have abortions. However, if physicians did not meet their "reproductive norms" they were taxed. In a few cases physicians who did not meet their norms were arrested and suffered through show trials. In order to meet their goals some physicians conducted 50 to 60 gynecological exams a day. This attempt to increase population was handled by Communist planners as if it were a routine "production plan" (Kligman, 1998:99-105, 149).

In economics the government followed the Stalinist model and focused on heavy industry. As a result of this it failed to produce enough consumer goods. In the 1980s Ceausescu decided to pay off Romania's foreign debts in order to become financially independent. He did this by imposing severe austerity measures. He also began exporting gas, oil, medicine, and food. This further exacerbated the situation. Ceausescu's obsession with industrialization, austerity, and his "attachment to an obsolete, rigid hypercentralized planning system" resulted in dramatically declining living standards and growing popular discontent (Tismaneanu, 2003:189).

Because of these shortages the typical day of the average Romanian consisted of long waits for milk in the morning, even longer waits for gasoline in the afternoon, and endless lines for scarce, and often poor quality meat, in the evening. Also, health care required bribes to secure treatment and medicine was often unavailable. "Luxury" items such as fresh fruit, vegetables, chocolate, nylons, and cigarettes were unavailable. This led citizens to become "hunters and gatherers of scarce goods" (Fitzpatrick, 1999:3; Kideckel, 1993:63, 136-7, 140-1).

The consequence of this was that workers often left work hours early in order to secure these consumer items. To meet this demand a black market emerged in order to secure these goods. Also, government workers extorted bribes for routine government services so they could afford inflated black market prices. Soon corruption became an endemic part of everyday life. This created dependency, cynicism, and powerlessness among the population. However, some Romanians overcame this by becoming highly manipulative (Kideckel, 1993:xiii, 168-70, 189).

Another institution that strongly influenced everyday life was the (secret) police. In the West, the primary focus of the police is crime control. They function within the rule of law and under legitimate (elected) officials. However, there are two other types of policing. One is colonial policing. Here, the police institution is created by an outside power to control a native population. Although this type of police force handles routine crime control matters its primary function is to keep the colonial power in control. Another type of policing is the continental model. This type was typical of the centralized premodern European state. Although these forces were concerned with crime control their primary function was to uphold the political power of their absolutist monarch. Czarist Russia adopted this type of policing (Shelley, 1996).

The Soviet regime inherited this type of policing. The only change that the police made was made was to shift from the protection of the monarch to the protection of the Communist Party. That is, they functioned as "political police." The Romanian government adopted this type of policing. Over time the police took on numerous administrative duties. Functions such as food inspections, public works planning, the regulation of public meetings, public health, fire prevention, and population registration, all became police functions. Also, the regulation of political, cultural, and religious life were all police responsibilities. Therefore, virtually all citizen behavior fell within the legitimate control of the police (Shelley, 1990, 1996; Liang, 1992:1-17; Brodeur, 1983; Marx, 1988:139).

In carrying out these duties the police did not simply monitor the ordinary activities of Soviet citizens. Instead, they actively attempted to change them in order to create the "new Socialist man." The ideology that drove this was the Marxist notion of inevitable class conflict. This led the police to often view citizens as class enemies. And force was considered to be a legitimate tool against such enemies.

In their administrative role the police continually monitored the minutiae of each citizens daily existence. They perpetually interfered in the economic, political, and social lives of citizens. In their control of large portions of civil society the police created a labyrinth of rules. No citizen could comply with all of these regulations. Therefore, no citizen could be truly law-abiding (Shelley, 1996:XV, 130). Even if one wished to follow the state's regulations this was difficult since the state was usually slow, cumbersome, corrupt, and arbitrary (Fitzpatrick, 1993:3).

Another component of everyday life was (petty) politics. One way to get ahead, or just get along, was to inform. By turning in someone to the (secret) police you improved your standing in the eyes of the regime. And if you were lucky you might even move up to the other person's position. However, informing did not need to be an active process. Simply not associating with "enemies of the people" or not defending friends made one complicit with the state (Fitzpatrick, 1999:219, 221, 191; Verdery, 1991:83-84; Anguelov, 2002).

Another characteristic inherent in everyday life in Communist states was terror. Terror, whether physical or psychological, was not an aberration. Terror was one of the political tools routinely used by the state. However, how it was applied changed over time. Communist regimes went through three stages of development. The first stage was the takeover stage. In this phase the regime relied heavily upon physical coercion in order to eliminate current or future enemies. In the second, or transformation stage, organized terror was used to "remold society." And, in the third, or post-mobilization stage, physical terror tended to fade since the regime was secure. However, in its place psychological terror was installed (Dallin and Breslauer, 1971; Adelman, 1984).

In Romania, the initial takeover by the Communists after World War II ushered in a period of Stalinist terror. The collectivization of agriculture in 1949 brought on violent protests. Hundreds of thousands of peasants were killed or imprisoned. The old cultural and political elite were liquidated. In the mid-1950s the terror began to abate because the regime had thoroughly penetrated society and eliminated all serious opposition. By the 1960s physical coercion greatly diminished. In 1964 almost all political prisoners were freed. However, by then, four hundred thousand people had perished in Romania. In the Soviet Union the victims of terror ran into the millions (Bacon, 1984; Treptow, 1995:52139).

When Ceausescu took over in the 1960s, he promoted nationalism. After 500 years of Ottomon and Russian control this was relatively well received. However, this good will quickly faded when the Communist regime could not produce material prosperity for its citizens. The regime then fell back on massive campaigns of political propaganda. However, this fell on deaf ears. As Ceausescu's popularity ebbed psychological terror emerged as the primary tool to keep the population under control (Bacon, 1984; Kideckel, 1993:52-5).

The Romanian secret police, the Securitate, carried out this program. The Securitate was formed in 1945. They were an elite force of up to 180,000 troops with the latest equipment. One of their functions was to be a counterbalance to the army, which had about the same number of troops. Many of the Securitate were recruited from orphanages and trained to be fanatically devoted to the Ceausescus. It was often said that "the best Communists came from the orphanages." The Securitate infiltrated every facet of Romanian life. It has been reported that they had planted up to 10 million microphones in a country of 23 million people. And the Securitate had handwriting samples on 60 percent of the population. Also, it is said that many writers who were suspected of dissidence received summons to report to a certain Securitate colonel. They waited for several hours at his office but never got to see him. It is believed that the room had a cobalt device which irradiated them. Later, many contracted cancer (Cullen, 1991:24; Cordrescu, 1991:137; Pacepa, 1987).

The four million members of the Communist Party served as the eyes and ears of the Securitate. There were also three million registered informants. However, the actual number of informers could have been as high as one third of the entire adult population (Pacepa, 1987:216).

The Securitate sent dissidents to mental hospitals. They tapped the phones of citizens, and even bugged their ashtrays. Individuals felt helpless. The fear of arbitrary punishment was pervasive. Under Ceausecu there was an all-pervasive paranoia (Bacon, 1984; Adelman, 1984; Pilon, 1992:1; Brogan, 1990; Fischer, 1989; Rollnick, 1990; *Gulag Gives Up Lost Patients*, 1991; see also King, 1980:106-9).

Ceausescu once was reported to have said, "We should not trust anyone . . . before checking on their thoughts." Ceausescu devoted a great deal of effort to monitoring these thoughts. When he came to power in 1965 the Romanian security forces had twelve electronic monitoring centers and five mail censorship units. By 1978 there were 1,258 electronic monitoring units and 48 mail censoring stations. In explaining his attempt to know every thought of every Romanian citizen Ceausescu is reported to have said: "In a very short time we will be the only country on earth able to know what every single one of its citizens is thinking. Five years is all that separates us . . . from a new, much more scientific form of government. . . . Why is American imperialism so unpopular? Because it does not know what its people think, because it is not scientific. What . . . [the Ceausescu government is] doing . . . is the real science of government. It is a true public opinion survey. The Communist system . . . is the most scientific . . . *ever* to be put at the service of mankind" (Pacepa, 1987, emphasis in the original; Doerner, 1990; Cordrescu, 1991; Bialer, 1980:14; see also Kundera, 1984; Verdery, 1991:85).

When citizens were arrested by the Securitate these apprehensions were either arbitrary or the result of informers. This broke down the bonds of trust between citizens and atomized them (Sofsky, 1993:257). The Securitate operated on a simple premise: "The . . . idea was to produce an atmosphere of uncertainty and suspicion, [an] . . . all enveloping fog, through which naked terror might suddenly loom to destroy the individual." The job of the police, or secret police, "was not so much to capture and punish individuals who had acted against the . . . State as to arrest on suspicion *before*" they could take action (Crankshaw, 1956:83, emphasis added; see also Delarue, 1964:97, 133, 135; Aronson, 1969:34, 37).

Sofsky notes that in such a system "equality was total;" that is, "the equality of universal powerlessness." The use of psychological terror was meant to intimidate, to crush resistance, and to spread fear. It could only come to an end when the last opponent had been eliminated and "the peace of the grave" held dominion (1993:16; Fitzpatrick: 1999).

Physical control of the population was not needed under such circumstances. Instead, the point was to make individuals "complicit in their own control." This control was to be "lodged in the brain of the obedient." Thus, the point of the terror was *self-control* (Shelley, 1996:16; Sofsky, 1993:17).

National: The Romanian Communist Party (RCP)

The Turks ruled Romania for 400 years. After the Romanians gained their independence the people remained politically passive. As a result of this the governments that grew up after independence were elitist, paternalistic, Byzantine, and focused on cults of personality. These governments were also centralized, incompetent, and corrupt. Whatever enthusiasm that existed for these governments was the product of a long suppressed nationalism. But, when this nationalism faded the state applied physical coercion to maintain control (Bacon, 1984; Fischer, 1989; Pilon, 1992:61).

The Germans invaded Romania in World War II. The Soviet army swept into Romania in 1944 and drove the Germans out. After a series of short-lived governments the Communists took official control in 1948. However, before 1944 the Communist Party never had more than a thousand members. In fact, they were "a tiny messianic" movement "unwaveringly committed" to Stalinism. In other words, Communism was an alien political ideology imposed upon Romania by Soviet troops (Tismaneanu, 2003:189).

From 1948 until the late 1950s the Romanian Communist Party* under Gheorghe Gheorghiu-Dej** followed the model and the directives of the Kremlin and forcibly sovietized Romania. For example in the late 1940s the Communist Party nationalized all factories, mines, banks, insurance companies, and major health care institutions. In the early 1950s, housing, private medical offices, restaurants, taxis, and retail shops were also nationalized. In 1949 the process of collectivization began in agriculture. Although violent protests occurred resistance proved futile. By the early 1960s, 90 percent of all land were under the control of state farms or collectives. Hundreds of thousands of peasants were killed or imprisoned during this process (Treptow, 1995:521-39; Kideckel, 1993:57).

In order to transform society, the state glorified labor and made it its central activity. Through the labor unions worker housing, shopping, social clubs, and even vacations were controlled. Thus, "by making the workplace the focus of social life . . . the party enhanced its ability to supervise workers' lives and thoughts" (Kideckel, 1993:78, 61).

After the Communist Party's power was consolidated the repression abated. They then attempted to establish their legitimacy by promoting nationalism (see Verdery, 1991:98-134). This paid off in 1958 when the Russians withdrew their troops from Romania. However, whatever legitimacy the Communists garnered was quickly eroded due to their harsh tactics and their inability to produce any material benefits for the Romanian people (Holmes, 1997:42-62: Tismaneanu, 2003:217; Treptow, 1995).

In 1965 Gheorghiu-Dej died. He was replaced by an *apparatchik*, a party functionary, named Nicolae Ceausescu. Ceausescu was described as a drab little man with a bushy pompadour, a warm smile, and pink lips. He was born in a small Romanian town. His father was an alcoholic. To escape this environment Nicolae left for Bucharest at the age of twelve. Bucharest was then a

---

* The Romanian Communist Party could simply be considered "an institution." However, since it reached into every facet of society it is more appropriate to perceive it as a national entity (see Gellner, 1991: 232).

** pronounced: Zhorje Zhor-jiu-Dej

cosmopolitan city that was known as the Paris of the East. However, Nicolae was too young, uneducated, and poor to participate in, or even appreciate, the cultural life of the city (Pacepa, 1987).

He became a cobbler's apprentice. But, it is said that he was too lazy to learn how to make shoes. It is reported that when he was asked what he would do when he got older he replied, "I'll become the Romanian Stalin." At 18 he was arrested for distributing leaflets for the Communist Party. He was so disruptive at his trial that he was given a harsh sentence—three years in jail. In prison he showed the other Communist prisoners that he was intelligent and devoted to the cause. Because of this he became the personal servant to Gheorghiu-Dej. However, his mental stability was questionable. He frequently flew into hysterical rages. Later, a Securitate official described him as "talkative, impulsive, violent, [and] hysterical" (Pacepa, 1987:24).

After the Communist Party took control in 1948, Ceausescu started his rise in the party. He soon murdered a bank manager who would not contribute to the party. However, this incident was ignored by the police, as well as, the Communist Party. He was soon appointed a political officer in the army. He eventually rose to general. However, his behavior was erratic and he was about to be replaced when Gheorghiu-Dej died in 1965. He was then appointed party chairman because others felt that they could control him. This, however, did not occur. Under the guise of political and cultural liberalization he soon purged his rivals. Then, in 1968 he opposed the Russian invasion of Czechoslovakia. This anti-Russian stance made him very popular at home; and, he also quickly became the West's favorite Communist. However, during a visit to North Korea in 1971 Ceausescu was impressed by the regimentation of the populace and Kim Il Sung's cult of personality. Upon his return to Romania he reestablished Stalinist policies—emphasis on heavy industry, centralization in agriculture, suppression of culture, and the creation of a cult of personality (Treptow, 1995; Calinescu and Tismaneanu, 1991).

Exacerbating these tendencies was the emergence of paranoia and grandiosity in Ceausescu. He began to employ food tasters and had a lab test his clothing. He installed radiation detectors in all his offices and washed his hands with alcohol after every contact with a stranger. And, every child he kissed had to have a medical certificate to prove that they were free of disease. Also, he never wore a suit twice. After one wearing his clothes were burned. In a warehouse next to his residence was a one-year supply of clothes sealed in plastic: 365 suits, 365 pairs of shoes, and so on. One day he proclaimed: "A man like me comes along only once in 500 years." Tismaneanu concludes that by then Ceausescu "had acquired the status of a Communist pharaoh, an infallible demigod, whose vanity seemed boundless" (Tismaneanu, 2003:224, 189).

After several years in power Ceausescu began to have mood swings and he became extremely suspicious. He refused to take medication and began to trust only his wife. Along with his paranoia, his grandiosity grew. One day he decided to build a huge palace for himself. He tore down one-fifth of the entire city of Bucharest to accomplish this task.

Elena, his wife, was portrayed as a scientific genius. However, this was far from reality. She had dropped out of school at the age of 14 and became a pharmaceutical factory worker. After her husband became the party leader she decided that she wanted a doctorate. She approached Professor Constin Nenitescu from the University of Bucharest and asked him to award her a doctorate in chemistry. He refused. Immediately he "retired." She then asked a professor from a provincial university. He agreed, although she didn't even know the formula for water. She soon was portrayed by government propaganda as a brilliant scientist.

Nicolae also considered himself a superior intellect. He wrote numerous books. For those who read them they were said to suffer from "stupefying dullness." As his ego grew, so did the number of his television appearances. However, the TV station had to edit out the stutters, pauses, facial grimaces, and grammatical errors in his speeches. He decided on state visits by sticking pins in a globe. And, when he visited one Western capital he stole everything from the apartment where he stayed. At home he had 40 palaces for his personal use. Most of them were decorated in what has been called "French Renaissance *kitsch*." In the end the Ceausescus came to believe *they* were Romania. This led Romanians to call them, *He* and *She*.

Kennan succinctly describes such a classic Stalinist regime. It was characterized by: The absolute power of a single man, his power over thoughts as well as actions; the impermanence and insubstantiality of all subordinate distinctions of rank and dignity—the instantaneous transition from lofty station to disgrace and oblivion; the indecent association of sycophancy upwards with brutality downwards, the utter disenfranchisement and helplessness of the popular masses . . . the neurotic relationship to the West; the frantic fear of foreign observation; the obsession with espionage; the secrecy; the systematic mystification; [and] the general silence of intimidation (1971:124 5).

Most importantly, the regime punished Romanians for offenses they *might* be capable of committing. This is the key to understanding the psychological terror that the regime employed. The terror that kept it in power.

Global

In 1989 communism collapsed in Romania. However, this was not a unique event. Communism also collapsed throughout Eastern Europe and the Soviet Union at the same time. Why did this occur? The answer is rather simple, because of Mikhail Gorbachev.

When Gorbachev came to power in 1985 he saw the Soviet Union disintegrating. The Russian citizenry had grown weary of dictatorship. They also had grown weary of material shortages, poor quality goods, a stagnant economy, and "pervasive squalor" (Gellner, 1991:234). By the 1980s there was also a growing population, increasing urbanization, higher levels of education, and an expanding intelligentsia (Lane, 1991). Because of these factors Gorbachev faced widespread demands for political and economic reform. Gorbachev attempted to achieve this political and economic transformation through *glasnost*, openness, and *perestroika*, restructuring. He felt that this was the only way he could save communism. Privately, however, Gorbachev confided to a Hungarian Communist official that the totality of the Soviet experience had been wrong. And, he believed that most Soviet practices were discredited. In a 1998 speech Gorbachev concluded: "*Perestroika* is our last chance" for "if we stop, it will be our death" (Brzezinski, 1990:44-5, 53).

Gorbachev began by attempting to reform the political system. Under Stalinism the Soviet state had been an engine of massive repression. By the time Gorbachev came to power the Soviet political system had become somewhat freer. It was what Brown (1996) has called a "post-totalitarian authoritarian" regime. Gorbachev first reform was *glasnost*. He felt that in order to transform the political system competitive elections, freedom of assembly, the rule of law, and freedom of the press all had to be established (McClarnand, 1998). Although *glasnost* came from above this was an attempt to generate social pressure from below. The *glasnost* policy unleashed a debate throughout society concerning the foundations of the Soviet system. "In the course of the debate, things once held to be sacred were publicly profaned; matters long ago swept under the rug [were] openly exposed; the seeming unanimity of the country [was] shattered; and in some eyes even the future of the system [was] placed in doubt." As a result of this the Soviet Union increasingly became a "volatile Soviet disunion" (Brzezinski, 1990:54, 1997; Garthoff, 1994b).

Gorbachev's second reform was *perestroika*, economic restructuring. This reform attempted to change the Soviet system from a command economy to a free market one. In order to accomplish this the state had to be stripped of much of its ownership in order to create private property. Gorbachev also saw a need to eliminate Russian domination over the 100 other ethnic groups in the Soviet Union. This was important since non-Russian groups made up almost half the population of the country (Brown, 1996; McFaul, 1999).

Gorbachev sought to change foreign policy, as well. He felt this was needed because military competition with the West had produced a military-industrial complex which consumed a disproportionate share of the national budget and distorted the economy. Because of this the consumer sector was starved. So, in order to improve the daily lives of Soviet citizens a major shift in spending had to occur. Such a shift could only occur if East-West relations improved and military spending was reduced.

Another drain on the Soviet economy were the regimes they propped up in Eastern Europe. Those regimes only existed because of the threat of Soviet military intervention. At a secret meeting in November 1986, Gorbachev told

Eastern European leaders that the Soviet Union would no longer intervene if their regimes were threatened (Garthoff, 1994a:574). Gorbachev's rationale for this was the people's "freedom to choose" a Communist or non-Communist regime. This has been called the Sinatra Doctrine after the crooner's hit, "I Did It My Way." As a result of Gorbachev's decision Communism collapsed throughout Eastern Europe in 1989. Thus, the overthrow of Ceausescu and other Communist dictators was a "direct consequence of the transformation of Soviet policy" at the hands of Gorbachev (Brown, 1996:116; Garthoff, 1994a:604n, 1994b; Brzezinski, 1997:26; Risen, 2001).

So, in an attempt to save the Soviet Union Gorbachev allowed Romania and the other Eastern European Communist states to break away and become free. And as a result of that I was able to adopt my babies.

Bibliography

Adoptive Families of America
   1993 "1993 Agency Update: Choosing an Adoption Agency," *Ours*, vol. 25 no. 6, Nov-Dec, 47.
Adelman, Jonathan R., ed.
   1984 *Terror and Communist Politics: the Role of the Secret Police in Communist States*. Boulder, CO: Westview Press.
Aitken, Lee
   1992 "The High Price of a Baby's Love," *Money*, January, 98 113.
Albrecht, Gary L., Ray Fitzpatrick and Susan C. Scrimshaw, eds.
   2000 *Handbook of Social Studies in Health and Medicine*. Thousand Oaks, CA: Sage Press.
Altstein, Howard
   1992 "Rescuing Romania's orphans," *New York Times*, November 28, 13.
Altstein, Howard, and Rita J. Simon, eds.
   1991 *Intercountry Adoption: a Multinational Perspective*. New York: Praeger.
Angrosino, Michael V.
   1998 *Opportunity House: Ethnographic Stories of Mental Retardation*. Walnut Creek, CA: Altamira Press.
   2002 "Babaji and Me: Reflections on a Fictional Ethnography," in *Ethnographically Speaking: Autoethnography, Literature, and Aesthetics*, Arthur P. Bochner and Carolyn Ellis eds. Walnut Creek, CA: Altamira Press.
Anguelov, Zlatko
   2002 *Communism and the Remorse of an Innocent Victimizer*. College Station, TX: Texas A&M University Press.
Ashraf, Haroom
   2000 "UK Allows Frozen Eggs for Fertility Treatment," *Lancet*, vol. 355 issue 9201, Jan 29, 387.
Associated Press
   1989 "Mass graves found in Romania; relatives of missing dig them up," *New York Times*, Dec 23, 1.
Atkinson, Paul, Amanda Coffey and Sara Delamont, eds.
   2003 *Key Themes in Qualitative Research: Continuities and Changes*. Walnut Creek, CA: Altamira Press.
Bachman, Ronald D., ed.
   1991 "Romania: Country Study," Washington, DC: Federal Research Division, Library of Congress.

Bacon, Walter
　1984　"Romanian Secret Police," in *Terror and Communist Politics*, Jonathan R. Adelman ed. Boulder, CO: Westview Press.
Bair, Frank E., ed.
　1991　"Romania," *Countries of the World*, vol. 2. Detroit: Gaia Research Service.
Bardescu, Andrei
　1991　"In Romania, anti-semitism stirs passions," *New York Times*, July 29, 1991, 10.
Barringer, Felicity
　1991　"Birth rates plummeting in Romanian province," *New York Times*, Dec 31, 3.
Battiata, Mary
　1990a　"A clash of culture in Romanian province," *The Washington Post*, March 29, 17.
　1990b　"Romania turns toward the sun," *Washington Post National Weekly Edition*, May 7 to May 13, 10-11.
Beaver, Paul
　1992　"Flash Points," *Jane's Defense Weekly*, November 7, 20.
Beck, Joan
　1994　"We should stop ignoring adoption as a viable solution," *Chicago Tribune*, Aug 7, 4-3.
　1995　"Interracial adoptions make loving sense," *Chicago Tribune*, April 20, 21.
Benjamin, Daniel
　1990　"Below the Speed Limit," *Time*, Jan 29, 34-36.
Bernstein, Elizabeth
　1994　"Giant Loss: Remembering Rabbi Moses Rosen," *Jewish United Fund (JUF) News*, July 21.
Bernstein, Linda
　1991　"Are the babies twins? Well, no. Not quite.," *New York Times*, Dec 26, 81.
Bialer, Seweryn
　1980　*Stalin's Successors: Leadership, Stability and Change in the Soviet Union*, Cambridge: Cambridge University Press, 1980.
Bjorklund, Diane
　1998　*Interpreting the Self: Two Hundred Years of American Autobiography*. Chicago, IL: University of Chicago Press.
Binder, David
　1989a　"At least 13 are reported killed in protest in Rumania's capital," *New York Times*, Dec 22. 1.
　1989b　"Bodies in streets," *New York Times*, Dec 24, 1.
　1990a　"Breaking the mold," *New York Times*, May 22, 6.
　1990b　"Ceausescu snipers at large, two former officials assert," *New York Times*, Aug 29, 10.

1990c "In East Europe, the police have gone the way of the police state," *New York Times*, Sept 2, E4.
1990d "Rallies criticize Rumania's new leaders," *New York Times*, Jan 8.
1990f "Romanian president says elements of secret police are still used to maintain order," *New York Times*, Oct 4, 4.
1990g "Romanian's hold sixth day of protest," *New York Times*, Aug 28, 3.
1990h "Romanian's lives quickly improve," *New York Times*, March 12, 9.
1990i "Romanian leaders outlaw ousted Communist Party," *New York Times*, Jan 13, 7.
1990j "The Old Guard in a new government," *New York Times*, Jan 26, 9.
1990k "With tears Romanians recall partition of 1940," *New York Times*, Sept 2, 5.
1991 "Slight thaw detected in U.S. - Romania ties," *New York Times*, April 18, 5.
1992a "Romanians and Hungarians building a bit of trust," *New York Times*, July 20, 5.
1992b "U.S. offers measure of approval to democratic trend in Romania," *New York Times*, April 1, 4.
1993a "European Gypsies issue call for human rights at meeting," *New York Times*, May 5, 9.
1993b "Romania is rebuked on move to imprison ex-spy for West," *New York Times*, June 30, 2.
1993c "Romanian mends his fences," *New York Times*, April 19, 4.
1993d "Romania's secret police fewer than believed," *New York Times*, April 19, 4.
1993e "Romanian mends his fences," *New York Times*, April 19, 4.
Birbaum, Susan
 1991 "Romania pledges to fight anti-semitism," *Wisconsin Jewish Chronicle*, July 12, 19.
Bird, Chloe E., Peter Conrad, and Allen M. Fremont, eds.
 2000 *Handbook of Medical Sociology* 5th Edition. Upper Saddle River, NJ: Prentice-Hall.
Blandiana, Ana
 1991 "A Sense of Solidarity," *Index on Censorship*, 5-6.
"Blood in the Square"
 1990 *Time*, April 2, 33.
Bochner, Arthur P. and Carolyn Ellis, eds.
 1996 "Talking Over Ethnography," *Composing Ethnography: Alternative Forms of Qualitative Writing*. Walnut Creek, CA: Altamira Press.
Bohlen, Celestine
 1989a "As Communist rule fades, Rumanian-Soviet ties grow," *New York Times*, Dec 30, 8.
 1989b "Hatred of security forces growing as Rumanian atrocities increase," *New York Times*, Dec 24, 1.
 1989c "Interim Romanian leaders named as fighting subsides," *New York Times*, Dec 27, 1.

1989d "Long-silenced, Rumanian artists break free," *New York Times*, Dec 31, 1.
1989e "Rumanians moving to abolish worst of repressive era," *New York Times*, Dec 28, 1.
1989f "Visitors horrified at protest scene," *New York Times*, Dec 20, 20.
1990a "Doubts and fears of Romania's lingering Germans," *New York Times*, Jan 12, 14.
1990b "Ethnic enmity governs a new Soviet Republic," *New York Times*, Oct 15.
1990c "Ex-dissidents will monitor Bucharest on rights," *New York Times*, Jan 6, 6.
1990e "Moscow promises to back Rumania in its new politics," *New York Times*, Jan 7, 1.
1990f "Romania struggles in battle against spread of AIDS," *New York Times*, May 9, 4.
1990g "Romania's AIDS babies: a legacy of neglect," *New York Times*, Feb 8, 1.
1990h "Rumania disbands rebellious forces," *New York Times*, Jan 2, 12.
1990i "The hurdles are many, but the reward is a child," *New York Times*, Nov 15, 12.
1990j "Whispered no longer, hearsay jolts Bucharest," *New York Times*, Jan 4.
1991 "Romania's leader vows freer reins," *New York Times*, Oct 3, 7.

Bohlen, Celestine and Clyde Haberman
 1989 "In Rumania a sense that no one's in charge," *New York Times*, Dec 25, 1.
 1990 "How the Ceausescus fell: harnessing popular rage," *New York Times*, Jan 7, 1.

Boroweic, Andres
 1990 "Agency launches program to save children warehoused by Ceausescu," *The Washington Post*, June 13.

Borrell, John
 1992 "Wild in the Streets," *Time*, June 25, 29.

Boyle, Tim
 1993 "Adoption rights," *Chicago Tribune*, Oct 4, 183.

Bohlen Celestine and Clyde Haberman
 1989 "In Rumania a sense that no one's in charge," *New York Times*, Dec 25, 1.

"Brazil Charges Israelis in Baby Scam"
 1993 *Forward*, Aug 20, 3.

Breslan, Karen
 1990 "Overplanned parenthood," *New York Times*, Dec 25, 1.

"Britons in baby-smuggling case go free"
 1994 *Chicago Tribune*, Nov 17, 20.

Brodeur, Jean-Paul
 1983 "High policing and low policing: remarks about the policing of political activities," *Social Problems*, vol. 30, 507-520.

Brogan, Patrick
 1990 *Eastern Europe, 1939-1989: The Fifty Years War*. Madison, WI: Bloomsbury.

Brown, Archie
  1996 *The Gorbachev Factor*. Oxford (Eng)/New York: Oxford University Press.
Brunner, Jerome
  1987 "Life as Narrative," *Social Research*, vol. 54 no. 1, 11-32.
Brzezinski, Zbigniew
  1990 *The Grand Failure: the birth and death of Communism in the Twentieth Century*. New York: Collier Books-Macmillan.
Burke, B. Meridith
  1990 "Ceausescu's main victims: women and children," *New York Times*, Jan 10, 27.
Burks, Richard Voyles
  1973 *East European History: an Ethnic Approach*. Washington, DC: American Historical Association.
Burrage, Michael and Rolph Torstendahl, eds.
  1990 *Professions in Theory and History: Rethinking the Study of the Professions*. Newbury Park, CA: Sage.
Butler, Lisa
  1991 "Hepatitis: A Nurse's Story," *RN*, April, 66.
Butler, Teresa
  1992 "The Prejudice Surrounding Romanian Adoptions," *Ours*, vol. 24 no. 6, Nov-Dec, 14.
Calinescu, Matei and Vladimir Tismaneanu
  1991 "The 1989 Revolution and Romania's Future," *Problems of Communism*, vol. 40 no. 12, 42-59.
Callahan, Daniel
  1993 "Pursuing a Peaceful Death," *Hastings Center Report*, vol. 23 no. 4, July-Aug, 33-9.
Campanella, Donna
  1993 "Adopting Andrew," *Glamour*, vol. 91, July.
Castelnau, Brigitte
  1990 "Kids' AIDS tragedy is Romania's latest horror," *Chicago Sun-Times*, Feb 5, 9.
Catchpole, Sarah
  1992 "Romania, a land of haunting fear and magnificent decay," *Chicago Tribune*, Jan 4, 12.
"Ceausescu's 'family' policy filled orphanages"
  1990 *Chicago Tribune*, Jan 4, 12.
Charalambous, Annie
  1994 "Baby market fetches top dollar in Cypress," *Chicago Sun-Times*, Feb 20, 45.
Chesler, Phyllis
  1988 *Sacred Bond: the Legacy of Baby M*. New York: Random House.
"Child prostitution growing in Bogotá"
  1990 *Chicago Tribune*, Nov 24, 15.
Chira, Susan
  1994 "Law proposed to end adoption horror stories," *New York Times*, Aug 24, 7.

Churchill, Caryl
　1991　*Mad Forest: A Play from Romania*. London: Nick Hern Books.
Cimons, Marlene
　1994　"Seeking a miracle for her son," *Los Angeles Times*, Sept 4, 1.
Clines, Frances X.
　1989a　"Gorbachev says he will confer with allies on aid to Rumanians," *New York Times*, Dec 24.
　1989b　"Romanian rebellion inspires proud Soviet relatives at the border," *New York Times*, Dec 31, 15.
　1990a　"Six killed in ethnic violence in Moldavia," *New York Times*, Nov 3, 4.
　1990b　"Strife averted in Moldova in protest against troops," *New York Times*, Nov 1, 4.
Clifford, James and George E. Marcus, eds.
　1986　*Writing Culture: the Poetics and Politics of Ethnography* (a School of American Research advanced seminar). Berkeley, CA: University of California Press.
Cohen, Anthony P.
　1994　*Self Consciousness: an Alternative Anthropology of Identity*. London: Routledge.
Cohen, Roger
　1992　"Paying for the fall of Communism," *New York Times*, Sept 27, 3-1.
Cole, Ardra L. and J. Gary Knowles
　2001　*Lives in Context: the Art of Life History Research*. Walnut Creek, CA: Altamira Press.
Cole, John W. and Judith A. Nyden
　1990　"Class, Gender, and Infertility: Contradictions of Social Life in Contemporary Romania," *East European Quarterly*, vol. 23 no. 4, Jan, 467-476.
Condurachi, Emil and Constantin Dalcoviciu; James Hogarth, trans. from French.
　1971　*Romania*. London: Barrie and Jenkins.
Codrescu, Andrei
　1991　*The Hole in the Flag: A Romanian Exile's Story of Return*. New York: William Morrow & Co.
　1992　"Gypsy tragedy, German amnesia," *New York Times*, Sept 23, 19.
　1993　"Fascism on a pedestal," *New York Times*, Dec 7, 11.
Corliss, Richard
　1992　"Adoption Fever," *Time*, Sept 7, 59.
Cowan, Alison Leigh
　1992a　"Can a baby-making venture deliver?," *New York Times*, June 1, C1.
　1992b　"A Swiss firm makes babies its bet," *New York Times*, April 19, F13.
Cowell, Alan
　1990a　"Catalyst of revolution still guarded by army," *New York Times*, Jan 8.
　1990b　"Officers say party in Rumania plans to dissolve itself," *New York Times*, Jan 1, 1.
　1990c　"Rumanian finds his file: 12 years of being watched," *New York Times*, Jan 2, 1.
　1990d　"Rumanians take stock of a tattered economy," *New York Times*, Jan 4.

Crankshaw, Edward
　1956　*Gestapo*. London: Putnam.
Crapanzano, Vincent
　1980　*Tuhami: Portrait of a Moroccan*. Chicago, IL: University of Chicago Press.
Crosette, Barbara
　1994　"U.N. study finds a free Eastern and Central Europe poorer and less healthy," *New York Times*, Oct 7, 7.
Crossen, Cynthia
　1989　"Hard Choices: In today's adoptions the biological parents are calling the shots," *New York Times*, Sept 14, 1.
Cullen, Robert
　1990　"Report from Romania," *New Yorker*, April 2, 94.
　1991　*Twilight of Empire: Inside the Crumbling Soviet Bloc*. New York: Atlantic Monthly Press.
Curley, John E. Jr.
　1992　"Romania's best hope is its people," *Chicago Tribune*, June 17, 13.
Daday, Eileen O.
　1993　"Young Russian orphan finds love with Palatine family," *Daily Herald*, July 20, 5-3.
Dallin, Alexander and George W. Breslauer
　1971　*Political Terror in Communist Systems*. Stanford, CA: Stanford University Press.
David, Henry P., et. al., eds.
　1988　*Born Unwanted: Developmental of Denied Abortion*. New York: Springer Publishing.
Dascalu, Roxana
　1991　"Romania cracks down on baby sales," *Chicago Sun-Times*, May 17, 24.
Davis, Robert
　1995　"Suits back interracial adoptions," *USA Today*, April 13, 3A.
Delarue, Jacques; Merigan Savil, trans. from French.
　1964　*Gestapo: A History of Horror*. New York: Paragon House.
Dellios, Hugh
　1993　"The lost pioneers of the West," *Chicago Tribune*. April 4, 5-1.
Denzin, Norman K.
　1989　*Interpretive Biography*. Newbury Park, CA: Sage.
　1997　*Interpretive Ethnography: Ethnographic Practices for the 21st Century*. Thousand Oaks, CA: Sage Press.
Denzin, Norman K. and Yvonna S. Lincoln, eds.
　2000　"Introduction: The Discipline and Practice of Qualitative Research," *Handbook of Qualitative Research*. Thousand Oaks, CA: Sage Press.
Dobbs, Michael
　1993　"Children of Tyranny," *Washington Post National Weekly Edition*, Jan 15-Jan 21, 8.
Doerner, William R.
　1990　"Vicious Keepers of the Faith," *Time*, Jan 8, 32-33.

Dugger, Celia W.
　1991　"Tougher adoptions: New York tries hard sell," *New York Times*, July 11, 1.
Dunphy, Cathy
　1990　"Trapped in Romanian nightmare," *Toronto Star*, Aug 4, A1.
Dwyer, Kevin
　1982　*Moroccan Dialogues: Anthropology in Question*. Prospect Heights, IL: Waveland Press.
Eakin, Paul John
　1992　*Touching the World: Reference in Autobiography*. Princeton, NJ: Princeton University Press.
Ehrlich, Eugene, et. al., comp.
　1980　*Oxford American Dictionary*. New York: Avon Books.
"Eight ex-Romanian officials get jail for slayings in Timisoara"
　1991　*New York Times*, Dec 10, 6.
Eisenberg, Bart
　1990　"Road to Foreign Adoptions Gets Rockier," *The Christian Science Monitor*, Feb 28, 13.
Ellis, Carolyn
　1997　"Evocative Autoethnography: Writing Emotionally About Our Lives," *Representation and the Text: Reframing the Narrative Voice*, William G. Tierney and Yvonna S. Lincoln, eds. Albany, NY: State University of New York Press.
Ellsworth, Raymond and John Stuart Martin
　1971　*A Picture History of Eastern Europe*. New York: Crown Publishers.
Engelberg, Stephen and Judith Ingram
　1993　"Now Hungary adds its voice to the ethnic tumult," *New York Times*, Jan 25, 3.
Engelberg, Stephen
　1991a　"Romania, still dark, is craving light bulbs," *New York Times*, Feb 25, 4.
　1991b　"Uneasy Romanians are asking: where have all the secret agents gone," *New York Times*, Feb 13, 4.
Engstrom, Marilyn and Rickey Greene
　1993　"Adult Daycare for Persons with Dementia: A Viable Community Option," *Generations*, vol. 17 no. 1, 75-76.
Enstad, Robert
　1993　"Adoption scam was born in jail," *Chicago Tribune*, June 20, 2-2.
Farberman, Harvey A.
　1994　"Symbolic Interaction and Postmodernism: close encounters of a dubious kind," *Symbolic Interaction*, vol. 14 no. 4, 471488.
Feeney, Sheila Anne
　1991　"Gifts of life," *Chicago Tribune*, June 19, 7-17.
Fieweger, Mary Ellen
　1991　"Stolen Children and International Adoptions," *Child Welfare*, vol. 70 no. 2, March-April, 285-291.

Fischer, Mary Ellen
 1989 "Romania," *United States-East European Relations in the 1990s*, Richard F. Staar ed. New York: Crane Russak.
Fishman, Katherine Davis
 1992 "Problem Adoptions," *The Atlantic Monthly*, vol. 270 no. 3, Sept, 37.
Fitzpatrick, Sheila
 1999 *Everyday Stalinism: Ordinary Life in Extraordinary Times, Soviet Russia in the 1930s*. New York: Oxford University Press.
Fleming, Anne Taylor
 1994 "Sperm in a Jar," *New York Times Magazine*, June 12, 52-55.
Fodors
 1989 *Fodor's Eastern Europe*. New York: Fodor's Travel Publications.
Franklin, Robert M.
 1990 "In Pursuit of a Just Society: Martin Luther King, Jr. and John Rawls," *The Journal of Religious Ethics*, vol. 18, fall, 5777.
Freeman, James M.
 1979 *Untouchable: an Indian Life History*. Stanford, CA: Stanford University Press.
Freidrich, Otto
 1990 "When Tyrants Fall," *Time*, Jan 8, 26.
Friedman, Thomas L.
 1989a "Baker gives U.S. approval if Soviets act on Romania," *New York Times*, Dec 25, 13.
 1989b "Bush promises to help if Romanians change," *New York Times*, Dec 23, 10.
 1989c "Rumania's suppression of protest condemned by the U.S. as 'brutal'," *New York Times*, Dec 20, 1.
Freddi, Giorgio and James Warner Björkman, eds.
 1989 *Controlling Medical Professionals: the Comparative Politics of Health Governance*. Newbury Park, CA: Sage.
Freidson, Eliot
 1970a *Profession of Medicine: a Study of the Sociology of Applied Knowledge*. New York: Dodd, Mead.
 1970b *Profession of Dominance: the Social Structure of Medical Care*. New York: Atherton.
Freidson, Eliot, ed.
 1973 *The Professions and Their Prospects*. Beverly Hills, CA: Sage Press.
 1993 "Gag rule in Romania," *New York Times*, March 9, 12.
Garthoff, Raymond L.
 1994a *The Great Transition: American-Soviet Relations and the End of the Cold War*. Washington, DC: The Brookings Institution.
 1994b "Looking Back: The Cold War in Retrospect," *The Brookings Review*, vol. 12, 10-13.
Geertz, Clifford
 1973 *The Interpretation of Cultures: Selected Essays*. New York: Basic Books.

"Germany deports 100 Romanians"
  1992 *Chicago Tribune*, Nov 14, 8.
Gellner, Ernest
  1991 "Conclusions," *Perestroika: the Historical Perspective*, Catherine Merridale and Chris Ward eds. London: Edward Arnold.
Gibbs, Nancy
  1989 "The Baby Chase," *Time*, Oct 9, 86.
Giddens, Anthony
  1991 *Modernity and Self-Identity: Self and Society in the Late Modern Age*. Cambridge: Polity Press.
Glaser, Barney G. and Anselm L. Strauss
  1967 *The Discovery of Grounded Theory: Strategies for Qualitative Research*. Chicago, IL: Aldine Publishing.
Glaser, Gabrielle
  1992 "Booming Polish market: blonde, blue-eyed babies," *New York Times*, April 19, 6.
Glenny, Misha
  1990 *The Rebirth of History: Eastern Europe in the Age of Democracy*. London: Penguin Books.
Godwin, Philip
  1990 "Adoption," *Better Homes and Gardens*, May, 33.
Goetz, Philip W.
  1990 "Romania," *The New Encyclopedia Britannica-Micropodia*, vol. 10. Chicago, IL: Encyclopedia Britannica.
Goldberg, Yemima
  1993 "Romania's Chief Rabbi Moshe Rosen Overcoming—And Surviving Communism," *Sentinel*, April 29, 24-25.
Good, Mary Jo Delvecchio and Byron J. Good
  2000 "Parallel Sisters: Medical Anthropology and Medical Sociology," *Handbook of Medical Sociology*, Fifth Edition, Chloe E. Bird, Peter Conrad, and Allen Fremont eds. Upper Saddle River, NJ: Prentice Hall.
Goodman, Ellen
  1993 "Racial matching bill for children sadly toned down," *Chicago Tribune*, Dec 20, 27.
Gordon, Meryl
  1991a "Handmaids' Tale," *Mirabella*, Jan, 92.
  1991b "Inconceivable?," *Mirabella*, July, 60-63.
Gorman, John and Robert Enstad
  1992 "Childless, they had to believe," *Chicago Tribune*, Oct 4, 2-1.
Gottesman, Andrew
  1992 "Polish adoptions seen as righting Romanian wrongs," *Chicago Tribune*, Nov 15, 2-1.
Gottschalk, Simon
  1998 "Postmodern Sensibilities and Ethnographic Possibilities," *Fiction and Social Research*, Anna Banks and Stephen P. Banks, eds. Walnut Creek, CA: Altamira Press.

Greenblatt, Samuel H. MD, et.al., ed.
  1997 *A History of Neurosurgery in its Scientific and Professional Contexts*. Park Ridge, IL: American Association of Neurological Surgeons.
Greenhouse, Steven
  1989 "Paris is pressing aid for Rumanians," *New York Times*, Dec 8, 13.
  1990a "In Romania, Ceausescu is gone but his crippling economic legacy endures," *New York Times*, Aug 6, 4.
  1990b "Reformers in Romania fight Ceausescu legacy," *New York Times*, Aug 6, 4.
  1990c "Romania isn't trusted, within or without," *New York Times*, July 7, E3.
  1990d "Romania struggles to improve its image after violence by miners against protesters," *New York Times*, July 16, 7.
  1993 "Dying hope," *Chicago Tribune*, May 2, 6-8.
Grotenant, Harold D.
  1997 "Coming to Terms with Adoption: the Construction of Identity from Adolescence into Adulthood," *Adoption Quarterly*, vol. 1 no. 1, 3-27.
Gubernick, Lisa
  1991 "How Much is that Baby in the Window?," *Forbes*, Oct 14, 90-98.
"Gulag Gives Up Lost Patients"
  1991 *The European*, Nov 15-Nov 21, 1.
Gullestad, Marianne
  1994 "Construction of Self and Society in Autobiographical Accounts: a Scandinavian Life Story," *Exploring the Written: the Anthropology of Written Identities*, Eduardo P. Archetti, ed. Oslo: Scandinavian University Press.
  1996 *Everyday Life Philosophers: Modernity, Morality, and Autobiography in Norway*. Oslo: Scandinavian University Press.
"Gypsies and Germans, wronged"
  1992 *New York Times*, Sept 27, E16.
Haberman, Clyde
  1989a "A community rushes to renounce its native son," *New York Times*, Dec 30, 8.
  1989b "Disclosure of the Ceausescus' riches appall many threadbare Rumanians," *New York Times*, Dec 27, 10.
  1990a "Romania averted massacre by executions, official says," *New York Times*, Jan 5, 14.
  1990b "New ruling group in Rumania to vie in April elections," *New York Times*, Jan 2, 1.
Hafferty, Frederic W. and John B. McKinlay, eds.
  1993 *The Changing Medical Profession: an International Perspective*. New York: Oxford University Press.
Hamilton, John M.
  1991 "Will Pollution Kill the Revolution?," *The Bulletin of the Atomic Scientists*, vol. 47 no. 4, June, 12-18.
Hanley, Robert
  1989 "A Jersey panel backs limits on surrogacy pacts," *New York Times*, March 13, 13.

Harden, Blaine
  1990a "Hungary protests Romanian mob action," *The Washington Post*, March 28, 17.
  1990b "Romanian clashes affect Hungarian elections," *The Washington Post*, March 23, 18.
Harder, Laura
  1990 "From Bucharest With Love," *People*, Sept 24, 34.
Harris, Marlys
  1988 "Where Have All the Babies Gone?," *Money*, Dec, 164.
Harsanyi, Doina P. and Nicolae Harsanyi
  1993 "Romania: Democracy and the Intellectuals," *Eastern European Quarterly*, vol. 27 no. 2, June, 243-260.
Harvey, Janet
  1996 "Achieving the Indeterminate: Accomplishing Degrees of Certainty in Life and Death Situations," *The Sociological Review*, vol. 44, 78-98.
  1997 "The Technological Regulation of Death with Reference to the Technological Regulation of Birth," *Sociology*, vol. 31 no. 4, 719-738.
Haynes, Karima A.
  1994 "Single Black Women Who Adopt," *Ebony*, May.
Heeg, Judy M. and Deborah A. Coleman
  1992 "Hepatitis Kills," *RN*, April, 60.
Henderson, C.W.
  2000 "Improved Fertility Treatments Increase Delivery Success Rates," *Women's Health Weekly*, Jan 22, 11.
Henney, Susan M., et.al.
  1998 "Changing Agency Practices Towards Openness in Adoption," *Adoption Quarterly*, vol. 1 no. 3, Jan 22, 11.
Hevesi, Dennis
  1990 "Romanian rebel predicts slow progress," *New York Times*, March 11, 8.
Hoibraaten, Helge
  1993 "Secular Society: an Attempt at Initiation," *Islamic Law Reform and Human Rights*, Tore Lindholm and Kari Vogt, eds. Copenhagen: Nordic Human Rights Publications.
Hoffman, Charles
  1992 *Gray Dawn: the Jews of Eastern Europe in the Post-Communist Era*. New York: Harper-Collins.
Holmes, Leslie
  1997 *Post-Communism: an Introduction*. Durham, NC: Duke University Press.
Holmes, Steven A.
  1995a "Bitter racial dispute rages over adoption," *New York Times*, April 13, 8.
  1995b "Texas approves couple's adoption of two black boys, official says," *New York Times*, April 15, 9.
Holstein, James A. and Jaber F. Gubrium
  2004 "Context: Working It Up, Down, and Across," *Qualitative Research Practice,* Clive Seale, et.al., eds. Thousand Oaks, CA: Sage Press.

Hope, Toni Gerber
1998 "The Ultimate Fertility Guide," *Redbook*, vol. 192 no. 1, Nov, 146-153.
Hopkins, Ellen
1992 "Tales from the Baby Factory," *New York Times Magazine*, March 15, 40.
Horowitz, Carl
1995 "White Parents, Black Children," *Investors Business Daily*, May 12, 1.
Hostetter, Margaret K., et.al.
1991 "Medical Evolution of Internationally Adopted Children," *The New England Journal of Medicine*, vol. 325 no. 7, 479485.
Howell, Signe
1994 "Reading Cultures or How Anthropological Texts Create Fieldwork Expectations and Shape Future Texts," *Exploring the Written: the Anthropology of Written Identities*, Eduardo P. Archetti, ed. Oslo: Scandinavian University Press.
Huckshorn, Kristin
1992 "Worldwide disorder sets stage for another baby market boom," *Chicago Tribune*, Jan 12, 13.
Humphrey, Peter
1993 "A culture ends in Romania," *Chicago Tribune*, May 6, p. 7.
Hundley, Tom
1995a "Fertility clinic sparks debate in Poland," *Chicago Tribune*, April 19, 6.
1995b "Romanian exodus: Jewish community dwindles away," *Chicago Tribune*, May 13, 1.
Hunt, Kathleen
1991 "The Romanian baby bazaar," *New York Times Magazine*, March 24, 24-53.
1998 *Abandoned to the State: Cruelty and Neglect in Russian Orphanage*. New York: Human Rights Watch.
Hupchick, Dennis P.
1994 *Culture and History in Eastern Europe*. New York: St. Martin's Press.
Husarska, Anna
1990 "Street Theater," *The New Republic*, Feb 5, 18.
Ingram, Judith
1991 "Romanians ostracize Gypsies," *Chicago Tribune*, June 18, 9.
1992a "At last a helping hand for Romanian Gypsies," *New York Times*, Oct 18, 5.
1992b "Little children come, for there is nowhere else," *New York Times*, Aug 4, 5.
1993a "Hungary's tiny immigrants: the new foundlings," *New York Times*, May 18, 4.
1993b "28 Romanian foundlings freed for adoption in U.S.," *New York Times*, July 6, 6.
Iherjirika, Maudlyne
1994 "The adoption connection," *Chicago Sun-Times*, Dec 14, 7.

"Intercountry Adoptions Up In FY 1994"
  1995 *Adoption Families*, Jan-Feb, 6.
"International Adoptions, 1982-1992"
  1993 *Ours*, vol. 25 no. 3, May-June, 11.
Isaacs, Mike
  1989 "Bringing Families Together," *Skokie Review*, March 16, 5.
"Israeli Couple, Six Brazilians Arrested for Alleged Baby Smuggling"
  1993 *Agency France-Presse (AFP-English Wire)*, Aug 11.
"Israelis hear about bribery in Latin American adoptions"
  1988 *New York Times*, July 17, 2.
ITIM News Agency
  1993 "Israel denies Rio arrests connected to baby smuggling," *The Jerusalem Post*, Aug 13, 16.
Jaffe, Eliezer D.
  1991 "Foreign Adoption in Israel: Private Paths to Parenthood," *Intercountry Adoption: a Multinational Perspective*, Howard Altstein and Rita J. Simon, eds. New York: Praeger
James, Frank
  1991 "Out of Romania's bleakness comes beacon of life," *Chicago Tribune*, May 20, 1.
Jenks, Elaine B.
  2002 "Searching for Autoethnographic Credibility: Reflections from a Mom with a Notepad," *Ethnographically Speaking: Autoethnography, Literature, and Aesthetics*, Arthur P. Bochner and Carolyn Ellis, eds. Walnut Creek, CA: Altamira Press.
Johnson, Harold J.
  1993 "Intercountry Adoption." Washington, DC: General Accounting Office.
Johnson, Steve
  1991 "Many in Chicago have their hearts in the Baltics," *Chicago Tribune*, Sept 1, 1.
Johnson, Terry, Gerry Larkin, and Mike Saks. eds.
  1995 *Health Professions and the State in Europe*. New York: Routledge.
Jones, Charisse
  1993 "Role of race in adoptions: old debate is being reborn," *New York Times*, Oct 24, 1.
Jordan, Mary
  1990 "Fairfax woman rescues orphan from Romania," *The Washington Post*, July 17, D1.
Jouzaitis, Carol and John Koss
  1991 "Lithuanian leader makes vow to Jews," *Chicago Tribune*, May 15, 2-2.
Kamm, Henry
  1991a "Romania's Jews shaken by rising verbal attacks," *New York Times*, June 19, 6.
  1991b "Romanian's see more woes ahead in move to a market economy," *New York Times*, April 7, 6.

1992a "Romanian leaders still face mistrust over their Communist past," *New York Times*, Dec 17, 11.
1992b "Romania's monuments make strange bedfellows," *New York Times*, Dec 15, 4.
1992c "Yiddish soil that once bred poets," *New York Times*, Feb 25, 6.
1993 "To the Gypsies, death is a neighbor and so is this implacable hatred," *New York Times*, Oct 27, 4.

Kaplan, Robert D.
1990 "Romania's Changeless Land," *New York Times Magazine*, Oct 21, 30-41.

Kaufman, Walter Arnold, ed.
1956 *Existentialism from Dostoevsky to Sartre*. New York: Meridian Books.

Kaufman, Sharon R.
1986 *The Ageless Self: Sources of Meaning in Late Life*. Madison: University of Wisconsin Press.
2000 "In the Shadow of 'Death with Dignity': Medicine and Cultural Quandaries of the Vegetative State," *American Anthropologist*, vol. 102 no. 1, 69-83.

Kennan, George F.
1971 *The Marquis de Custine and his Russia in 1839*. Princeton, NJ: Princeton University Press.

Kenny, Timothy
1990 "Mission of mercy begins to save Romanian children," *USA Today*, July 12, 7.

Kideckel, David A.
1989 "Romania's Revolution Isn't Over," *Hartford Courant*, Dec 31, D1.
1993 *The Solitude of Collectivism: Romanian Villagers to the Revolution and Beyond*. Ithaca, NY: Cornell University Press.

Kifner, John
1989a "Bucharest tension," *New York Times*, Dec 25, 1.
1989b "For the victims in Rumania, flowers and places of honor," *New York Times*, Dec 27, 1.
1989c "Romanian revolt, live and uncensored," *New York Times*, Dec 28, 1.
1989d "Rumanians finding a bounty of food they long missed," *New York Times*, Dec 29, 1.
1990 "With 3 dead, soldiers break up Romanian and Hungarian mobs," *New York Times*, March 22, 17.

King, Robert R.
1980 *A History of the Romanian Communist Party*. Stanford, CA: Hoover Institution Press.

Kinzer, Stephen
1992 "Germany cracks down; Gypsies come first," *New York Times*, Sept 27, E5.

Klein, George C.
2000 "Terrible Events: a Sociological Analysis of War Crimes in the Former Yugoslavia," *Sociological Imagination*, vol. 37, 731-752.

Kligman, Gail
   1998 "The Technological Imperative in Ethical Practice: the Social Creation of a 'Routine' Treatment," *Biomedicine Examined*, Margaret Lock and Deborah Gordon, eds. Boston, MA: Kluver.

Kozma, Anna-Liza
   1995 "Going batty," *Chicago Tribune*, Aug 6, 6-1.

Krause, Elliot A.
   1996 *Death of the Guilds: Professions, States, and the Advance of Capitalism - 1930 to the Present*. New Haven, CT: Yale University Press.

Laslett, Barbara
   1999 "Personal Narratives as Sociology," *Contemporary Sociology*, vol. 28 no. 4, 391-401.

Lawson, Carol
   1991 "A doctor acts to heal Romania's wound of baby trafficking," *New York Times*, Oct 3, B1.

Lewin, Tamar
   1990 "South Korea slows export of babies for adoption," *New York Times*, Feb 12, 15.
   1992 "Undelivered adoptions investigated in three states," *New York Times*, March 22, 10.
   1994 "Study of adopted finds nothing unusual," *New York Times*, June 23, 8.

Lewis, Neil A.
   1989 "Rumania aides in U.S. switch, but emigrees aren't satisfied," *New York Times*, Dec 24, 1.

Lewis, Paul
   1989 "U.N. Rights Report indicts Ceausescu," *New York Times*, Aug 30, 6.

Lewthwaite, Gilbert A.
   1990a "Romanian medical care creates kids AIDS crisis," *Chicago Sun-Times*, Feb 2, 6.
   1990b "Romanian trial heavy on drama," *Chicago Sun-Times*, Feb 2, 36.

Liang, Hsi-huey
   1992 *The Rise of Modern Police and European State System from Metternich to the Second World War*. Cambridge: Cambridge University Press.

Little, Heather M.
   1993 "Taking up the fight," *Chicago Tribune*, June 27, pp. 6-3.
   1994 "Open hearts," *Chicago Tribune*, July 10, pp. 6-1.

Lock, M. and C. Honde
   1990 "Reaching Consensus about Death: Heart Transplants and Cultural Identity in Japan," *Social Science Perspectives on Medical Ethics*, George Weisz, ed. Philadelphia, PA: University of Pennsylvania Press.

Longman, Jere
   1991 "Romania's new ambassadors," *New York Times*, May 8, 23.

Longworth, R.C.
   1990 "Miners leave after sowing fear in Bucharest," *Chicago Tribune*, June 16, 3.

1991 "Romanians still staggered by burden of brutal past," *Chicago Tribune,* Oct 24, 1.
Lopez, Laura
1994 "Dangerous Rumors," *Time,* April 18, 48.
Louie, Elaine
1995 "Abandoned Chinese girls find families in America," *New York Times,* April 27, B1.
Love, Gail Backman
1991 "For the love of children," *The Washington Post,* Jan 29, B5.
Luft, Kerry
1995 "For Bogotá's street children, death is just around the corner," *Chicago Tribune,* Jan 15, 12.
Lynch, Mike
1990 "Pediatrician Delivers Hope to Romanian Orphans," *AAP News,* vol. 6 no. 11, Nov, p. 1.
Madison, Cathy
1992 "Adoption action," *Chicago Tribune,* April 19, 6-1.
Maines, David R.
2001 *The Faultline of Consciousness: a View of Interactionism in Sociology.* New York: A. de Gruter.
Mandelbaum, David G.
1973 "The Study of Life History: Gandhi," *Current Anthropology,* vol. 14 no. 3, 177-206.
Mandelbaum, Michael
1990 "The Trouble with Independence," *Time,* Jan 29, p. 33.
Manea, Norman; Linda Coverdale, trans. from French.
1993 *Compulsory Happiness.* New York: Farrar, Straus & Giroux.
Mansnerus, Laura
1989 "Private adoptions aided by expanding network," *New York Times,* Oct 5, 1.
Marcus, George E.
1986 "Contemporary Problems of Ethnography in the Modern World System," *Writing Culture,* James Clifford and George E. Marcus, eds. Berkeley, CA: University of California Press.
Marsh, Virginia and Robert Corzine
1993 "Feet Drag on Road to Market," *Financial Times,* July 27, 3-1.
Marks, Jane
1993 "How We Adopted Me," *New York Times Magazine,* May 23, 32-34.
Marx, Gary T. and Cyrille Fijnaut, eds.
1988 *Undercover: Police Surveillance in Comparative Perspective.* Berkeley, CA: University of California Press.
McArdle, Thomas
1994 "Exploring the adoption option," *Investor's Business Daily,* Aug 4, 1.

McClarnand, Elaine
   1998   "The Politics of History and Historical Revisionism: De-Stalinization and the Search for Identity in Gorbachev's Russia 1985-1991," *The History Teacher*, vol. 3, Feb, 153-179.

McCurdy, David B.
   1998   "Creating an Ethical Organization," *Generations*, vol. 23 no. 2, Fall, 26-31.

McFadden, Robert D.
   1989   "Transylvania casts off Rumania's tall shadow," *New York Times*, Dec 19.

McFaul, Michael
   1999   "Lessons from Russia's Protracted Transition from Communist Rule," *Political Science Quarterly*, vol. 114 no. 1, 103130.

McHugh, James T.
   1995   "Last of the Enlightened Despots: a Comparison of President Mikhail Gorbachev and Emperor Joseph II," *Social Science Journal*, vol. 32 no. 1, 69-85.

McKay, Nina
   1989   "Desperately Seeking Baby!," *New Women*, April, 80-84.

McNamara, Joan
   1975   *The Adoption Adviser*. New York: Hawthorn Books.

McNamee, Tom
   1989a   "Fast-track adoption," *Chicago Sun-Times*, Sept 10, 1.
   1989b   "Infant imports soar in state," *Chicago Sun-Times*, Sept 12, 5.
   1989c   "Open adoptions gain support," *Chicago Sun-Times*, Sept 11, 5.

McPherson, William
   1990   "William McPherson in Romania," *Granta*, vol. 33, summer, 10-58.

McRoberts, Flynn
   1989   "Lithuanians open push for freedom," *Chicago Tribune*, Nov 24, 2-1.

Melosh, Barbara
   2002   *Strangers and Kin: the American Way of Adoption*. Cambridge: Harvard University Press.

Mercer, Pamela
   1993   "In the street urchins dark haunt, no ray of hope," *New York Times*, Aug 6, 4.

Micheletti, Eric; Alex McCall trans.
   1990   "Puppet Revolution," *Soldier of Fortune*. July, 49-55.

Michelman, Stanley B. and Meg Schneider
   1988   *The Private Adoption Handbook*. New York: Villard Books.

Mihaesco, Eugene
   1990   "Essay," *Time*, Jan 8, 78.

Miller, Bryan
   2000   "Babies Wanted," *Reader*, May 12, 11.

Miller, Robert L. MA
   2000   *Researching Life Stories and Family Histories*. Thousand Oaks, CA: Sage Press.

Mills, Steve
   1995   "Couples rush in to adopt abandoned Chinese baby girls," *Chicago Tribune*, May 18, 2-1.

Mitchell, Rosas
   1999   "Home from Home: A Model of Daycare for People with Dementia," *Generations*, vol. 23 no. 3, fall, 78-81.

Modell, Judith and Naomi Dambacher
   1997   "Making a 'Real' Family: Matching and Cultural Biologism in American Adoption," *Adoption Quarterly*, vol. 1 no. 2, 333.

"Mud and Democracy"
   1990   *The Economist*, April 28, 54.

Munroe, Robin and Jeff Rigby
   1996   "Death by Default: Policy of Fatal Neglect in China's State Orphanages," *Human Rights Watch*, January.

Nachtway, James and Kathleen Hunt
   1990   "Romania's Lost Children," *New York Times Magazine*, June 24, 28-33.

National Committee for Adoption
   1989   *Adoption Factbook*. Washington, DC: National Committee for Adoption.

Neeley, Anthony
   1991   "Adopting from Romania," *Ours*, vol. 24 no. 1, Jan-Feb, 13.

Nelan, Bruce W.
   1990a   "Slaughter in the Streets," *Time*, Jan 1, 34-37.
   1990b   "Unfinished Revolution," *Time*, Jan 8, 28-33.

Nelkin, Dorothy
   1973   *Methadone Maintenance: a Technological Fix*. New York: Braziller.

Neubauer, Rita and Willi Germund
   1988   "Babies For Sale," *World Press Review*, vol. 35, Aug, 57.

Neuman, Johanna
   1990   "Culture clash turns adopting into 'ordeal'," *USA Today*, July 12, 1.

"New Romanian law will curb lucrative black market in babies"
   1991   *Chicago Tribune*, July 17, 8.

"New rules try to ease interracial adoption"
   1995   *New York Times*, April 27, 12.

Nydon, Judith
   1984   "Public Policy and Private Fertility Behavior: the Case of Pronatalist Policy in Socialist Romania," PhD dissertation. University of Massachusetts.

Okely, Judith
   1992   "Anthropology and Autobiography: Participatory Experience and Embodies Knowledge," *Anthropology and Autobiography*, Judith Okely and Helen Callaway, eds. London: Routledge.

Ogintz, Eileen
   1998   "Babies wanted," *Chicago Tribune*, Dec 21, 5-1.

Oloroso, Arsenio Jr.
   1994   "A Baby Boom for Adoption Big," *Crain's Chicago Business*, vol. 17 no. 8, Feb 21-Feb 27, 17-19.

"Once blackballed, Romania is allowed to join aid club"
 1991 *New York Times*, Jan 31, 10.
Pace, Eric
 1989 "Two Romanians defend the leader's execution and secret trial," *New York Times*, Dec 29.
Pacepa, Ion Mihai
 1987 *Red Horizons: Chronicles of a Communist Spy Chief*. Washington, DC: Regnery Gateway.
Page, Clarence
 1993 "Black adoption myths and mistakes," *Chicago Tribune*, Nov 28, 4-3.
Pahz, James A.
 1987 "Building Families Through Intercountry Adoption," *International Quarterly of Community Health Education*, vol. 8 no. 1, 91-97.
Perlez, Jane
 1993 "Bleak Romanian economy growing ever bleaker," *New York Times*, Nov 24, 3.
 1994a "No love and little care: Romania's sad orphans," *New York Times*, Oct 27, 4.
 1994b "Uprising or coup? Romanian ask five years later," *New York Times*, Dec 25, 3.
 1995a "A grown-up mess, and children pay," *New York Times*, May 12, 6.
 1995b "Cradle of revolution still apart in Romania," *New York Times*, June 18, 7.
Peters, Ann
 1988a "Adoption," *UPI*, June 29.
 1988b "Adoption," *UPI*, July 11.
Petrakos, Chris
 1994 "A perfect match," *Chicago Tribune*, July 14, 6-1.
Peucelle, Nicholas
 1990 "Rummaging through the Ruins of the Securitate," *Soldier of Fortune*, July, 54-55.
Pilon, Juliana Geran
 1992 *The Bloody Flag: Post-Communist Nationalism in Eastern Europe: Spotlight on Romania*. New Brunswick, NJ: Transaction Publishers.
Porter, Bruce.
 1993 "I Met My Daughter at the Wuhan Foundling Hospital," *New York Times Magazine*, April 11, 224-226.
Price, Monroe E.
 1993 "Letter from Cluj: Meeting Agnes," *Forward*, July 9, 1.
"Promise cools Romanian rally"
 1990 *Chicago Sun-Times*, March 23, 5.
Protzman, Ferdinand
 1992 "Germany reaches a deal to send thousands of Romanians home," *New York Times*, Sept 19, 1.
Quinn, Hal
 1990 "A Cruel Legacy," *Macleans*, vol. 103, Aug 20, 48.

"Rabbi Moses Rosen, 81, leader of Romanian Jews"
  1994 *New York Times*, May 7, 11.
Rabinow, Paul
  1997 *Reflections on Fieldwork in Morocco*. Berkeley, CA: University of California Press.
Rasmussen, Douglas B.
  1990 "Liberalism and Natural End Ethics," *American Philosophical Quarterly*, vol. 27 no. 2, April, 153161.
Ratesh, Nestor
  1993 "Romania: Slamming on the Brakes," *Current History*, vol. 92 no. 577, Nov, 390-395.
Rawls, John
  1971 *A Theory of Justice*. Cambridge, MA: Harvard University Press.
Reaves, Joseph A.
  1990a "Coroner: Romanian massacre never happened," *Chicago Tribune*, March 13, 1.
  1990b "Iliescu elected Romanian leader," *Chicago Tribune*, May 23, 1.
  1990c "Legalization of abortion brings throngs to Romanian hospitals," *Chicago Tribune*, March 8, 13.
  1990d "Romania says army didn't plot overthrow," *Chicago Tribune*, Jan 4, 12.
  1990e "Romanians rally for bigger voice in running nation," *Chicago Tribune*, Jan 8, 1.
"Recount is called in Romanian vote"
  1992 *New York Times*, Oct 1, 3.
Reitz, Miriam and Kenneth W. Watson
  1992 *Adoption and the Family System: Strategies for Treatment*. New York: Guilford Press.
"Revolution was stolen; Romanian priest says"
  1991 *Chicago Tribune*, Dec 16, 8.
Revzin, Philip
  1990 "Ceausescu's palace, a monument to ego, has new landlords," *Wall Street Journal*, April 4, 1.
Richards, Cindy
  1992 "In Romania, take nothing for granted," *Chicago Sun-Times*, May 3, D5.
Richardson, Laurel
  2000 "Writing: a Method of Inquiry," *Handbook of Qualitative Research*, Norman K. Denzin and Yvonna S. Lincoln, eds. Thousand Oaks, CA: Sage Press.
Richardson, Lynda
  1993 "Adoptions that lack papers, not purpose," *New York Times*, Nov 25, B1.
Richman, Ruth
  1993a "Homeless: conference to examine special needs adoptions," *Chicago Tribune*, July 25, 6-1.
  1993b "Unfair, harmful?," *Chicago Tribune*, April 4, 6-1.
Riniker, Theresa
  1991 "Hendricks adopt Romanian child," *The Galena Gazette*, April 7, 2.

Rios-Kohn, Rebeca
   1998   "Intercountry Adoption: an International Perspective on the Practices and Standards," *Adoption Quarterly*, vol. 1 no. 4, 332.
"Riots in Romania after miners protest"
   1991 *New York Times,* Sept 26, 3.
Risen, James
   2001   "Documents shed new light on CIA's view of the Soviets," *New York Times*, March 10, 5.
Rocks, David
   1990   "Room for improvement," *Chicago Tribune*, March 24, 5-1.
Rollnick, Roman
   1990   "Moment of Romania's Rebels," *The European,* Dec 7, 3.
"Romania: Amnesty Delegation Discusses Concerns with Government"
   1990 *Amnesty Action*, Nov-Dec, 4.
"Romania and Moldova chiefs see economic ties, but no early union"
   1992 *New York Times*, Jan 26, 6.
"Romania looks to vote to erase Communist ties"
   1992 *New York Times,* Sept 27, 11.
"Romania OK's laws outlining new government, free elections"
   1990   *Chicago Tribune,* March 15, 8.
"Romania premier steps down"
   1991   *Chicago Tribune,* Sept 27, 3.
"Romania tightens regulations on adoptions"
   1991   *Chicago Tribune,* Feb 6, 5.
"Romania vows order after riots"
   1991   *Chicago Tribune,* Sept 26, 3.
"Romanian Gypsies are skeptical about Germany's financial help"
   1991 *New York Times,* Sept 26, 3.
"Romanian land reform falters"
   1994 *Wall Street Journal,* Feb 18, 8.
"Romanian: Miners Attack Protesters"
   1990   *Amnesty Action,* Sept-Oct, 4.
"Romanian miners club citizens indiscriminately"
   1990   *Chicago Tribune,* June 15, 1.
"Romanian opposition parties win local elections"
   1991 *New York Times,* Feb 25, 6.
"Romanian 'orphans' find homes"
   1991   *Chicago Tribune,* Feb 17, 24.
"Romanian sentenced and commits suicide"
   1992 *New York Times,* April 22, 7.
"Romanian's can't afford to farm their lands"
   1992 *New York Times,* Feb 12, 4.
"Romanian's condemn uprisings observance"
   1992 *New York Times,* Dec 23, 4.
"Romanian's OK multiparty system"
   1991   *Chicago Tribune,* Dec 14, 16.

"Romanian's re-elect ex-Communist leader"
  1992 *New York Times,* Oct 13, 6.
"Romanian's salute Ceausescu at his grave"
  1991 *New York Times,* Dec 12, 12.
"Romanian's talk turns to economy"
  1991 *New York Times,* Dec 5, 4.
"Romanian's vote but runoff is expected"
  1992 *New York Times,* Sept 28, 6.
"Romanian's opposition finds revolution's hero a liability"
  1992 *New York Times,* Sept 13, 8.
"Romania's ruling front makes concessions to critics"
  1990 *Chicago Tribune,* Jan 31, 4.
Roos, J.P.
  1985 "Life Stories of Social Changes: Four Generations in Finland," *International Journal of Oral History,* vol. 6 no. 3, 179190.
Rothman, David J. and Sheila M. Rothman
  1990 "How AIDS came to Romania," *New York Review of Books,* vol. 37 no. 18, Nov 8, 5.
Rummler, Gary C.
  1991 "Reaching out," *The Milwaukee Journal,* Jan 13, G1.
Ruston, Ursula
  1991 "Romania: Lost Planet in the Guttenberg Galaxy," *Index on Censorship,* 5-6.
Sacharow, Fredda
  1990 "Romania, Romania," *JUF News,* June, 8.
Sammons, Mary Beth
  1992 "Adoption adapts: multi-ethnic families increase," *Chicago Tribune,* Aug 23, 1-3.
Sandstrom, Kent L., Daniel D. Martin, and Gary Alan Fine
  2003 *Symbols, Selves, and Social Reality: a Symbolic Interactionist Approach to Social Psychology and Sociology.* Los Angeles, CA: Roxbury.
Sartre, Jean-Paul
  1989 "An Existential Ethic," *Philosophy: History and Problems* 4th Edition, Samuel E. Stumpf ed. New York: McGraw-Hill.
Schmemann, Serge
  1990 "In cradle of revolt, anger quickly overcame fear," *New York Times,* Dec 30, 1.
Schmetzer, Uli
  1995a "Grisly orphanages haunting China on eve of U.N. meeting," *Chicago Tribune,* Aug 23, 1.
  1995b "Sweet home Chicago for Chinese tots," *Chicago Tribune,* June 1, 1.
Schoofs, Mark
  1990 "Romania miners rampage," *Chicago Sun-Times,* June 15, 5.

Schwandt, Thomas A.
  2000   "Three Epistemological Stances for Qualitative Inquiry," *Handbook of Qualitative Research* 2nd Edition, Norman K. Denzin and Yvonna S. Lincoln, eds. Thousand Oaks, CA: Sage Press.
Sennett, Richard
  1978   *The Fall of Public Man.* New York: Vintage Books.
Serrill, Michael S.
  1991   "Going Abroad to Find a Baby," *Time*, Oct 21, 86.
Sexton, James D., ed.
  1981   *Son of Tecún Umán: a Maya Indian Tells His Life Story.* Tuscon, AZ: University of Arizona Press.
Shafir, Michael
  1993   "Romania: the Rechristening of the National Salvation Front," *Radio Free Europe/Radio Liberty Research Report*, vol. 2 no. 27, July, 22-26.
Sheehy, Gail
  1990   *The Man Who Changed the World: the Lives of Mikhail S. Gorbachev.* New York: HarperCollins.
Shelley, Louise I.
  1990   "The Soviet Militia: Agents of Political and Social Control," *Policing and Society*, vol. 1, 39-56.
Shelton, Allen
  1994   "My Bloody Valentine," *Studies in Symbolic Interaction*, vol. 16, 191-211.
  1995   "Foucault's Madonna: The Secret Life of Carolyn Ellis," *Symbolic Interaction*, vol. 16, 191-211.
Sheppard, Nathaniel Jr.
  1991   "The victimizers—and victims," *Chicago Tribune*, Aug 22, 29.
"Shooting continues in the western city where the uprising against Ceausescu began"
  1989   *New York Times*, Dec 26, 17.
Simon, Rita J. and Howard Altstein
  1992   *Adoption, Race, and Identity: From Infancy through Adolescence.* New York: Praeger.
Simon, Rita J., Howard Altstein and Marygold S. Melli
  1992   *The Case for Transracial Adoption.* Washington, DC: American University Press.
Simons, Marlise and Antonin Kratochvil
  1990   "The Polluted Lands," *New York Times Magazine*, April 29, 30.
Singer, Natasha
  1993   "In Orphanage #5, Darkness Falls on Children," *Forward*, Aug 27, 12.
Smolowe, Jill
  1995   "Adoption in Black and White," *Time*, Aug 14, 50-51.
Snead, Bill
  1991   "The abandoned children of Romania's orphanages," *The Washington Post*, Sept 17.

Sofsky, Wolfgang; William Templer trans.
1993 *The Order of Terror: the Concentration Camp*. Princeton, NJ: Princeton University Press.
Sonnenberg, Joachim
1992 "Romanian economy sinking," *Chicago Tribune*, Jan 19, 7-8.
Sparkes, Andrew C.
2002 "Autoethnography: Self-Indulgence or Something More?," *Ethnographically Speaking*, Arthur P. Bochner and Carolyn Ellis, eds. Walnut Creek, CA: Altamira Press.
Star, Susan L.
1991 "The Sociology of the Invisible: the Primacy of Work in the Writings of Anselm Strauss," *Social Organization and Social Process*, David A. Maines, ed. New York: A. deGruyter.
Stark, David C. and László Bruszt
1998 *Postsocialist Pathways: Transforming Politics and Property in East Central Europe*. Cambridge: Cambridge University Press.
Stavrianos, Leften Stavros
1958 *The Balkans Since 1453*. New York: Holt, Rinehart and Winston.
Stein, Sharman
1990 "Parents often helpless if adoption goes bad," *Chicago Tribune*, April 15, 1.
1994 "10 years, 220 miracles," *Chicago Tribune*, March 15, 1.
Stephenson, Patricia, Marsden Wagner, Mihaela Badea and Florina Serbanescu
1992 "Commentary: the Public Health Consequences of Restricted Induced Abortion—Lessons From Romania," *American Journal of Public Health*, vol. 81 no. 19, Oct, 1328-1331.
Stout, Janis P.
1983 *The Journey Narrative in American Literature: Patterns and Departures*. Westport, CT: Greenwood Press.
Strauss, Anselm, and Juliet M. Corbin
1998 *Basics of Qualitative Research: Grounded Theory Procedures and Techniques* 2nd Edition. Thousand Oaks, CA: Sage Press.
Stumpf, Samuel E.
1989 "Existentialism," *Philosophy: History and Problems* 4th Edition. New York: McGraw-Hill.
Sudetic, Chuck
1990 "Expelling former king, Romanians cite stunt," *New York Times*, Dec 27, 2.
1991a "Romania seeks to reduce abortions," *New York Times*, Jan 17, 3.
1991b "Who'll love these cast-off children," *New York Times*, Jan 11, 8.
Sullivan, Barbara
1991 "Wanted: a baby to love," *Chicago Tribune*, Feb 1, 5-1.
1994 "Adoption network," *Chicago Tribune*, April 25, 5-1.
Szulc, Tad
1991 *The Secret Alliance: the Extraordinary Story of the Rescue of the Jews since World War II*. New York: Farrar, Straus & Giroux.

Tagliabue, John
   1991   "Critics view Ceausescu works and, well, despair," *New York Times*, Dec 5, 6.

Talaly, Sarah
   1994a   "From Russia with love," *Chicago Tribune*, July 26, 2-1.
   1994b   "Parents for sale in baby market," *Chicago Tribune*, Feb 8, 2-1.

Talaly, Sarah and Julie Irwin
   1994   "Red flags raised on baby scams," *Chicago Tribune*, May 6, 2-1.

Tanner, Adam
   1989   *Frommer's Eastern Europe and Yugoslavia on $25 a Day*. New York: Prentice Hall.

Taylor, Charles
   1991   *The Ethics of Authenticity*. Cambridge, MA: Harvard University Press.

Tedlock, Barbara
   1991   "From Participant Observation to the Observation of Participation: the Emergence of Narrative Ethnography," *Journal of Anthropological Research*, vol. 37, 69-94.
   2000   "Ethnography and Ethnographic Representation," *Handbook of Qualitative Research*, Norman K. Denzin and Yvonna S. Lincoln, eds. Thousand Oaks, CA: Sage Press.

Tessler, Richard C., Gail Gamache and Liming Liu
   1999   *West Meets East: Americans Adopt Chinese Children*. Westport, CT: Bergin & Garvey.

Thomas, Jerry
   1991a   "Adoption isn't as simple as black, white," *Chicago Tribune*, June 2, 2-1.
   1991b   "Should white parents adopt black children?," *Chicago Tribune*, June 23, 2-1.

Thompson, Jon
   1991   "East Europe's Dark Dawn," *National Geographic*, vol. 179 no. 6, June, 37.

Tillman-Healy, Lisa M.
   2002   "Men Kissing," *Ethnographically Speaking*, Arthur P. Bochner and Carolyn Ellis, eds. Walnut Creek, CA: Altamira Press.

Tismaneanu, Vladimir
   1990   "New Masks, Old Faces," *The New Republic*, Feb 5, 17.
   2003   *Stalinism For All Seasons: a Political History of Romanian Communism*. Berkeley, CA: University of California Press.

Torstendahl, Rolf and Michael Barrage, eds.
   1990   *The Formation of Professions: Knowledge, State, and Strategy*. Newbury Park, CA: Sage.

Treptow, Kurt W., ed.
   1995   *A History of Romania*. Iasi: The Romanian Cultural Foundation, Center for Roman Studies.

Tugend, Tom
   1992a   "The Dwindling Jewish Community in Romania," *Sentinel*, Jan 16, 12.
   1992b   "The Jews of Bucharest," *Sentinel*, Jan 23, 13.

United Kingdom-Department of Health, Welsh Office and Scottish Office
   1992 "Background Paper No. 3," *Inter-Departmental Review of Adoption Law: Intercountry Adoption*, Jan.
United Nations Development Programme
   1994 *Human Development Report*. New York: Oxford University Press.
"U.S. moves to curb adoptions of Romanians"
   1991 *New York Times*, July 28, 8.
"U.S. urges Americans seeking babies not to go to Romania"
   1981 *Chicago Tribune*, May 31, 9.
Van Maanen, John
   1988 *Tales of the Field: On Writing Ethnography*. Chicago, IL: University of Chicago Press.
Waller, C.L.
   1991 "Adoption brings Romanian baby a happy future," *Daily Herald*, Aug 5, 4.
Warren, Ellen
   1995 "Adopted kids bring instant chaos, joy from native Russia, with love," *Chicago Tribune*, April 14, 2-2.
Warren, James
   1989 "Editor brings glimpse of Lithuania to city," *Chicago Tribune*, Feb, 2-1.
Watson, Lawrence C. and Maria-Barbara Watson-Franke
   1985 *Interpreting Life Histories: an Anthropological Inquiry*. New Brunswick, NJ: Rutgers University Press.
Wattenberg, Ruth
   1989 "Ceausescu's Schools," *American Educator*, Fall, 11-23.
Waxman, Sharon
   1990 "Ceausescu's legacy of distrust stays alive," *Chicago Tribune*, June 15, 6.
Wegar, Katarina
   1997 *Adoption, Identity, and Kinship: the Debate Over Sealed Birth Records*. New Haven, CT: Yale University Press.
Weir, Kyle N.
   2003 *Coming Out of the Adoptive Closet*. Lanham, MD: University Press of America.
Weiss, Steven
   1993 "New Status of Nazi Collaborator Sparks Concern for Romanian Jews," *Sentinel*, Dec 23, 24.
Westhues, Anne and Joyce C. Cohen
   1998 "Ethnic and Racial Identity of Internationally Adopted Adolescents and Young Adults: Same Issues in Relation to Children's Rights," *Adoption Quarterly*, vol. 1 no. 4, 33-55.
Williams, Lena
   1995 "Transracial adoption: the truth comes in shades of gray," *New York Times*, March 23, B1.
Wills, Kendall J.
   1994 "From Russia with love: a couple from New York find son in Moscow," *Daily Herald*, Dec 26, 3-6.

Wisby, Gary
   1991   "Pairs dream of a child comes true a world away," *Chicago Sun-Times*, May 17, 24.

Wolf, Margery
   1982   *A Thrice-Told Tale: Feminism, Postmodernism, and Ethnographic Responsibility*. Stanford, CA: Stanford University Press.

WuDunn, Sheryl
   1991   "The castaway babies of the Chinese: heartless feudal practice lives on," *New York Times*, Feb 26, 4.

Zabell, Martin
   1991   "In Lemont, a Lithuanian voice," *Chicago Tribune*, Sept 2, 2-7.

Zabell, Martin and Louise Kiernan
   1992   "Lithuanian festival symbol of new world," *Chicago Tribune*, July 6, 2-3.

Television

"A Miracle for Michael"
   1991   *20/20*, ABC, Dec 20.

"Children For Sale"
   1991   *60 Minutes*, CBS.

"Nobody's Children"
   1990   *20/20*, ABC, April 27.

"Shame of a Nation"
   1990   *20/20*, ABC, Oct 5.

"The Greatest Gift of All"
   1990   *20/20*, ABC, Dec 21.

"Death of a Dictator"
   1990   *The Koppel Report*, ABC.

"The Rise and Fall of Ceausescu: a Personal Investigation of Edward Behr"
   1991   PBS.

Radio

Interview: Dr. Barbara Bascombe
   1991   *Morning Edition*, National Public Radio, March 12.

Index

abortions, banned 1966 140
accidental ethnography 121
Adelman 1984 143
Adelman, 1984 142
adoption
agencies 7
adoption
  arbitrary limits 8
  adoption donation 7
  adoption, identified 8
  adoption law 9
  adoption, regular 4
  adoption stigma 5
  adoption, typical cost 7
  adoption ads 7
  adoption, black market 12
  adoption, gray market 12
  adoption, large scale 3
  adoption of non-relatives 5
  adoption, post WWI 3
Adoptive Families of America (AFA) 9
advertising 7
agro-industrial complexes, Romania 129
AIDS babies, Romania 33
AIDS conference canceled 34
Aitkin, Lee 115
Alexandru 53, 59
Amerasian children 15
American Embassy 115
Anguelov, 2002 142
Antonescu, Marshal 26
Appalachia 13
apparatchik, a party functionary 146
Arad 50, 53
Aronson, 1969 143
autobiography 121

Babies 'R Us 14

Baby M 16, 17
baby selling, felony 11
Bacon, 1984 142, 143, 146
Bair, 1991 27
Baneasa Airport, revolution 134
Barringer, 1991 32
Bascombe, Dr. Barbara 32
Battiata, 1990b 32, 35, 140
baube 21, 61
bazuco, cocaine 6
Beck, 1995 5
Bernstein, 1991 42
Bessarabia 26
Bialer, 1980 143
Bill, barber 10
biological mother 17
birth father 11
birth mothers 8
Bjorkland, 1998 124
black children 4
black market adoptions 12
Black Sea 35
Blaiken, Mr. Council 18
Blandiana, Ana 131, 134
blonde boy 58
blondeh 58
Bochner and Ellis, 1996 124
Bogotá 6
Bohlen 33
  1990f 35
  1990g 33, 34
  1990g, 1990f 35, 140
  1990i 37, 140
Boyle, 1992 15
"Brazil Charges Israelis in Baby Scam,"
  1993 11
Bread and Newspapers 49
Breslan, 1990 33, 140

bribe 46
"Britons in Baby-Smuggling Case Go Free," 1994 115
Brodeur, 1983 142
Brogan, 1990 128, 143
bronchita, the bronchitis 112
Brooke, 1994 6
Brown, 1996 147
Brucan, Silviu 128, 134
Brzezinski, 1990 147
Bucharest 27, 46, 49
    Municipal Hospital 32
    revolution 131
    Virology Institute 34
Burke, 1990 31, 140
Byzantine 146
Bzezinski, 1990/1997 147

Calinescu and Tismaneanu, 1991 146
Candurachi and Dricoviciu, 1971 24
CAP Book 3
Castantsa 140
Castelnau, 1990 35
Ceausescu 29
    Elena 25, 128, 134, 147
    Marin 134
    Nicolae 134
    Nicolae (apparatchik) 146
    Nicoli 23, 25, 62, 129, 131, 140, 142
    Nicu 134
    October 1966 Decree 131, 140
    oppression 129
    trial & execution 30
Central Committee 131
    Building 29
    Building, revolution 131
Cerevoda 35
Charalambous, 1994 115
Chesler, 1988 17
Chicago Council on Foreign Relations 27
Child Prostitution Growing in Brazil," 1993 6
Children Awaiting Parents, Inc. 3
China Doll Syndrome 15
Chira, 1994 5
Churchill, 1991 33, 140

Cole and Knowles, 2001 121
Cole and Nyden, 1990 140
Communist Era 50
Communist, everyday life 142
Communist Party, Romania 146
Communist Youth League 33
Communisti 44
congenital anomalies 3
Congress of Berlin 25
consent 10
Continent of Meaning 124
contraceptives, banned (Romania) 140
Cordrescu, Andrei 128, 143
Cornea, Doina 134
Costanta 35
Count Dracula 25
Crankshaw, 1956 143
Crapanzano, 1980 125
Crossen, 1989 8
Cullen, 1991 143
cult of personality 25, 146

Dacian, native 24
Daday, 1993 6
Dallin and Breslauer, 1971 142
David, 1988 140
Davis, 1995 5
decree babies 131
Delarue, 1964 143
Dellios, 1993 3
Denzin, 1997 124, 125
    and Lincoln, 2000 124
difficult behaviors 4
Dinescu, Mircea 131, 134, 136
DNP, Do Not Publish 5
DNS, Do Not Show 5
Dobbs, 1990 32
Dobruja 26
Doerner, 1990 143
Don Coolman 2
Dowagiac, MI 3
Dracula, Tour to his Homeland for Halloween 27
Drell, 1994 11
Dressler, Dr. Milan 136
Dugger, 1991 3

Eakin, 1992 121

eanu 23
Ecuador 12
Ehrlich, 1980 121
Eisenberg, 1990 6
Ellis, Carolyn 125
Emperor Trajan 24
Enstad, 1993 11
Era of Light 35
escu 23
Evangelical Christian agencies 9
evocative autoethnography 125

facilitators 7, 8
FBI fingerprint clearance 39
Fieweger, 1991 11
First Contact 23
Fischer, 1989 143, 146
Fishman, 1992 4
Fitzpatrick, 1993 142
Fitzpatrick, 1999 142, 143
Floriescu, Elena 92
   Floriana 47, 50, 56
   Elena 23
   Raymond 46, 92
Fodors, 1989 24, 25, 26, 27
foreign adoption, Korea 6
Fotografie 60
Francez 60
Franks, 1993 11
Free Romanian Television 30, 134
Freeman, 1979 125
French Embassy 19
Friends of Romania 56
Friends of Seudis 23

Garthoff, 1994 147
Geertz, 1973 124
geharget 21
Gellner, 1991 147
Germans, ethnic 50
Gheorghe (translator) 47, 51, 54
Gheorgiu-Dej, Gheorje 146
Gibbs, 1989 5, 7
Giddens, 1991 124
gift 46
glasnost 147
   openness 147
Glasser, 1992 115

Global, analysis level 147
Godwin, 1989 7
Goetz, 1990 27
Goodman, 1993 5
Gorbachev, Mikhail 131, 147
   Era 25
Gordon, 1991a 14
Gottesman, 1992 115
goyem 21
grandmother 21
gray market adoptions 12
Gubernick, 1991 14
Gulag Gives Up Lost Patients, 1991 143
Gullestad, 1996 121, 124
Gusa, General Stefan 134
Gypsies 57, 60, 61
   babies 20

Hanley, 1989 17
hard to place 3
Harris, 1988 3
Haynes, 1994 3
He and She 134
high risk adoptions 4
Higher Council on Health, Romania 140
Historical Context 129
history of Communist policing 119
Hitler-Stalin Pact 26
Hoibraaten, 1993 124
Holmes, 1995 5
Holmes, 1997 146
Holstein and Gubrium, 2004 124
home study 10
Horowitz, 1995a, 1995b 5
Huckshorn, 1992 6
Hungarian minority 29
Hungarians, ethnic 129
Hunt, 1991 115
Hunt, Kathleen 115

I-600 39
I-600A 39
IDC&FS, international adoption
   coordinator 8
identified adoption 8
Iherjirika, 1994 6
Iliescu, Ion 134
Illinois Department of Children and

Family Service 4
Immigration Service 39
incorrigibles 140
Individuals, analysis level 140
Ingram, 1992b 32
Ingram, 1993a, 1993b 115
initial service fee. nonrefundable 7
INS application 40
institutional racism 5
Institutions, analysis level 140
"Intercountry Adoptions Up in FY 1994," 1995 6
international adoptions 5
interstate compact 10
Ion (driver) 47, 49
Iron Guard 25, 26
irrecoverable orphanages 140
irrecoverables 36
Isaacs, 1989 15
"Israeli Couple, Six Brazilians Arrested For Alleg 11
"Israelis Hear About Bribery In Latin American Ado 11
Izzy from Indianapolis 11

Jaffe, 1991 11
Jenks, 2002 124
Jewish babies 12
Jewish Children's Bureau 8
Jewish Family Services 40
Jewish Federation 22
Johnson, 1991 21
Johnson, 1993 17, 115
Jones, 1993 5
Jouzaitis and Kass, 1991 22

Kaufman, 1956 46
Kenny, 1990 140
Kideckel, 1993 142, 146
King, 1980 143
King Carol 25
King Michael 26
Klein, Susie
    4, 8, 16, 41, 46, 57, 59, 72, 115
Kligman, 1998 140
Korea 14
Korean adoptions 14
Kovno 22

Kozma, 1995 25
Kundera, 1984 143
Kundrup 121

Lacayo, 1989 4, 5
Lane, 1991 147
Langness and Franke, 1965 124
Lawson, 1991 115
leagane 36
Leaganul Pentru Copii Arad 53
lei 41
Leontin, Viorel 58, 59
Lethwaite, 1990 33
Lewin, 1990 6
Lewin, 1994 4, 5
Liang, 1992 142
life cycle approach 124
life history 121
    evocative autoethnography 125
    messy text 124
    narrative ethnography 125
    study 124
    thick description 124
life passage approach 124
Lindblad 27
Lithuania, SSR 22
Lithuanian American Cultural Center 21
Lithuanian American social agency 21
Lithuanian Consul General, Honorary 21
Lithuanian Jews 21
Little, 1994 6
little blond boy 58
Litvaks 21
long-term foster care 5
Louie, 1995 6
Luft, 1995 6
Lugens 21
Lynch, 1990 140

Maines, 2001 121, 124
Mandelbaum, 1973 124
Mansnerus, 1989 6
Marx, 1988 142
Maximum Leader 131
Mazilu, Dumitru 136
McClarnand, 1998 147
McKay, 1989 8, 10

McNamara, 1975; 75-84 12
McNamee, 1989a; 1989c 6
McNamee, 1989b 5
McRoberts, 1989 21
menstrual police 33
Mercer, 1993 6
Metzenbaum, Senator Howard 5
Micheletti, 1990 128
Michelman and Schneider, 1988 5, 7, 9
Michelman, Stanley (atty) 9
Michigan agency 16
Micro-infusions, AIDS 140
micro-transfusions, AIDS 37
Milgram, Stanley 13
Militaru, General Nicolae 128, 134
Miller, 1989 7, 8
Miller, 2000 125
Mills, 1995 6
Moldavia 24
Money magazine 3
Morning Edition, 1991 32

Nachtway and Hunt, 1990 35
narrative ethnography 125
National Adoption Committee 115
National, analysis level 143
National Association of Black Social
  Workers 4
National Salvation Front 30, 128, 131
National Urban League study 5
Neeley, 1991 115, 140
Nenitescu, Professor Constin 147
Neubauer and Germund, 1988 11
New Rules Try To Ease Interracial
  Adoption, 1995 5
non-agency adoptions 6
Northern Bucovina 26
NWI (Normal White Infant) 12
  market value 12

Official Romanian Tour Company 27
Ogintz, 1989 8
Oloroso, 1994 6
Opera Square 129
  Cathedral 131
orphan train 3
Orphanage
  For Babies in Arad 53

No. 1 50
over-three
under-three 53
Plataresti 31
Otopeni International Airport 46
  revolution 134
over the hill 8

Pacepa, 1987 128, 143, 146
Page, 1993 5
Pahz, 1987 5
Paris of the Balkans 27
Paris of the East 49
Party Congress 131
Peoples Congress 136
  revolution 136
Perestroika 147
  restructuring 147
permanent legal termination 9
personal choice 124
Personal introspection 125
Peters, 1988a, 1988b 11
Petrakis, 1994 6
Pilon, 1992 143, 146
political police
  Romanian 142
  Soviet 142
post-totalitarian authoritarian regime
  147
problems 7
Proctor & Gamble 62

racial genocide 4
racial matching 4
Radio Free Europe 129
Reaves, 1990 128
Reaves, 1990c 31, 32, 140
Reitz and Watson, 1992 4
RESOLVE: The National Infertility
  Association 9
Revolution 29, 129
Richardson, 1993 5
Richardson, 2000 125
Richman, 1993a, 1993b 3, 5
rickette, the rickets 112
Rocketeer 44
Rocks, 1993 49
role of the researcher 125

Rollnick, 1990 143
Roman conquest 24
Roman, Prime Minister Petre 115, 134, 136
Romania 24, 25, 136
  Axis 25
  1980s exports 140
  coup d'etat 136
  daily life 121
  shortages 26
  program suspended 18
  Turk rule 146
  WWII 146
Romanian
  adoption 39
  adoption scandal 24
  Communist Party 146
  Communist Party (RCP) 143
  Communist Party, abolished 136
  Embassy 18
  flag 30
  history 24
  names 23
  National Tourist Office 27
  Orthodox Church 36
  public housing projects 49
  television 115
Romanian-American newspaper 40
Romanian-Americans 45
Romanians, daily lives 142
Rothman, 1990 35, 36, 37, 140
Russian Embassy, Lithuanian representative 22

Saint Sybarite by the Lake 13
San Antonio 13
Sandstrom, Martini and Fine, 2003 121
Sarajevo 46
Satre, 1989 46
Schiene kind, starker! 57
schmaltz 21
Schmetzer, 1995 11
Schmetzer, 1995a, 1995b 6
Schwandt, 2000 121
Securitate 29, 51, 129, 131, 134, 143
  abolished 136
  base 134
  revolution 128

self and data 125
Sennett, 1978 124
Serrill, 1991 6
Seudis 23
Shelley, 1990, 1996 142
Shelley, 1996 142, 143
Shelton, 1995 124, 125
Sheppard, 1991 6
Simon and Altstein, 1992 4
Singer, 1993 115
Smolowe, 1995 4, 5
social cleansing 6
socialism in the family 25
Socialist man 142
socialist principles 25
Socialist Republic 136
Sofsky, 1993 143
Soviet policing 142
Sparkes, 2002 125
special needs 3
sperm donor 17
Stalinism 146, 147
Stalinist
  model 140
  terror, Romania 142
Stanculescu, General Victor 134
Stark and Bruszt, 1998 128
Stars of David International, Inc. 9
Stein, 1990 3
Stepheson, et.al., 1992 32
Stern, William & Elizabeth 17
Stevens and Tennison, 1993 11
street children 6
Stumpf, 1989 46
subculture of adoption 9
Sudetic, 1991a 32
Sudetic, 1991b 32
Sullivan, 1991 7
Sullivan, 1994 8
support group, Jewish adoptive parents 9
surrogacy 17
surrogates 16
systemization, Romania 129

Talaly, 1994b 8
Tanner, 1989 24, 25
TAROM, 40

Taylor, 1991 124
Tedlock, 1991, 2000 125
television 62
Tepes, Prince Vlad 25
Texas 13
The Adoption Services Associates, ASA 14
The East European Grand Tour 27
The State 49
Thomas, 1991a, 1991b 5
Tillman-Healy, 2002 125
Timisoara 29, 51
  1989 riots 29
  revolution 129
Tismaneanu, 2003 140, 146
Tokes, Rev. Laszlo 29, 129, 134
transracial adoption 4
transracial placement 5
Transylvania 24
Treaty of Berlin 26
Treptow, 1995 146
TWA 44

United Nations Human Development Report, 1992 140
University of Bucharest 147
  revolution 131
University Square 50
unknown life expectancy 3
unsafe abortions 32

Vasile Milea, Defense Minister 131
Verdery, 1991 142, 143, 146
Victor Babes Hospital 34, 35
Viorel Leontin 58, 59
Vlad, General (revolution) 134
Vlad the Impaler 25
Vlahs 24
Vlahs, Land of the 24
Voice of America 129

waiting children 3, 16
Wallachia 24
Warren, 1989 21
Warren, 1995 6
Warsaw Pact 25
Watson and Watson-Franke, 1985 121
Welcome to the Balkans 39
Whitehead, Mary Beth 17
Williams, 1995 5
Wills, 1994 6
Wolf, 1992 121
World Health Organization 34
WuDunn, 1991 6

Zabell, 1991 21
Zabell and Kiernan, 1992 22
Zadek 52
Zugravescu, Dr. Alexandra 115

www.ingramcontent.com/pod-product-compliance
Lightning Source LLC
Chambersburg PA
CBHW021407290426
44108CB00010B/418